Learn Rails 5.2

Accelerated Web Development with Ruby on Rails

Stefan Wintermeyer

Apress®

Learn Rails 5.2: Accelerated Web Development with Ruby on Rails

Stefan Wintermeyer
Bochum, Germany

ISBN-13 (pbk): 978-1-4842-3488-4   ISBN-13 (electronic): 978-1-4842-3489-1
https://doi.org/10.1007/978-1-4842-3489-1

Library of Congress Control Number: 2018939414

Managing Director, Apress Media LLC: Welmoed Spahr
Acquisitions Editor: Steve Anglin
Development Editor: Matthew Moodie
Coordinating Editor: Mark Powers

Cover designed by eStudioCalamar

Cover image designed by Freepik (www.freepik.com)

Distributed to the book trade worldwide by Springer Science+Business Media New York, 233 Spring Street, 6th Floor, New York, NY 10013. Phone 1-800-SPRINGER, fax (201) 348-4505, e-mail orders-ny@springer-sbm.com, or visit www.springeronline.com. Apress Media, LLC is a California LLC and the sole member (owner) is Springer Science + Business Media Finance Inc (SSBM Finance Inc). SSBM Finance Inc is a **Delaware** corporation.

For information on translations, please e-mail editorial@apress.com; for reprint, paperback, or audio rights, please email bookpermissions@springernature.com.

Apress titles may be purchased in bulk for academic, corporate, or promotional use. eBook versions and licenses are also available for most titles. For more information, reference our Print and eBook Bulk Sales web page at www.apress.com/bulk-sales.

Any source code or other supplementary material referenced by the author in this book is available to readers on GitHub via the book's product page, located at www.apress.com/9781484234884. For more detailed information, please visit www.apress.com/source-code.

Printed on acid-free paper

Für Oma und Opa.

I dedicate this book to my grandparents.

Table of Contents

About the Author

Stefan Wintermeyer is a freelance web developer, trainer, and consultant. Prior to this position, he was a founder and managing director at AMOOMA GmbH, cofounder and managing director at OTRS GmbH, and vice president at Techspan Enterprise and SuSE Linux AG. He was also a project manager for Lufthansa Systems.

About the Technical Reviewer

Eldon Alameda is a web developer who currently resides in the harsh climates of Kansas. He works as a regional webmaster for the U.S. National Weather Service; prior to this, he did development for a variety of companies including local startups, advertising firms, Sprint PCS, and IBM. During the 1990s, he also acquired a nice stack of worthless stock options by working for dot-com companies.

Preface

I write for developers who learn best by following short, clean examples. I don't like the idea of coding one big application over the course of a book; I much prefer smaller, stand-alone code. Therefore, you can skip a couple of pages or even complete chapters without losing context. On the other hand, I'll frequently be asking you to create another new Rails application.

A word of warning: I'm not going to sprinkle in CSS beauty anywhere.

Don't let people fool you into believing that Ruby on Rails is easy to learn. It's not! It's one of the best and most effective frameworks to develop web applications, but it takes time to understand and master. The worst mistake of all is to not learn Ruby *before* diving into Ruby on Rails. To avoid this, the book starts with the basics of Ruby. You will not become a Ruby guru after reading it, but you'll understand the basic ideas, which is most important.

Newsletter and Updates

I publish a free Ruby on Rails e-mail newsletter that offers news and general information about Rails. You can subscribe at `https://www.wintermeyer-consulting.de/newsletters/`.

Additionally, you can follow me on Twitter at `https://twitter.com/wintermeyer`.

Consulting and Training

I provide Rails consulting and training anywhere in the world, on-site or remote. If you are interested, please contact me by e-mail at `sw@wintermeyer-consulting.de`.

Meetups and Conferences

Please don't be shy if you'd like me to speak or offer a training session at your local meetup or conference; send me an e-mail, and I'll try to make it happen.

Feedback

Two things in particular highlight my work as an author: five-star Amazon reviews and reader feedback offered by e-mail or Twitter. Please reach out and let me know what you thought of this book.

Have fun with Ruby on Rails!

—Stefan Wintermeyer

Introduction

This book requires basic knowledge of HTML, plus the reader (you, in other words!) should have a basic understanding of programming. I'm not going to teach you what variables are. I'm just using them. I work a lot with example code and not so much with abstract definitions.

 This is a technical book. Therefore, there are parts that are mind-blowingly boring. But I try to keep them to a minimum.

Each chapter and most sections work autarkic. You don't have to read the book in order, and you can skip chapters if they are not important to you. All code examples work without any dependencies on earlier chapters. I'm not going to build a gigantic application to show how cool Rails is. I prefer the approach of small projects to analyze and discuss specific topics.

CHAPTER 1

Ruby Introduction

This chapter is a tightrope walk between oversimplification and a degree of detail that is unnecessary for a Rails newbie. After all, the objective is not to become a Ruby guru but to understand Ruby on Rails. I will elaborate on the most important points, and the rest is then up to you. If you would like to know more about Ruby, I recommend the book *The Ruby Programming Language* by David Flanagan and Yukihiro Matsumoto.

> *"It is easy to program in Ruby, but Ruby is not a simple language."*
>
> —Yukihiro Matsumoto

Ruby 2.5

I'm going to use Ruby 2.5, but for most part of this book you can use older versions too. Ruby 2.5 is just a bit faster. You can check the installed Ruby version by running the command `ruby -v`, as shown here:

```
$ ruby -v
ruby 2.5.0p0 (2017-12-25 revision 61468) [x86_64-darwin17]
$
```

ℹ️ If your system is running an older version and you want to upgrade it, take a look at `https://rvm.io`, which is my preferred way of installing and using different Ruby versions.

© Stefan Wintermeyer 2018
S. Wintermeyer, *Learn Rails 5.2*, https://doi.org/10.1007/978-1-4842-3489-1_1

Basics

Ruby is a scripting language. So, it is not compiled and then executed; instead, it is read by an interpreter and then processed line by line.

Hello World

A simple `hello-world.rb` program consists of one line of code, as shown in Listing 1-1.

Listing 1-1. hello-world.rb

```
puts 'Hello World!'
```

Use your favorite editor to open a new file with the filename `hello-world.rb` and insert the previous line into it. You can then execute this Ruby program at the command line as follows:

```
$ ruby hello-world.rb
Hello World!
$
```

ℹ️   A program line in a Ruby program does not have to end with a semicolon. The Ruby interpreter is even so intelligent that it recognizes if a program line was split over two or more lines for the sake of readability. Indenting code is also not necessary. But it does make it much easier to read for human beings!

---

puts and print

If you look for examples on Ruby on the Internet, you will find two typical ways of printing text on the screen.

- `puts` prints a string, followed by a newline.
- `print` prints a string (without a newline).

Listing 1-2 shows an example program (an extension of the program `hello-world.rb`).

Listing 1-2. hello-world.rb

```ruby
puts 'Hello World!'
puts
puts 'zzz'
print 'Hello World!'
print
puts 'zzz'
```

On the screen, you will see this:

```
$ ruby hello-world.rb
Hello World!

zzz
Hello World!zzz
```

Comments

A comment in a Ruby program starts with a # sign and ends with a newline. As an example, I added a comment to the earlier `hello-world.rb` program; see Listing 1-3.

Listing 1-3. hello-world.rb

```ruby
# Program for displaying "Hello World!"
# by Stefan Wintermeyer

puts 'Hello World!'
```

A comment can also follow a program line, as shown in Listing 1-4.

Listing 1-4. hello-world.rb

```ruby
puts 'Hello World!'  # Example comment
```

A # sign within strings in a single quote mark is not treated as the start of a comment, as shown in Listing 1-5.

Listing 1-5. hello-world.rb

```
# Example program
# by Stefan Wintermeyer

puts 'Hello World!'
puts '############'
puts
puts '1#2#3#4#5#6#'    # Comment on this
```

Help via ri

When programming, you do not always have a Ruby handbook available. Fortunately, the Ruby developers thought of this and provided a built-in help feature in form of the program `ri`.

 Of course, you must have installed the documentation, which is the default. If you used `rvm` to install Ruby, you can run `rvm docs generate` to generate the documentation.

This is a typical chicken-and-egg situation. How can I explain the Ruby help feature if you are only just getting started with Ruby? So, I am going to jump ahead a little and show you how you can search for information on the class `String`.

```
$ ri String
  [...]
$
```

Many times it is easier and more informative to use Google instead of `ri`.

irb

`irb` stands for "**I**nteractive **Ruby**" and is a kind of sandbox where you can play around with Ruby at your leisure. You can launch `irb` by entering `irb` on the shell and end it by entering `exit`.

4

An example is worth a thousand words.

```
$ irb
irb(main):001:0> puts 'Hello World!'
Hello World!
=> nil
irb(main):002:0> exit
$
```

> **ℹ** In future examples, I use IRB.conf[:PROMPT_MODE] = :SIMPLE in my
> .irbrc config file to generate shorter irb output (without the irb(main):001:0>
> part). You can do the same by using irb --simple-prompt.

Ruby Is Object-Oriented

Ruby only knows objects. Everything is an object (sounds almost like Zen). Every object is an instance of a class. You can find out the class of an object via the method .class.

An object in Ruby is encapsulated and can be reached from the outside only via the methods of the corresponding object. What does this mean? You cannot change any property of an object directly from the outside. The corresponding object has to offer a method with which you can do so.

> **ℹ** Please do not panic if you have no idea what a class or an object is. I won't
> tell anyone, and you can still work with them just fine without worrying too much.
> This topic alone could fill whole volumes. Roughly speaking, an *object* is a
> container for something, and a *method* changes something in that container.
>
> Please go on reading and take a look at the examples. The puzzle will gradually get
> clearer.

Methods

In other programming languages, the terms you would use for Ruby methods would be *functions*, *procedures*, *subroutines*, and of course *methods*.

    Here I go with the oversimplification. You cannot compare non-object-oriented programming languages with object-oriented ones. Plus, there are two kinds of methods (class methods and instance methods). I do not want to make it too complicated. So, I simply ignore those "fine" distinctions.

At this point, you probably want to look at a good example, but all I can think of are silly ones. The problem is the assumption that you are only allowed to use knowledge that has already been described in this book.

So, let's assume that you use the code sequence in Listing 1-6 repeatedly (for whatever reason).

Listing 1-6. hello-worldx3a.rb

```
puts 'Hello World!'
puts 'Hello World!'
puts 'Hello World!'
```

So , you want to output the string "Hello World!" three times in separate rows. As this makes your daily work routine much longer, you are now going to define a method (with the meaningless name three_times), with which this can all be done in one go, as shown in Listing 1-7.

    Names of methods are always written in lowercase.

Listing 1-7. hello-worldx3b.rb

```
def three_times
  puts 'Hello World!'
  puts 'Hello World!'
  puts 'Hello World!'
end
```

Let's test this by starting `irb` and loading the program with the command `load './ hello-worldx3b.rb'`. After that, you have access to the `three_times` method.

```
$ irb
>> load './hello-worldx3b.rb'
=> true
>> three_times
Hello World!
Hello World!
Hello World!
=> nil
>> exit
```

When defining a method, you can define required parameters and use them within the method. This enables you to create a method to which you pass a string as a parameter, and you can then output it three times, as shown in Listing 1-8.

Listing 1-8. hello-worldx3c.rb

```
def three_times(value)
  puts value
  puts value
  puts value
end
$ irb
>> load './hello-worldx3c.rb'
=> true
>> three_times('Hello World!')
Hello World!
Hello World!
Hello World!
=> nil
```

Incidentally, you can omit the brackets when calling the method.

```
>> three_times 'Hello World!'
Hello World!
Hello World!
Hello World!
=> nil
```

💡 Ruby gurus and would-be gurus are going to turn up their noses on the subject of "unnecessary" brackets in your programs and will probably pepper you with more or less stupid comments of comparisons to Java and other programming languages.

There is one simple rule in the Ruby community: the fewer brackets, the cooler you are!

But you won't get a medal for using fewer brackets. Decide for yourself what makes you happy.

If you do not specify a parameter with the previous method, you will get this error message: `wrong number of arguments (0 for 1)`.

```
>> three_times
ArgumentError: wrong number of arguments (given 0, expected 1)
    from /Users/.../hello-worldx3c.rb:1:in `three_times'
    from (irb):2
    from /Users/stefan/.rvm/rubies/ruby-2.5.0/bin/irb:11:in `<main>'
>> exit
```

You can give the variable `value` a default value, and then you can also call the method without a parameter, as shown in Listing 1-9.

Listing 1-9. hello-worldx3d.rb

```ruby
def three_times(value = 'blue')
  puts value
  puts value
  puts value
end

$ irb
>> load './hello-worldx3d.rb'
=> true
>> three_times('Example')
Example
```

8

```
Example
Example
=> nil
>> three_times
blue
blue
blue
=> nil
>> exit
```

Classes

For now you can think of a class as a collection of methods. The name of a class always starts with an uppercase letter. Let's assume that the method belongs to the new class This_and_that. It would then be defined as shown in Listing 1-10 in a Ruby program.

Listing 1-10. hello-worldx3e.rb

```ruby
class This_and_that
  def three_times
    puts 'Hello World!'
    puts 'Hello World!'
    puts 'Hello World!'
  end
end
```

Let's play it through in irb.

```
$ irb
>> load './hello-worldx3e.rb'
=> true
```

Now you try to call the method three_times.

```
>> This_and_that.three_times
NoMethodError: undefined method `three_times' for This_and_that:Class
    from (irb):2
    from /Users/stefan/.rvm/rubies/ruby-2.5.0/bin/irb:11:in `<main>'
>>
```

This results in an error message because `This_and_that` is a class and not an instance. As you are working with instance methods, it works only if you have first created a new object (a new instance) of the class `This_and_that` with the class method new. Let's name it abc.

```
>> abc = This_and_that.new
=> #<This_and_that:0x007fb01b02dcd0>
>> abc.three_times
Hello World!
Hello World!
Hello World!
=> nil
>> exit
```

I will explain the difference between instance and class methods in more detail in the section "Class Methods and Instance Methods" (another chicken-and-egg problem).

Private Methods

Quite often it makes sense to only call a method within its own class or own instance. Such methods are referred to as *private* methods (as opposed to public methods), and they are listed after the keyword `private` within a class, as shown in Listing 1-11.

Listing 1-11. pm-example.rb

```ruby
class Example
  def a
    puts 'a'
  end

  private
  def b
    puts 'b'
  end
end
```

You run this in `irb`, first the public and then the private method, which raises an error.

```
$ irb
>> load './pm-example.rb'
=> true
>> abc = Example.new
=> #<Example:0x007fa530037910>
>> abc.a
a
=> nil
>> abc.b
NoMethodError: private method `b' called for #<Example:0x007fa530037910>
    from (irb):4
    from /Users/stefan/.rvm/rubies/ruby-2.5.0/bin/irb:11:in `<main>'
>> exit
```

Method initialize()

If a new instance is created (by calling the method new), the method that is processed first and automatically is the method `initialize`. The method is automatically a private method, even if it not listed explicitly under `private`, as shown in Listing 1-12.

Listing 1-12. pm-example-a.rb

```
class Room
  def initialize
    puts 'abc'
  end
end
```

Here is an `irb` test of it:

```
$ irb
>> load './initialize-example-a.rb'
=> true
>> kitchen = Room.new
abc
=> #<Room:0x007f830704edb8>
>> exit
```

11

The instance kitchen is created with Room.new, and the method initialize is processed automatically.

The method new accepts the parameters specified for the method initialize, as shown in Listing 1-13.

Listing 1-13. initialize-example-b.rb

```
class Example
  def initialize(value)
    puts value
  end
end

$ irb
>> load './initialize-example-b.rb'
=> true
>> abc = Example.new('Hello World!')
Hello World!
=> #<Example:0x007fbb0b845f30>
>> exit
```

return

puts is nice to demonstrate an example in this book, but normally you need a way to return the result of something. The return statement can be used for that, as shown in Listing 1-14.

Listing 1-14. circle-a.rb

```
def area_of_a_circle(radius)
  pi = 3.14
  area = pi * radius * radius
  return area
end
```

```
$ irb
>> load './circle-a.rb'
=> true
>> area_of_a_circle(10)
=> 314.0
>> exit
```

But it wouldn't be Ruby if you couldn't do it shorter, right? You can simply skip `return`, as shown in Listing 1-15.

Listing 1-15. circle-b.rb

```ruby
def area_of_a_circle(radius)
  pi = 3.14
  area = pi * radius * radius
  area
end
```

You can actually even skip the last line because Ruby returns the value of the last expression as a default, as shown in Listing 1-16.

Listing 1-16. circle-c.rb

```ruby
def area_of_a_circle(radius)
  pi = 3.14
  area = pi * radius * radius
end
```

Obviously you can go one step further with this code, as shown in Listing 1-17.

Listing 1-17. circle-d.rb

```ruby
def area_of_a_circle(radius)
  pi = 3.14
  pi * radius * radius
end
```

`return` is sometimes useful to make a method easier to read. But you don't have to use it if you feel more comfortable with out.

Inheritance

A class can inherit from another class. When defining the class, the parent class must be added with a less-than (<) sign.

```
class Example < ParentClass
```

Rails makes use of this approach frequently (otherwise I would not be bothering you with it).

In Listing 1-18, you define the class Abc that contains the methods a, b, and c. Then you define a class Abcd and let it inherit the class Abc and add a new method d. The new instances example1 and example2 are created with the class method new and show that example2 has access to the methods a, b, c, and d but example1 only to a, b, and c.

Listing 1-18. inheritance-example-a.rb

```ruby
class Abc
  def a
    'a'
  end

  def b
    'b'
  end

  def c
    'c'
  end
end

class Abcd < Abc
  def d
    'd'
  end
end
```

Run it in `irb`.

```
$ irb
>> load './inheritance-example-a.rb'
=> true
>> example1 = Abc.new
=> #<Abc:0x007fac5a845630>
>> example2 = Abcd.new
=> #<Abcd:0x007fac5a836630>
>> example2.d
=> "d"
>> example2.a
=> "a"
>> example1.d
NoMethodError: undefined method `d' for #<Abc:0x007fac5a845630>
    from (irb):6
    from /Users/stefan/.rvm/rubies/ruby-2.5.0/bin/irb:11:in `<main>'
>> example1.a
=> "a"
>> exit
```

It is important to read the error messages. They tell you what happened and where to search for the problem. In this example, Ruby says that there is an `undefined method` for `#<Abc:0x007fac5a845630>`. With that information you know that the class Abc is missing the method that you were trying to use.

Class Methods and Instance Methods

There are two important kinds of methods: class methods and instance methods.

You now already know what a class is. An *instance* of such a class is created via the class method new. A class method can only be called in connection with the class (for example, the method new is a class method). An instance method is a method that works only with an instance. So, you cannot apply the method new to an instance.

Let's first try to call an instance method as a class method, as shown in Listing 1-19.

Listing 1-19. pi-a.rb

```
class Knowledge
  def pi
    3.14
  end
end
```

Run it in irb.

```
$ irb
>> load 'pi-a.rb'
=> true
>> Knowledge.pi
NoMethodError: undefined method `pi' for Knowledge:Class
    from (irb):2
    from /Users/stefan/.rvm/rubies/ruby-2.5.0/bin/irb:11:in `<main>'
>>
```

So, that does not work. Well, then let's create a new instance of the class and try again.

```
>> example = Knowledge.new
=> #<Knowledge:0x007fe620010938>
>> example.pi
=> 3.14
>> exit
```

Now you just need to find out how to define a class method. Hard-core Rails gurus would now whisk you away into the depths of the source code and pick out examples from ActiveRecord. I will spare you this and show an abstract example; see Listing 1-20.

Listing 1-20. pi-b.rb

```
class Knowledge
  def self.pi
    3.14
  end
end

$ irb
>> load './pi-b.rb'
=> true
>> Knowledge.pi
=> 3.14
>>
```

Here is the proof to the contrary:

```
>> example = Knowledge.new
=> #<Knowledge:0x007fa8da045198>
>> example.pi
NoMethodError: undefined method `pi' for #<Knowledge:0x007fa8da045198>
    from (irb):4
    from /Users/stefan/.rvm/rubies/ruby-2.5.0/bin/irb:11:in `<main>'
>> exit
```

There are different notations for defining class methods. The two most common ones are `self.xyz` and `class << self`.

```
# Variant 1
# with self.xyz
#
class Knowledge
  def self.pi
    3.14
  end
end
```

```ruby
# Variant 2
# with class << self
#
class Knowledge
  class << self
    def pi
      3.14
    end
  end
end
```

The result is always the same.

Of course, you can use the same method name for a class and an instance method. Obviously that doesn't make code easier to read. Listing 1-21 shows an example with pi as a class and an instance method.

Listing 1-21. pi-c.rb

```ruby
class Knowledge
  def pi
    3.14
  end

  def self.pi
    3.14159265359
  end
end
```

```
$ irb
>> load './pi-c.rb'
=> true
>> Knowledge.pi
=> 3.14159265359
>> example = Knowledge.new
=> #<Knowledge:0x007f8379846f30>
>> example.pi
=> 3.14
>> exit
```

List of All Instance Methods

You can read all the defined methods for a class with the method `instance_methods`. Try it with the class `Knowledge` (first you create it once again in `irb`), as shown in Listing 1-22.

Listing 1-22. pi-a.rb

```
class Knowledge
  def pi
    3.14
  end
end
```

```
$ irb
>> load './pi-a.rb'
=> true
>> Knowledge.instance_methods
=> [:pi, :instance_of?, :kind_of?, :is_a?, :tap, :public_send,
:remove_instance_variable, :singleton_method, :instance_variable_set,
:define_singleton_method, :method, :public_method, :extend, :to_enum,
:enum_for, :<=>, :===, :=~, :!~, :eql?, :respond_to?, :freeze,
:inspect, :object_id, :send, :display, :to_s, :nil?, :hash, :class,
:singleton_class, :clone, :dup, :itself, :taint, :tainted?, :untaint,
:untrust, :untrusted?, :trust, :frozen?, :methods, :singleton_methods,
:protected_methods, :private_methods, :public_methods,
:instance_variable_get, :instance_variables,
:instance_variable_defined?, :!, :==, :!=, :__send__, :equal?,
:instance_eval, :instance_exec, :__id__]
>>
```

But that is much more than you have defined! Why? It's because Ruby gives every new class a basic set of methods by default. If you want to list only the methods that you have defined, then you can do it like this:

```
>> Knowledge.instance_methods(false)
=> [:pi]
>> exit
```

Basic Classes

Many predefined classes are available in Ruby. For a newbie, probably the most important ones handle numbers and strings.

Strings

Let's experiment a little bit in `irb`. The method `.class` tells you which class you are dealing with.

```
$ irb
>> "First test"
=> "First test"
>> "First test".class
=> String
```

That was easy. As you can see, Ruby "automagically" creates an object of the class String. You can also do this by explicitly calling the method new.

```
>> String.new("Second test")
=> "Second test"
>> String.new("Second test").class
=> String
```

If you call `String.new` or `String.new()` without a parameter, this also creates an object of the class `String`. But it is an empty `String`.

```
>> String.new
=> ""
>> String.new.class
=> String
>> exit
```

Single and Double Quotations Marks

Strings can be defined either in single quotes or in double quotes.

There is a special feature for the double quotes: you can integrate expressions with the construct #{}. The result is then automatically inserted in the corresponding place in the string.

To show this, you have to jump ahead and use variables in the example.

```
$ irb
>> a = "blue"
=> "blue"
>> b = "Color: #{a}"
=> "Color: blue"
>> exit
```

If the result of the expression is not a string, Ruby tries to apply the method to_s to convert the value of the object into a string. Let's try that by integrating an Integer into a String.

```
$ irb
>> a = 1
=> 1
>> b = "A test: #{a}"
=> "A test: 1"
>> a.class
=> Integer
>> b.class
=> String
>> exit
```

ℹ️   If I mention *single* or *double quotation marks* in the context of strings, I do not mean typographically correct curly quotation marks (see `wikipedia.org/wiki/Quotation_mark`); instead, I mean the ASCII symbols referred to as *apostrophe* (') or *quotation mark* (").

Built-in Methods for String

Most classes already come with a bundle of useful methods. These methods are always written after the relevant object, separated by a dot.

Here are a few examples for methods of the class String:

```
$ irb
>> a = 'A dog'
=> "A dog"
>> a.class
=> String
>> a.size
=> 5
>> a.downcase
=> "a dog"
>> a.upcase
=> "A DOG"
>> a.reverse
=> "god A"
>> exit
```

With instance_methods(false), you can get a list of the built-in methods.

```
$ irb
>> String.instance_methods(false)
=> [:include?, :%, :*, :+, :to_c, :unicode_normalize, :unicode_normalize!,
:unicode_normalized?, :count, :partition, :unpack, :unpack1, :sum, :next,
:casecmp, :casecmp?, :insert, :bytesize, :match, :match?, :succ!, :+@,
:-@, :index, :rindex, :<=>, :replace, :clear, :upto, :getbyte, :==, :===,
:setbyte, :=~, :scrub, :[], :[]=, :chr, :scrub!, :dump, :byteslice,
:upcase, :next!, :empty?, :eql?, :downcase, :capitalize, :swapcase,
:upcase!, :downcase!, :capitalize!, :swapcase!, :hex, :oct, :split,
:lines, :reverse, :chars, :codepoints, :prepend, :bytes, :concat, :<<,
:freeze, :inspect, :intern, :end_with?, :crypt, :ljust, :reverse!, :chop,
:scan, :gsub, :ord, :start_with?, :length, :size, :rstrip, :succ, :center,
:sub, :chomp!, :sub!, :chomp, :rjust, :lstrip!, :gsub!, :chop!, :strip,
:to_str, :to_sym, :rstrip!, :tr, :tr_s, :delete, :to_s, :to_i, :tr_s!,
:delete!, :squeeze!, :each_line, :squeeze, :strip!, :each_codepoint,
:lstrip, :slice!, :rpartition, :each_byte, :each_char, :to_f, :slice,
:ascii_only?, :encoding, :force_encoding, :b, :valid_encoding?, :tr!,
:encode, :encode!, :hash, :to_r]
>> exit
```

Numbers

Let's discuss numbers.

Integers

Ruby used to have different types of integers depending on the length of the number. Since Ruby version 2.4, things are easier; you just deal with `Integer`.

```
$ irb
>> 23.class
=> Integer
>> 23000000000000000000.class
=> Integer
>> (23*10000).class
=> Integer
>> exit
```

Floats

`Float` is a class for real numbers ("floating-point numbers"). The decimal separator is a dot.

```
$ irb
>> a = 20.424
=> 20.424
>> a.class
=> Float
>> exit
```

Mixed Class Calculations

Adding two integers will result in an integer. Adding an integer and a float will result in a float.

```
$ irb
>> a = 10
=> 10
>> b = 23
```

```
=> 23
>> (a + b).class
=> Integer
>> (a + 3.13).class
=> Float
>> exit
```

Boolean Values and nil

For Boolean values (`true` and `false`) and for `nil` (no value), there are separate classes.

```
$ irb
>> true.class
=> TrueClass
>> false.class
=> FalseClass
>> nil.class
=> NilClass
>> exit
```

nil (no value) is, by the way, the contraction of the Latin word *nihil* (nothing); or if you look at it in terms of programming history, the term derives from "not in list" from the legacy of the programming language Lisp (the name is an acronym of "list processing").

Variables

Let's discuss variables.

Naming Conventions

Normal variables are written in lowercase. Please use snake_case. The same goes for symbols and methods.

```
$ irb
>> pi = 3.14
=> 3.14
>> exit
```

Constants

Constants start with an uppercase letter.

⚠️   A constant can also be overwritten with a new value since Ruby 2.3 (but you will get a warning message). So, please do not rely on the constancy of a constant.

```
$ irb
>> Pi = 3.14
=> 3.14
>> Pi = 123
(irb):2: warning: already initialized constant Pi
(irb):1: warning: previous definition of Pi was here
=> 123
>> puts Pi
123
=> nil
>> exit
```

You are on the safe side if you are using only ASCII symbols. But with Ruby 2.5 and the right encoding, you could also use special characters (for example, the German umlaut) more or less without any problems in a variable name. But if you want to be polite toward other programmers who probably do not have those characters directly available on their keyboards, it is better to stick to pure ASCII.

Scope of Variables

Variables have a different scope (or "reach") within the Ruby application and therefore also within a Ruby on Rails application.

! You need to keep this scope in mind while programming. Otherwise, you can end up with odd effects.

Local Variables (aaa or _aaa)

Local variables start with either a lowercase letter or an underscore (_). Their scope is limited to the current environment (for example, the current method). Listing 1-23 defines two methods that use the same local variable radius. Because they are local, they don't interact with each other.

Listing 1-23. variable-a.rb

```ruby
def area(radius)
  3.14 * radius * radius
end

def circumference(radius)
  2 * 3.14 * radius
end

$ irb
>> load './variable-a.rb'
=> true
>> area(10)
=> 314.0
>> circumference(1)
=> 6.28
>> exit
```

Global Variables ($aaa)

A global variable starts with a $ sign and is accessible in the entire program. Listing 1-24 shows an example program.

Listing 1-24. variable-b.rb

```
$value = 10

def example
  $value = 20
end

puts $value
example
puts $value
$ ruby variable-b.rb
10
20
```

Global variables are used rarely! You wouldn't harm yourself by forgetting that they exist right now.

Instance Variables (@aaa)

Instance variables ("attributes," which is why there's an @ sign) apply only within a class, but they apply *everywhere* in it—they're mini versions of global variables, so to speak. Unlike global variables, you will find instance variables all over the place in a Rails application. Let's tackle them in form of an example program with the name color.rb, as shown in Listing 1-25.

Listing 1-25. color.rb

```
class Wall
  def initialize
    @color = 'white'
  end
```

```ruby
  def color
    @color
  end

  def paint_it(value)
    @color = value
  end
end

my_wall = Wall.new
puts my_wall.color

my_wall.paint_it('red')
puts my_wall.color
```

If you start this program, you will see the following output:

```
$ ruby color.rb
white
red
$
```

In the method `initialize`, you set the instance variable `@color` to the value `white`. The method `paint_it(value)` changes this instance variable.

With the method `color` you can access the value of `@color` outside of the instance. This kind of method is called a *setter* method.

Methods Once Again

To keep the amount of chicken-and-egg problems in this chapter at a manageable level, you need to go back to the topic of methods and combine what you have learned so far.

Method Chaining

You may not think of it straightaway, but once you have gotten used to working with Ruby, then it makes perfect sense (and is perfectly logical) to chain different methods.

```
$ irb
>> a = 'a blue car'
=> "a blue car"
>> a.upcase
=> "A BLUE CAR"
>> a.upcase.reverse
=> "RAC EULB A"
>> exit
```

Getters and Setters

As instance variables (attributes) exist only within the relevant instance, you always need to write a "getter" method for exporting such a variable. If you define a class Room that has the instance variables @doors and @windows (for the number of doors and windows in the room), then you can create the getter methods doors and windows. Listing 1-26 shows an example program called room.rb.

Listing 1-26. room.rb

```ruby
class Room
  def initialize
    @doors   = 1
    @windows = 1
  end

  def doors
    @doors
  end
end
```

```
  def windows
    @windows
  end
end

kitchen = Room.new

puts "D: #{kitchen.doors}"
puts "W: #{kitchen.windows}"
```

Here is the output from the execution of the program:

```
$ ruby room.rb
D: 1
W: 1
$
```

Because this scenario—wanting to simply return a value in identical form—is so common, there is already a ready-made getter method for it with the name `attr_reader`, which you would apply as follows in the program `room.rb`, as shown in Listing 1-27.

Listing 1-27. room.rb

```
class Room
  def initialize
    @doors   = 1
    @windows = 1
  end

  attr_reader :doors, :windows
end

kitchen = Room.new

puts "D: #{kitchen.doors}"
puts "W: #{kitchen.windows}"
```

`attr_reader` is a method called on the Room class. That is the reason why you use symbols (e.g., `:doors` and `:windows`) instead of variables (e.g., @doors and @windows) as parameters.

> ℹ️ `attr_reader` is a good example for metaprogramming in Ruby. When working with Rails, you will frequently come across metaprogramming and be grateful for how it works "automagically."

If you want to change the number of doors or windows from the outside, you need a setter method. It can be implemented as shown in Listing 1-28.

Listing 1-28. room.rb

```ruby
class Room
  def initialize
    @doors   = 1
    @windows = 1
  end

  attr_reader :doors, :windows

  def doors=(value)
    @doors = value
  end

  def windows=(value)
    @windows = value
  end
end

kitchen = Room.new

kitchen.windows = 2

puts "D: #{kitchen.doors}"
puts "W: #{kitchen.windows}"
```

The corresponding output is as follows:

```
$ **ruby room.rb**
D: 1
W: 2
$
```

As you can probably imagine, there is also a ready-made and easier way of doing this. Via the setter method `attr_writer`, you can simplify the code of `room.rb` as shown in Listing 1-29.

Listing 1-29. room.rb

```ruby
class Room
  def initialize
    @doors   = 1
    @windows = 1
  end

  attr_reader :doors, :windows
  attr_writer :doors, :windows
end

kitchen = Room.new

kitchen.windows = 2

puts "D: #{kitchen.doors}"
puts "W: #{kitchen.windows}"
```

And (who would have thought?) there is even a method `attr_accessor` that combines getters and setters. The code for `room.rb` would then look like Listing 1-30.

Listing 1-30. room.rb

```ruby
class Room
  def initialize
    @doors   = 1
    @windows = 1
  end
```

```
    attr_accessor :doors, :windows
end

kitchen = Room.new

kitchen.windows = 2

puts "D: #{kitchen.doors}"
puts "W: #{kitchen.windows}"
```

Converting from One to the Other: Casting

There is a whole range of useful instance methods for converting (*casting*) objects from one class to another. First, let's use the method .to_s to convert a Fixnum to a String.

```
$ irb
>> a = 10
=> 10
>> a.class
=> Integer
>> b = a.to_s
=> "10"
>> b.class
=> String
>> exit
```

> ℹ Incidentally, that is exactly what puts does if you use puts to output a Fixnum or a Float (for nonstrings, it simply implicitly adds the method .to_s and outputs the result).

Now you use the method `.to_i` to change a `Float` to a `Fixnum`.

```
irb
>> c = 10.0
=> 10.0
>> c.class
=> Float
>> d = c.to_i
=> 10
>> d.class
=> Integer
>> exit
```

Method `to_s` for Your Own Classes

Integrating a `to_s` method is often useful. Then you can simply output a corresponding object via `puts` (`puts` automatically outputs an object via the method `to_s`).

Listing 1-31 shows an example.

Listing 1-31. person-a.rb

```ruby
class Person
  def initialize(first_name, last_name)
    @first_name = first_name
    @last_name = last_name
  end

  def to_s
    "#{@first_name} #{@last_name}"
  end
end

$ irb
>> load './person-a.rb'
=> true
>> sw = Person.new('Stefan', 'Wintermeyer')
=> #<Person:0x007fa95d030558 @first_name="Stefan",
   @last_name="Wintermeyer">
```

```
>> puts sw
Stefan Wintermeyer
=> nil
>> exit
```

Is + a Method?

Why is there also a plus symbol in the list of methods for String? Let's find out by looking it up in ri.

```
$ ri -T String.+
String.+

(from ruby site)
------------------------------------------------------------------------------
  str + other_str    -> new_str

------------------------------------------------------------------------------


Concatenation---Returns a new String containing other_str
concatenated to str.

  "Hello from " + self.to_s    #=> "Hello from main"
```

Let's see what it says for Integer.

```
$ ri -T Integer.+
Integer.+

(from ruby site)
------------------------------------------------------------------------------
  int + numeric  ->  numeric_result

------------------------------------------------------------------------------


Performs addition: the class of the resulting object depends on the class of
numeric and on the magnitude of the result. It may return a Bignum.
```

Let's play around with this in `irb`. You should be able to add the + to an object, just as any other method, separated by a dot and then add the second number in brackets as a parameter.

```
$ irb
>> 10 + 10
=> 20
>> 10+10
=> 20
>> 10.+10
=> 20
>> 10.+(10)
=> 20
>> exit
```

Aha! The plus symbol is indeed a method, and this method takes the next value as a parameter. Really, you should put this value in brackets, but thanks to Ruby's well-thought-out syntax, this is not necessary.

Can You Overwrite the Method +?

Yes, you can overwrite any method. Logically, this does not make much sense for methods such as +, unless you want to drive your fellow programmers mad. I am going to show you a little demo in `irb` so you will believe me.

The aim is overwriting the method + for `Fixnum`. You want the result of every addition to be the number 42. You can write a so-called monkey patch, as shown in Listing 1-32.

Listing 1-32. monkey-patch-a.rb

```
class Integer
  def +(name, *args, &blk)
    42
  end
end
```

Now you use the + method before and after that monkey patch.

```
irb
>> 10 + 10
=> 20
>> load './monkey-patch-a.rb'
=> true
>> 10 + 10
=> 42
>> exit
```

First you perform a normal addition. Then you redefine the method + for the class Integer, and after that you do the calculation again. But this time, you get different results.

if Condition

An abstract if condition looks like this:

```
if expression
  program
end
```

The program between the expression and end is executed if the result of the expression is not false and not nil.

    You can also use a then after the expression, as shown here:

```
if expression then
  program
end
```

The construct for a simple `if` branch in a Ruby program looks like the following example program:

```
a = 10

if a == 10
  puts 'a is 10'
end
```

 The `==` is used to compare two values. Please don't mix it up with the single `=`.

You can test an *expression* really well in `irb`.

```
$ irb
>> a = 10
=> 10
>> a == 10
=> true
>> exit
$
```

Shorthand

The following code shows a frequently used shorthand notation of an `if` condition:

```
a = 10

# long version
#
if a == 10
  puts 'a is 10'
end

# short version
#
puts 'a is 10' if a == 10
```

else

You can probably imagine how this works, but for the sake of completeness, here is a little example:

```
a = 10

if a == 10
  puts 'a is 10'
else
  puts 'a is not 10'
end
```

elsif

Again, most programmers will know what this is all about. Here's an example:

```
a = 10

if a == 10
  puts 'a is 10'
elsif a == 20
  puts 'a is 20'
end
```

Loops

There are different ways of implementing loops in Ruby. The iterator variation is used particularly often in the Rails environment.

while and until

An abstract while loop looks like this:

```
while expression do
  program
end
```

The do that follows `expression` is optional. Often you will also see this:

```
while expression
  program
end
```

Here is an `irb` example:

```
$ irb
>> i = 0
=> 0
>> while i < 3 do
?>   puts i
>>   i = i + 1
>> end
0
1
2
=> nil
>> exit
```

You build until loops similarly.

```
until expression
  program
ends
```

Again, here is the corresponding `irb` example:

```
$ irb
>> i = 5
=> 5
>> until i == 0
>>   i = i - 1
>>   puts i
>> end
4
```

```
3
2
1
0
=> nil
>> exit
```

Blocks and Iterators

Block and *iterator* are some of the favorite words of many Ruby programmers. Now I am going to show you why.

In the following loop, i is the iterator, and puts i is the block.

```
5.times { |i| puts i }
```

You can also express the whole thing in the following syntax:

```
5.times do |i|
  puts i
end
```

Iterators

Iterators are just a specific type of method. As you probably know, the word *iterate* means to repeat something. For example, the class Integer has the iterator times(). Let's see what help ri Integer.times offers:

```
$ ri -T Integer.times
Integer.times

(from ruby site)
------------------------------------------------------------------------
  int.times {|i| block }  ->  self
  int.times               ->  an_enumerator

------------------------------------------------------------------------

Iterates the given block int times, passing in values from zero to int - 1.
```

If no block is given, an Enumerator is returned instead.

```
5.times do |i|
  print i, " "
end
#=> 0 1 2 3 4
```

It also gives a nice example that you can try in irb.

```
$ irb
>> 5.times do |i|
?>   puts i
>> end
0
1
2
3
4
=> 5
>> exit
```

There is also a single-line notation for small blocks.

```
$ irb
>> 5.times { |i| puts i }
0
1
2
3
4
=> 5
>> exit
```

By the way, an iterator does not necessarily have to pass a variable to the block.

```
$ irb
>> 5.times { puts 'example' }
example
example
```

```
example
example
example
=> 5
>> exit
```

Blocks

A block is the code that is triggered by an iterator. In the block, you have access to the local variable (or variables) passed by the iterator.

Method upto

In addition to `times`, there is also the method `upto` for easily implementing a loop. `ri` offers a nice example for this, too.

```
$ ri -T Integer.upto
Integer.upto

(from ruby site)
-----------------------------------------------------------------------
  int.upto(limit) {|i| block }  ->  self
  int.upto(limit)               ->  an_enumerator

-----------------------------------------------------------------------

Iterates the given block, passing in integer values from int up to and
including limit.

If no block is given, an Enumerator is returned instead.

For example:

  5.upto(10) { |i| print i, " " }
  #=> 5 6 7 8 9 10
```

Arrays and Hashes

As in many programming languages, *arrays* and *hashes* are popular structures in Ruby for storing data.

Arrays

An array is a list of objects. Let's play around in `irb`.

```
$ irb
>> a = [1,2,3,4,5]
=> [1, 2, 3, 4, 5]
>> a.class
=> Array
>> exit
```

That is simple and easy to understand.

Let's see if it also works with strings in the array.

```
$ irb
>> a = ['Test', 'Banana', 'blue']
=> ["Test", "Banana", "blue"]
>> a.class
=> Array
>> a[1]
=> "Banana"
>> a[1].class
=> String
>> exit
```

That also works.

So, all that's missing now is an array with a mixture of both. Obviously that will work, too, because the array stores objects, and it does not matter which kind of objects they are (i.e., `String`, `Integer`, `Float`, …). But a little test can't hurt.

```
$ irb
>> a = [1, 2.2, 'House', nil]
=> [1, 2.2, "House", nil]
```

```
>> a.class
=> Array
>> a[0]
=> 1
>> a[0].class
=> Integer
>> a[1].class
=> Float
>> a[2].class
=> String
>> a[3].class
=> NilClass
>> exit
```

Arrays can also be created via the method new (like any class). Individual new elements can then be added at the end of an array via the method <<. Here is the corresponding example:

```
$ irb
>> a = Array.new
=> []
>> a << 'first item'
=> ["first item"]
>> a << 'second item'
=> ["first item", "second item"]
>> exit
```

Iterator each

You can work your way through an array piece by piece via the method each. Here's an example:

```
$ irb
>> cart = ['eggs', 'butter']
=> ["eggs", "butter"]
>> cart.each do |item|
?>   puts item
>> end
```

```
eggs
butter
=> ["eggs", "butter"]
>> exit
```

   ri Array.each provides help and an example in case you forget how to use each.

Hashes

A *hash* is a list of *key-value pairs*. Here is an example with strings as keys:

```
$ irb
>> prices = { 'egg' => 0.1, 'butter' => 0.99 }
=> {"egg"=>0.1, "butter"=>0.99}
>> prices['egg']
=> 0.1
>> prices.count
=> 2
>> exit
```

   Of course, hashes can store not just strings as objects in the values but, as with arrays, also classes that you define yourself (see the section "Arrays").

Symbols

Symbols are a strange concept and difficult to explain. But they are useful and used frequently with hashes, among others.

   Normally, variables always create new objects.

```
$ irb
>> a = 'Example 1'
=> "Example 1"
>> a.object_id
=> 70124141350360
>> a = 'Example 2'
=> "Example 2"
>> a.object_id
=> 70124141316700
>> exit
```

In both cases, you have the variable a, but object_id is different. You could carry on in this way indefinitely. Each time, it would generate a different object ID and therefore a new object. In principle, this is no big deal and entirely logical in terms of object orientation. But it is also rather a waste of memory space.

A symbol is defined by a colon before the name and cannot store any values itself, but it always has the same object ID, so it is very well suited to be a *key*.

```
$ irb
>> :a.class
=> Symbol
>> :a.object_id
=> 702428
>> exit
```

Let's do another little experiment to make the difference clearer. Use a string object with the content white three times in a row and then the symbol :white three times in a row. For white, a new object is created each time. For the symbol :white, it's created only the first time.

```
$ irb
>> 'white'.object_id
=> 70342874305700
>> 'white'.object_id
=> 70342874300640
>> 'white'.object_id
=> 70342874271720
>> :white.object_id
=> 1088668
>> :white.object_id
=> 1088668
>> :white.object_id
=> 1088668
>> exit
```

Using symbols as key for hashes is much more memory efficient.

```
$ irb
>> colors = { black: '#000000', white: '#FFFFFF' }
=> {:black=>"#000000", :white=>"#FFFFFF"}
>> puts colors[:white]
#FFFFFF
=> nil
>> exit
```

You will frequently see symbols in Rails. If you want to find out more about symbols, go to the help page about the class Symbol via ri Symbol.

Iterator each

With the method each you can work your way through a Hash step-by-step. Here's an example:

```
$ irb
>> colors = {black: '#000000', white: '#FFFFFF' }
=> {:black=>"#000000", :white=>"#FFFFFF"}
>> colors.each do |key, value|
?>   puts "#{key} #{value}"
>> end
black #000000
white #FFFFFF
=> {:black=>"#000000", :white=>"#FFFFFF"}
>> exit
```

Again, ri Hash.each offers help and an example in case you cannot remember one day how to use each.

Range

The class Range represents an interval. The starting and ending points of the interval are defined enclosed in normal brackets and separated by two dots in between them. Here is an example in which you use a range like an iterator with each:

```
$ irb
>> (0..3)
=> 0..3
>> (0..3).class
=> Range
>> (0..3).each do |i|
?>   puts i
>> end
0
1
2
3
=> 0..3
>>
```

Via the method to_a, you can generate an array from a range.

```
>> (0..3).to_a
=> [0, 1, 2, 3]
>>
```

A range can be generated from objects of any type. It's only important that the objects can be compared via <, >, == and can use the method succ for counting on to the next value. So, you can also use Range to represent letters.

```
>> ('a'..'h').to_a
=> ["a", "b", "c", "d", "e", "f", "g", "h"]
>>
```

As alternative notation, you may sometimes come across Range.new(). In this case, the starting and ending points are not separated by two dots but by a comma. This is what it looks like:

```
>> (0..3) == Range.new(0,3)
=> true
>> exit
```

CHAPTER 2

First Steps with Rails

Now that you have painstakingly read your way through the basics of Ruby in Chapter 1, you can move on to a more exciting topic. In this chapter, you will create your first small Ruby on Rails project.

Environment (Development)

By default a Rails project offers three environments to work in.

- Development

- Test

- Production

In this chapter, you will be working only with the Development environment. Once you have gained a better feeling for Rails, you will start using tests, and then you will need the corresponding environment (where, for example, the test database is populated when you start a test and then cleared). Later, I will explain the various scenarios to show how you can roll out your Rails application from the Development environment to the Production environment.

The Development environment has everything you need for developing, besides an editor and a web browser. You do not need to install a special web server but can use the integrated Rails web server. It does not have extremely high performance, but you do not need that for developing. Later, you can switch to big web servers like Apache or Nginx. The same applies to the database.

© Stefan Wintermeyer 2018
S. Wintermeyer, *Learn Rails 5.2*, https://doi.org/10.1007/978-1-4842-3489-1_2

SQLite3 Database

In terms of the database, the main focus in this chapter is once more not on optimum performance but on showing you a simple and quick way of getting started. That's why Rails uses the SQLite3 database. You already have everything you need installed, and you don't need to worry about anything. Later I will explain how you can use other databases (e.g., PostgreSQL).

Why Is It All in English?

If you are not a native English speaker, you should try to accept and even adopt Rails' love for the English language. Much of it will then be much easier and more logical. Most of the code reads just like a normal English sentence. For example, many mechanisms "automagically" use plural or singular forms of normal English words. If you get used to naming database fields and tables with English terms (even if you are programming in a different language), then you can make use of the whole power of this magic. This mechanism is referred to as `Inflector` or *inflections*.

If you are programming in a language other than English, it still makes sense to use English names for variables, classes, and methods. You can write the comments in your own language, but if you take part in international projects, you should obviously write the comments in English as well.

Static Content (HTML and Graphics Files)

Let's first create a new Rails project.

Create a Rails Project

Before you even get going, please check that you are using Rails 5.2.

```
$ rails -v
Rails 5.2.0
```

That's looking good. If you have an older version of Ruby or Rails installed, please install the 5.2 version before you read any further. The command gem install rails installs the current Rails version, and gem install rails --pre installs the beta of the next version.

Now you start by creating a new Rails project with the name testproject. Ruby on Rails is a framework, so you first need to set up the corresponding directory structure and basic configuration, including several scripts. It's as easy as pie; just use the command rails new testproject to create everything you need.

```
$ rails new testproject
    create
    create  README.md
    create  Rakefile
    create  .ruby-version
    create  config.ru
    [...]
```

Next, you cd into the new directory and run the first migration to create Active Storage tables.

```
$ cd testproject
$ rails db:migrate
```

> ℹ️ You don't need to run rails db:migrate, which runs open database migrations at this time, but it is a good habit to make sure all database migrations are done.

You can check whether the new Rails application is working by launching the integrated web server.

> 💡 Depending on the operating system (for example, macOS) and on your firewall settings, you may see a pop-up window when first starting a Rails application asking you if the firewall should permit the corresponding connection.

```
$ rails server
=> Booting Puma
=> Rails 5.2.0 application starting in development
=> Run `rails server -h` for more startup options
Puma starting in single mode...
* Version 3.11.0 (ruby 2.5.0-p0), codename: Love Song
* Min threads: 5, max threads: 5
* Environment: development
* Listening on tcp://0.0.0.0:3000
Use Ctrl-C to stop
```

The start of the Rails application is looking good, so go to the URL
http://localhost:3000 in your web browser (see Figure 2-1).

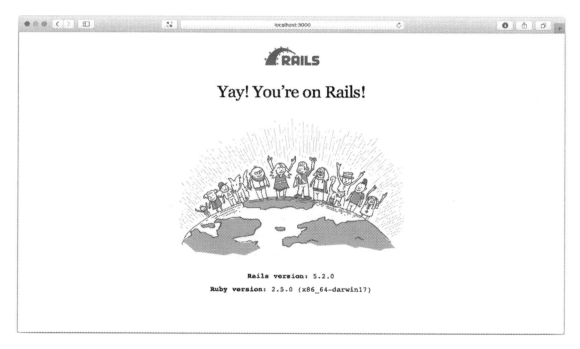

Figure 2-1. *Rails*

Looks good. Rails works fine.

 You can stop the web server with the key combination Ctrl+C.

54

Static Pages

There are certain static pages, images, and JavaScript files that are automatically delivered by Rails. Remember the following part of the output of the command `rails new testproject`?

```
[...]
create  public
create  public/404.html
create  public/422.html
create  public/500.html
create  public/apple-touch-icon-precomposed.png
create  public/apple-touch-icon.png
create  public/favicon.ico
create  public/robots.txt
[...]
```

The directory name `public` and the files it contains already look very much like static pages. Let's create the file `public/hello-world.html` with the content shown in Listing 2-1.

Listing 2-1. public/hello-world.html

```
<html>
<head>
  <title>Hello World!</title>
</head>
<body>
  <h1>Hello World!</h1>
  <p>An example page.</p>
</body>
</html>
```

Now start the Rails web server with `rails server`.

```
$ rails server
=> Booting Puma
=> Rails 5.2.0 application starting in development on http://localhost:3000
=> Run `rails server -h` for more startup options
```

```
Puma starting in single mode...
* Version 3.11.0 (ruby 2.5.0-p0), codename: Love Song
* Min threads: 5, max threads: 5
* Environment: development
* Listening on tcp://0.0.0.0:3000
Use Ctrl-C to stop
```

You can take a look at this web page at the URL http://localhost:3000/hello-world (see Figure 2-2).

Figure 2-2. *Hello!*

No output in the log means that this page was not handled by the Rails framework. It was delivered directly from the web server, which is Puma in this case.

ℹ   You can of course also use the URL http://localhost:3000/hello-world.html. But Rails regards HTML and therefore the file ending .html as standard output format, so you can omit the .html extension here.

Now you know how you can integrate fully static pages in Rails. This is useful for pages that never change and that you want to work even if Rails is not currently working, for example because of an update. In a production environment, you would usually put a classic web server such as Apache or Nginx in front of the Rails server, which is capable of autonomously delivering static files from the `public` directory.

Creating HTML Dynamically with erb

The content of an `erb` file will probably seem familiar to you. It is a mixture of HTML and Ruby code (`erb` stands for "embedded Ruby"). `erb` pages are rendered as views. This is the first time for you to get in touch with the MVC model. You need a controller to use a view, and that can be created via the generator `rails generate controller`. Let's take a look at the onboard help of this generator, shown here:

```
$ rails generate controller
Running via Spring preloader in process 11125
Usage:
  rails generate controller NAME [action action] [options]
[...]

Description:
    Stubs out a new controller and its views. Pass the controller name, either
    CamelCased or under_scored, and a list of views as arguments.
[...]

Example:
    `rails generate controller CreditCards open debit credit close`

    CreditCards controller with URLs like /credit_cards/debit.
        Controller: app/controllers/credit_cards_controller.rb
        Test:       test/controllers/credit_cards_controller_test.rb
        Views:      app/views/credit_cards/debit.html.erb [...]
        Helper:     app/helpers/credit_cards_helper.rb
```

Nice! You are kindly provided with an example further down:

```
rails generate controller CreditCard open debit credit close
```

This doesn't really fit the bill for this case, but I am feeling brave and suggest that you simply try rails generate controller Example test.

```
$ rails generate controller Example test
Running via Spring preloader in process 35388
      create  app/controllers/example_controller.rb
       route  get 'example/test'
      invoke  erb
      create    app/views/example
      create    app/views/example/test.html.erb
      invoke  test_unit
      create    test/controllers/example_controller_test.rb
      invoke  helper
      create    app/helpers/example_helper.rb
      invoke    test_unit
      invoke  assets
      invoke    coffee
      create      app/assets/javascripts/example.coffee
      invoke    scss
      create      app/assets/stylesheets/example.scss
```

Phew...that's a lot of stuff being created. Among others, the file app/views/example/test.html.erb is created. Let's take a closer look at it; see Listing 2-2.

Listing 2-2. app/views/example/test.html.erb

```
<h1>Example#test</h1>
<p>Find me in app/views/example/test.html.erb</p>
```

It's HTML, but for it to be a valid HTML page, something is "missing" at the top and bottom. The missing part can be found in the file app/views/layouts/application. html.erb. You are going to take a look into it later in the chapter.

Please launch the web server to test it.

```
$ rails server
```

Take a look at the web page in the browser at the URL http://localhost:3000/example/test.

In the log file log/development.log, you will find the following lines:

```
Started GET "/example/test" for 127.0.0.1 at 2018-01-17 16:59:41 +0100
   (0.1ms)  SELECT "schema_migrations"."version" FROM "schema_migrations"
ORDER BY "schema_migrations"."version" ASC
Processing by ExampleController#test as HTML
  Rendering example/test.html.erb within layouts/application
  Rendered example/test.html.erb within layouts/application (0.8ms)
Completed 200 OK in 833ms (Views: 823.0ms | ActiveRecord: 0.0ms)
```

This is an HTTP GET request for the URI /example/test. This was then apparently rendered as HTML by the controller ExampleController using the method test.

Now you just need to find the controller. It's a good thing you bought this book. All controllers are in the directory app/controllers, and there you go, you indeed find the corresponding file app/controllers/example_controller.rb.

```
$ tree app/controllers
app/controllers
├── application_controller.rb
├── concerns
└── example_controller.rb
```

Please open the file app/controllers/example_controller.rb with your favorite editor, as shown in Listing 2-3.

Listing 2-3. app/controllers/example_controller.rb

```
class ExampleController < ApplicationController
  def test
  end
end
```

That is very clear. The controller ExampleController is a descendant of the controller ApplicationController and contains currently just one method with the name test. This method has no program logic (it's empty).

You will probably ask yourself how Rails knows that for the URL path /example/test it should process the controller ExampleController and the method test. This is not determined by some magical logic but by a *routing* configuration. All routings can be listed with the command `rails routes`.

```
$ rails routes
      Prefix Verb URI Pattern               Controller#Action
example_test GET  /example/test(.:format) example#test
```

These routes are configured in the file `config/routes.rb`, which has been autofilled by the controller generator with a route to `example/test`. The line that is important is the second one, as shown in Listing 2-4.

Listing 2-4. config/routes.rb

```
Rails.application.routes.draw do
  get 'example/test'

  # For details on the DSL available within this file, see
  # http://guides.rubyonrails.org/routing.html
end
```

Later in the book you are going to dive more into routes.

!   A static file in the directory `public` always has higher priority than a route in `config/routes.rb`! So, if you were to save a static file in `public/example/test`, that file would be delivered.

Programming in an erb File

erb pages can contain Ruby code. You can use `erb` to program and give these pages dynamic content.

Let's start with something simple: adding 1 and 1. First try the following code in `irb`:

```
$ irb
>> 1 + 1
=> 2
>> exit
```

That was easy.

> **!** If you want to output the result of Ruby code in erb, enclose the code within `<%= ... %>`.

Fill the erb file `app/views/example/test.html.erb` as shown in Listing 2-5.

Listing 2-5. app/views/example/test.html.erb

```
<h1>First experiment with erb</h1>
<p>Addition:
  <%= 1 + 1 %>
</p>
```

Then use `rails server` to launch the web server.

```
$ rails server
```

Visit that page with the URL `http://localhost:3000/example/test`, as shown in Figure 2-3.

Figure 2-3. *Experimenting with erb*

You may ask yourself, how can the result of adding two Integers be displayed as a String? Let's first look up in irb if it really is an Integer.

```
$ irb
>> 1.class
=> Integer
>> (1 + 1).class
=> Integer
```

Yes, both the number 1 and the result of 1 + 1 is an Integer. What happened? Rails is intelligent enough to automatically call all objects in a view (that is, the file test.html.erb) that aren't already strings via the method .to_s, which always converts the content of the object to a string. Let's take a brief trip to irb.

```
>> (1 + 1).to_s
=> "2"
>> (1 + 1).to_s.class
=> String
>> exit
```

You are now going to learn the finer points of erb step-by-step. Don't worry, it's neither magic nor rocket science.

<% ... %> vs. <%= ... %>

In the .html.erb file, there are two kinds of Ruby code instructions in addition to the HTML elements.

- <% ... %>: Executes the Ruby code it contains but does not output anything (unless you explicitly use something like print or puts in special ways).

- <%= ... %>: Executes the Ruby code it contains and outputs the result as a String. If it's not a String, the method to_s will be called.

❗   The output of <%= ... %> is automatically escaped. So, you don't need to worry about "dangerous" HTML.

Let's use an example to make sure it all makes sense. You use each to iterate through the range (0..5). Edit app/views/example/test.html.erb as shown in Listing 2-6.

Listing 2-6. app/views/example/test.html.erb

```
<p>Loop from 0 to 5:
<% (0..5).each do |i| %>
  <%= "#{i}, " %>
<% end %>
</p>
```

Open this view in the browser (see Figure 2-4).

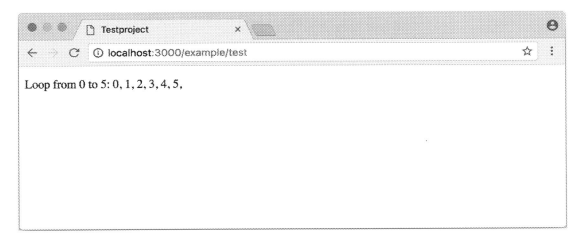

Figure 2-4. *Iterating through a range*

Let's now take a look at the HTML source code in the browser.

```
<!DOCTYPE html>
<html>
  <head>
    <title>Testproject</title>
[...]
  </head>

  <body>
```

```
    <p>Loop from 0 to 5:
  0,
  1,
  2,
  3,
  4,
  5,
</p>

  </body>
</html>
```

Now you understand how Ruby code is used in the view.

Q & A

1. *I don't understand anything. I can't cope with the Ruby code. Could you please explain it again?*

   Is it possible that you have not completely worked your way through Chapter 1? Please do take your time with it and have another thorough look. Otherwise, the rest won't make any sense here.

2. *I can understand the Ruby code and the HTML output. But I don't get why some HTML code was rendered around it if I didn't even write that HTML code. Where does it come from, and can I influence it?*

   Excellent question! I will get to that in the next section.

Layouts

The erb file in the directory app/views/example/ only forms the core of the later HTML page. By default, an automatically generated app/views/layouts/application.html.erb is always rendered around it. Take a closer look at it in Listing 2-7.

Listing 2-7. app/views/layouts/application.html.erb

```
<!DOCTYPE html>
<html>
  <head>
    <title>Testproject</title>
    <%= csrf_meta_tags %>

    <%= stylesheet_link_tag    'application', media: 'all', 'data-
    turbolinks-track': 'reload' %>
    <%= javascript_include_tag 'application', 'data-turbolinks-track':
    'reload' %>
  </head>

  <body>
    <%= yield %>
  </body>
</html>
```

The interesting bit is the following line:

```
<%= yield %>
```

With `<%= yield %>`, the view file is included here. The lines with the stylesheets, the JavaScript, and `csrf_meta_tags` can stay as they are for now. You'll take a look into that in the asset pipeline in Chapter 13. There's no need to bother with that right now.

The file `app/views/layouts/application.html.erb` enables you to determine the basic layout for the entire Rails application. If you want to enter a `<hr>` for each page and above it some header text, then you can do this between `<%= yield %>` and the `<body>` tag, as shown in Listing 2-8.

Listing 2-8. app/views/layouts/application.html.erb

```
<!DOCTYPE html>
<html>
  <head>
    <title>Testproject</title>
    <%= csrf_meta_tags %>
```

```
  <%= stylesheet_link_tag    'application', media: 'all', 'data-
  turbolinks-track': 'reload' %>
  <%= javascript_include_tag 'application', 'data-turbolinks-track': 'reload' %>
</head>

<body>
  <h1>My Header</h1>
  <hr>
  <%= yield %>
</body>
</html>
```

You can also create other layouts in the directory app/views/layouts/ and apply these layouts depending on the relevant situation. But let's leave it for now. The important thing is that you understand the basic concept.

Passing Instance Variables from a Controller to a View

One of the cardinal sins in the MVC model is to put too much program logic into the view. That's more or less what used to be done frequently in PHP programming. I'm guilty of having done it myself. But one of the aims of MVC is that any HTML designer can create a view without having to worry about the programming. Yeah, yeah…if only it were always that easy. But let's just play it through in our minds. If I have a value in the controller that I want to display in the view, then I need a mechanism for this. This is referred to as an *instance variable* and always starts with @. If you are not 100 percent sure which variable has which *scope,* then please take another quick look at "Scope of Variables" in Chapter 1.

In the following example, you insert an instance variable for the current time that you get by Time.now in the controller and then insert it in the view. You're taking programming intelligence from the view to the controller.

The controller file app/controllers/example_controller.rb looks like Listing 2-9.

Listing 2-9. app/controllers/example_controller.rb

```ruby
class ExampleController < ApplicationController
  def test
    @current_time = Time.now
  end
end
```

In the view file `app/views/example/test.html.erb`, you can then access this instance variable, as shown in Listing 2-10.

Listing 2-10. app/views/example/test.html.erb

```erb
<p>
The current time is
<%= @current_time %>
</p>
```

With the controller and the view, you now have a clear separation of programming logic and presentation logic. Now you can automatically adjust the time in the controller in accordance with the user's time zone, without the designer of the page having to worry about it. As always, the method `to_s` is automatically applied in the view.

I am well aware that no one will now jump up from their chair and shout, "Thank you for enlightening me! From now on, I will only program neatly in accordance with MVC." The previous example is just the first small step in the right direction and shows how you can easily get values from the controller to the view with instance variables.

Partials

Even with small web projects, there are often elements that appear repeatedly, for example, a footer on the page with contact info or a menu. Rails gives you the option of encapsulating this HTML code in the form of partials and then integrating it within a view. A partial is also stored in the directory structure under `app/views/`. But its file name must start with an underscore (_).

As an example, you now add a mini footer to your page in a separate partial. Copy the content shown in Listing 2-11 into the new file `app/views/example/_footer.html.erb`.

Listing 2-11. app/views/example/_footer.html.erb

```
<hr>
<p>
  Copyright 2009 - <%= Date.today.year %> the Easter Bunny.
</p>
```

> 🛈　　Yes, this is not the MVC way of doing it right. `Date.today.year` should be defined in the controller. I'm glad that you caught this mistake.

You can edit the file `app/views/example/test.html.erb` as shown in Listing 2-12 and insert the partial via the command render.

Listing 2-12. app/views/example/test.html.erb

```
<p>Loop from 0 to 5:
<% (0..5).each do |i| %>
  <%= "#{i}, " %>
<% end %>
</p>

<%= render "footer" %>
```

So, now you have the following files in the directory `app/views/example`:

```
$ tree app/views/example/
app/views/example/
├── _footer.html.erb
└── test.html.erb
```

The new web page now looks like Figure 2-5.

Figure 2-5. *Web page*

!   The name of a partial in the code is always specified *without* the preceding underscore (_) and *without* the file extensions `.erb` and `.html`. But the actual file must have the underscore at the beginning of the file name and end with the file extensions `.erb` and `.html`.

Partials can also be integrated from other areas of the subdirectory `app/views`. For example, you can create a directory `app/views/shared` for recurring and shared content and create a file `_footer.html.erb` in this directory. You would then integrate this file into the erb code via the following line:

```
<%= render "shared/footer" %>
```

Passing Variables to a Partial

Partials are great in the sense of the Don't Repeat Yourself (DRY) concept. But what makes them really useful is the option of passing variables. Let's stick with the copyright example. If you want to pass the start year as a value, you can integrate this by adding the code in Listing 2-13 in the file `app/views/example/_footer.html.erb`.

Listing 2-13. app/views/example/_footer.html.erb

```
<hr>
<p>
Copyright <%= start_year %> - <%= Date.today.year %> the Easter Bunny.
</p>
```

So, let's change the file app/views/example/test.html.erb as shown in Listing 2-14.

Listing 2-14. app/views/example/test.html.erb

```
<p>Loop from 0 to 5:
<% (0..5).each do |i| %>
  <%= "#{i}, " %>
<% end %>
</p>

<%= render partial: "footer", locals: {start_year: '2000'} %>
```

If you now go to the URL http://localhost:3000/example/test, you see the 2000.

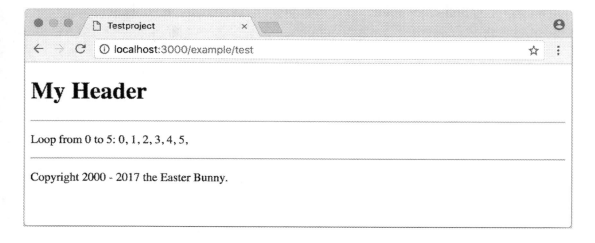

Sometimes you need a partial that uses a local variable and need the same partial but without the local variable somewhere else. You can take care of this in the partial with an `if` statement, as shown here:

```
<hr>
<p>
  Copyright
  <%= "#{start_year} - " if defined? start_year %>
  <%= Date.today.year %>
  the Easter Bunny.
</p>
```

 defined? can be used to check whether an expression has been defined.

Now you can call this partial with `<%= render partial: "footer", locals: {start_year: '2000'} %>` and with `<%= render 'footer' %>`.

Further Documentation on Partials

You have really only barely scratched the surface here. Partials are powerful tools. You can find the official Ruby on Rails documentation on partials at `http://guides.rubyonrails.org/layouts_and_rendering.html#using-partials`.

The Rails Console

The *console* in Rails is nothing more than an `irb` session (see the section "irb" in Chapter 1) built around the Rails environment. The console is useful both for developing and for administration purposes because the whole Rails environment is represented and available.

I'll show you how to work with it in this example application:

```
$ rails new pingpong
  [...]
$ cd pingpong
```

```
$ rails db:migrate
$ rails generate controller Game ping pong
  [...]
$
```

Start the Rails console with the command `rails console`.

```
$ rails console
Running via Spring preloader in process 18395
Loading development environment (Rails 5.2.0)
irb(main):001:0>
```

You can use exit to get back out.

```
irb(main):001:0> exit
$
```

As mentioned in Chapter 1, I use the configuration file shown in Listing 2-15 to save some real estate in the console.

Listing 2-15. ~/irbrc

```
IRB.conf[:PROMPT_MODE] = :SIMPLE
```

In the console, you have access to all variables that are also available later in the proper application.

```
$ rails console
Running via Spring preloader in process 19371
Loading development environment (Rails 5.2.0)
>> Rails.env
=> "development"
>> Rails.root
=> #<Pathname:/Users/stefan/pingpong>
>> exit
$
```

In Chapter 3, you are going to be working with the console a lot and will soon begin to appreciate the debugging possibilities it offers.

One of my best buddies when developing Rails applications is the Tab key. Whenever you are looking for a method for a particular problem, re-create it in the Rails console and then press the Tab key twice to list all the available methods. The names of the methods are usually self-explanatory.

app

app is useful if you want to analyze things having to do with routing.

```
$ rails console
Running via Spring preloader in process 19799
Loading development environment (Rails 5.2.0)
>> app.url_for(controller: 'game', action: 'ping')
=> "http://www.example.com/game/ping"
>> app.get '/game/ping'
Started GET "/game/ping" for 127.0.0.1 at 2018-01-17 17:14:50 +0100
   (0.2ms)  SELECT "schema_migrations"."version" FROM "schema_migrations"
ORDER BY "schema_migrations"."version" ASC
Processing by GameController#ping as HTML
  Rendering game/ping.html.erb within layouts/application
  Rendered game/ping.html.erb within layouts/application (54.4ms)
Completed 200 OK in 898ms (Views: 884.8ms | ActiveRecord: 0.0ms)

=> 200
>> exit
```

What Is a Generator?

You have already used the command rails generate controller. It starts the generator with the name controller. There are other generators as well. You can use the command rails generate to display a list of available generators.

```
$ rails generate
Running via Spring preloader in process 19901
Usage: rails generate GENERATOR [args] [options]
```

[...]

```
Rails:
  application_record
  assets
  channel
  controller
  encrypted_file
  encryption_key_file
  generator
  helper
  integration_test
  jbuilder
  job
  mailer
  master_key
  migration
  model
  resource
  scaffold
  scaffold_controller
  system_test
  task

ActiveRecord:
  active_record:application_record

Coffee:
  coffee:assets

Js:
  js:assets

TestUnit:
  test_unit:generator
  test_unit:plugin
```

What does a generator do? A generator makes a programmer's job easier by doing some of the mindless tasks for you. It creates files and fills them with default code, depending on the parameters passed. You could do the same manually, without the generator. So, you do not have to use a generator. It is primarily intended to save you work and avoid potential errors that can easily arise from mindless repetitive tasks.

Someday you might want to create your own generator. Take a look at `http://guides.rubyonrails.org/generators.html` to find a description of how to do that.

Helper

A helper method takes care of recurring tasks in a view. For example, if you want to display stars (*) for rating a restaurant and not numbers from 1 to 5, you can define the helper shown in Listing 2-16 in the file app/helpers/application_helper.rb.

Listing 2-16. app/helpers/application_helper.rb

```ruby
module ApplicationHelper

  def render_stars(value)
    output = ''
    if (1..5).include?(value)
      value.times { output += '*'}
    end
    output
  end

end
```

With this helper, you can then apply the following code in a view:

```erb
<p>
  <b>Rating:</b> <%= render_stars(5) %>
</p>
```

You can also try the helper in the console.

```
$ rails console
Running via Spring preloader in process 23849
Loading development environment (Rails 5.2.0)
>> helper.render_stars(5)
=> "*****"
>> helper.render_stars(3)
=> "***"
>> exit
```

There are lots of predefined helpers in Rails, and you will use some of them in the next chapters. But you can also define your own custom helpers. Any of the helpers from the file app/helpers/application_helper.rb can be used in any view. Helpers that you want to be available only in certain views must be defined for each controller. When creating a controller, a file for helpers of that controller is automatically created in app/helpers. This gives you the option of defining helpers only for this controller or for the views of this controller.

All helpers are in the directory app/helpers/.

Debugging

Rails provides a couple of debug tools to make a developer's live easier.

debug

In any view you can use the debug helper to render an object with the YAML format within a <pre> tag. To display the value of @foo, you can use the following line in your view:

```
<%= debug @foo %>
```

Web Console

The web-console gem provides a way to render Rails console views. When you browse to a specific URL, at the end of that page you'll get a console.

Let me show you this by example with this simple Rails application:

```
$ rails new testapp
  [...]
$ cd testapp
$ rails db:migrate
$ rails generate controller page index
```

Rails 5.2 introduces a strict content security policy (CSP) that has to be configured to use the web console first. Please take a look at https://developer.mozilla.org/en-US/docs/Web/HTTP/Headers/Content-Security-Policy to understand the concept of a CSP. You find your CSP configuration in the file config/initializers/content_security_policy.rb. Please configure it according to your security needs. Listing 2-17 shows a quick-and-dirty hack to display the use of web console. Please do not use this in production.

Listing 2-17. config/initializers/content_security_policy.rb

```
Rails.application.config.content_security_policy do |p|
  # p.default_src :self, :https
  p.font_src     :self, :https, :data
  p.img_src      :self, :https, :data
  p.object_src   :none
  # p.script_src  :self, :https
  p.style_src    :self, :https, :unsafe_inline

  # Specify URI for violation reports
  # p.report_uri "/csp-violation-report-endpoint"
end
```

In app/controllers/page_controller.rb, you'll add the code shown in Listing 2-18.

Listing 2-18. app/controllers/page_controller.rb

```
class PageController < ApplicationController
  def index
    @foo = 'bar'
  end
end
```

In the view `app/views/page/index.html.erb`, you'll add the `console` command shown in Listing 2-19.

Listing 2-19.   app/views/page/index.html.erb

```
<h1>Page#index</h1>
<p>Find me in app/views/page/index.html.erb</p>

<% console %>
```

After starting the Rails application with `rails server` and browsing to the URL `http://localhost:3000/page/index`, you get a web console at the bottom of the page (see Figure 2-6). In it you have access to the instance variable `@foo`.

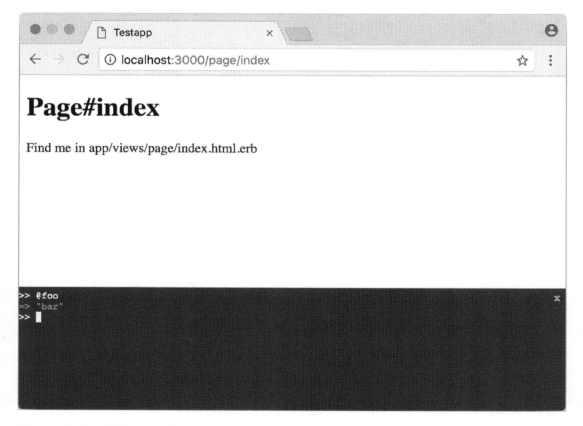

Figure 2-6. *Web console*

Other Debugging Tools

There are a couple of other built-in debugging tools that are out of the scope of this chapter. Please take a look at `http://guides.rubyonrails.org/debugging_rails_applications.html` to get an overview.

Rails Lingo

Here I'll cover a couple of words that you'll often find in the Ruby on Rails universe.

Don't Repeat Yourself

Many Rails programmers are big fans of DRY. DRY means purely and simply that you should try to place repeated programming logic into separate methods.

Refactoring

You'll often hear the word *refactoring* in the context of DRY. This involves functioning applications that are further improved. The application in itself remains unchanged in its interface. But its core is optimized through, among other principles, DRY.

Convention Over Configuration

Convention over configuration (also known as coding by convention; see `http://en.wikipedia.org/wiki/Convention_over_configuration`) is an important pillar of a Rails application. It states that the programmer does not need to decide in favor of certain features when starting a project and set these via configuration parameters. It specifies an underlying basic consensus, and this is set by default. But if you want to work outside of this conventional basic consensus, then you will need to change the corresponding parameters.

Model View Controller Architecture

You have already created a simple Rails application, and in the next chapter you will dive deeply into the topic of `ActiveRecord`. So, now is a good time to briefly introduce a few terms that often surface in the world of Rails.

According to Wikipedia (`http://en.wikipedia.org/wiki/Model-view-controller`), MVC is a design pattern that separates the representation of information from the user's interaction with it.

MVC is a structure for software development. It was agreed that it makes sense to have one part of the software in one place and another part of the software in another place. Nothing more, nothing less.

This agreement has the enormous advantage that once you are used to this concept, you know exactly where you can find or need to integrate a certain functionality in a Rails project.

Model

Model in this case means data model. By default, Rails applications are an `ActiveRecord` data model (see Chapter 3).

All models can be found in the directory `app/models/`.

View

The *view* is responsible for the presentation of the application. It takes care of rendering the web page, an XML file, or a JSON file. A view could also render a PDF or an ASCII text. It depends entirely on your application.

You will find all the views in the directory `app/views/`.

Controller

Once a web page call has ended up in a route (see Chapter 5), it goes from there to the controller. The route specifies a certain method (action) as a target. This method can then fulfil the desired tasks (such as finding a specific set of data and saving it in an instance variable) and render the desired view.

All controllers can be found in the directory `app/controllers/`.

Abbreviations

There are a handful of abbreviations that can make your life as a developer much easier if you know them. In the rest of this book, I always use the full version of these commands to make it clearer for beginners, but in practice, you will soon find that the abbreviations are easier to use.

- `rails console`

    Shorthand notation: `rails c`

- `rails server`

    Shorthand notation: `rails s`

- `rails generate scaffold`

    Shorthand notation: `rails g scaffold`

CHAPTER 3

ActiveRecord

ActiveRecord is a level of abstraction that offers access to a SQL database. ActiveRecord implements the architectural pattern *Active Record*.

ℹ️ This is referred to as *object-relational mapping* (ORM). I find it rather dry and boring, but if you have trouble going to sleep tonight, take a look at `http://en.wikipedia.org/wiki/Object_relational_mapping`.

One of the recipes for the success of Rails is surely the fact that it uses ActiveRecord. The programming and use "feels Ruby-like," and it is much less susceptible to errors than pure SQL. When working with this chapter, it helps if you have some knowledge of SQL, but this is not required and also not essential for working with ActiveRecord.

ℹ️ This chapter is only about ActiveRecord. I am not going to integrate any tests so I can keep the examples as simple as possible.

Creating a Database/Model

Model in this context refers to the data model of Model-View-Controller (MVC).

As a first example, let's take a list of countries in Europe. First, create a new Rails project.

```
$ rails new europe
  [...]
$ cd europe
```

© Stefan Wintermeyer 2018
S. Wintermeyer, *Learn Rails 5.2*, https://doi.org/10.1007/978-1-4842-3489-1_3

Next, let's take a look at the help page for rails generate model, as shown here:

```
$ rails generate model
Running via Spring preloader in process 21883
Usage:
  rails generate model NAME [field[:type][:index] field[:type][:index]]
  [options]

[...]

Description:
    Stubs out a new model. Pass the model name, either CamelCased or
    under_scored, and an optional list of attribute pairs as arguments.

[...]

Available field types:

    Just after the field name you can specify a type like text or boolean.
    It will generate the column with the associated SQL type. For instance:

        `rails generate model post title:string body:text`

will generate a title column with a varchar type and a body column with
a text type. If no type is specified the string type will be used by
default.
You can use the following types:

        integer
        primary_key
        decimal
        float
        boolean
        binary
        string
        text
        date
        time
        datetime
[...]
```

The usage description `rails generate model NAME [field[:type][:index]` `field[:type][:index]] [options]` tells you that after `rails generate model` comes the name of the model and then the table fields. If you do not put `:type` after a table field name, it is assumed to be a `string`.

Let's create the *model* called `country`.

```
$ rails generate model Country name population:integer
Running via Spring preloader in process 22053
      invoke  active_record
      create    db/migrate/20170322165321_create_countries.rb
      create    app/models/country.rb
      invoke  test_unit
      create      test/models/country_test.rb
      create      test/fixtures/countries.yml
```

The generator has created a database migration file with the name `db/migrate/20170322165321_create_countries.rb`. It provides the code shown in Listing 3-1.

Listing 3-1. db/migrate/20170322165321_create_countries.rb

```
class CreateCountries < ActiveRecord::Migration[5.1]
  def change
    create_table :countries do |t|
      t.string :name
      t.integer :population

      t.timestamps
    end
  end
end
```

A migration contains database changes. In this migration, a class called `CreateCountries` is defined as a child of `ActiveRecord::Migration`. The method change is used to define a migration and the associated rollback.

With the command `rails db:migrate`, you can apply the migrations, in other words, create the corresponding database table.

```
$ rails db:migrate
== 20170322165321 CreateCountries: migrating ===============================
-- create_table(:countries)
   -> 0.0010s
== 20170322165321 CreateCountries: migrated (0.0011s) =====================
```

> ℹ️ You will find more details on migrations in the section "Migrations."

Let's take a look at the file app/models/country.rb; see Listing 3-2.

Listing 3-2. app/models/country.rb

```
class Country < ApplicationRecord
end
```

The class `Country` is a child of `ApplicationRecord` that inherits from `ApplicationRecord`. In `ApplicationRecord` you'll find all the `ActiveRecord` magic.

The Attributes `id`, `created_at`, and `updated_at`

Even if you cannot see it in the migration, you also get the attributes `id`, `created_at`, and `updated_at` by default for each `ActiveRecord` model. In the Rails console, you can output the attributes of the class `Country` by using the class method `column_names`.

```
$ rails console
Running via Spring preloader in process 22303
Loading development environment (Rails 5.2.0)
>> Country.column_names
=> ["id", "name", "population", "created_at", "updated_at"]
>> exit
```

The attribute `created_at` stores the time when the record was initially created. `updated_at` stores the time of the last update for this record.

`id` is used as a central identification of the record (primary key). The `id` value is automatically incremented by 1 for each new record.

Getters and Setters

To read and write values of a SQL table row, you can use getters and setters based on ActiveRecord-provided getters and setters. These `attr_accessors` are automatically created. The getter of the field `updated_at` for a given `Country` with the name germany would be `germany.updated_at`.

Possible Data Types in ActiveRecord

ActiveRecord is a *layer* between Ruby and various relational databases. Unfortunately, many SQL databases have different perspectives regarding the definition of columns and their content. But you do not need to worry about this because `ActiveRecord` solves this problem transparently for you.

To generate a model, you can use the field types shown in Table 3-1.

Table 3-1. *Field Types*

Name	Description
binary	This is a *Binary Large Object* (BLOB) in the classical sense. Never heard of it? Then you probably won't need it. See also `http://en.wikipedia.org/wiki/Binary._large_object`.
boolean	`true`, `false`, or `nil`.
date	You can store a date here.
datetime	Here you can store a date including a time.
integer	This is for storing an integer. See also `http://en.wikipedia.org/wiki/Integer_(computer_science)`.
decimal	This is for storing a decimal number.
primary_key	This is an integer that is automatically incremented by 1 by the database for each new entry. This field type is often used as key for linking different database tables or models. See also `http://en.wikipedia.org/wiki/Unique_key`.
string	This is a string, in other words, a sequence of any characters, up to a maximum of $2^8 -1$ (= 255) characters. See also `http://en.wikipedia.org/wiki/String_(computer_science)`.

(continued)

Table 3-1. (*continued*)

Name	Description
text	This is also a string but is considerably bigger. By default, up to 2^16 -1 (= 65535) characters can be saved here.
time	This is for storing a time.
timestamp	This is for storing a time with a date, filled in automatically by the database.

Decimal

You can also define a decimal with the model generator. But you need to observe the special syntax (you have to use ' if you are using the Bash shell).

Here's an example of creating a price with a decimal:

```
$ rails generate model product name 'price:decimal{7,2}'
  [...]
$
```

That would generate the migration shown in Listing 3-3.

Listing 3-3. db/migrate/20170322170623_create_products.rb

```
class CreateProducts < ActiveRecord::Migration[5.1]
  def change
    create_table :products do |t|
      t.string :name
      t.decimal :price, precision: 7, scale: 2

      t.timestamps
    end
  end
end
```

In the section "Migrations," I will provide more information on the individual data types and discuss the available options.

Naming Conventions (**Country** vs. **country** vs. **countries**)

ActiveRecord automatically uses the English plural forms. So, for the class Country, it's countries. If you are not sure about a term, you can also work with the class and method names.

```
$ rails console
Running via Spring preloader in process 23132
Loading development environment (Rails 5.2.0)
>> Country.name.tableize
=> "countries"
>> Country.name.foreign_key
=> "country_id"
>> exit
```

Database Configuration

Which database is used by default? Let's take a quick look at the configuration file for the database (config/database.yml), as shown in Listing 3-4.

Listing 3-4. config/database.yml

```
# SQLite version 3.x
#   gem install sqlite3
#
#   Ensure the SQLite 3 gem is defined in your Gemfile
#   gem 'sqlite3'
#
default: &default
  adapter: sqlite3
  pool: <%= ENV.fetch("RAILS_MAX_THREADS") { 5 } %>
  timeout: 5000

development:
  <<: *default
  database: db/development.sqlite3
```

```
# Warning: The database defined as "test" will be erased and
# re-generated from your development database when you run "rake".
# Do not set this db to the same as development or production.
test:
  <<: *default
  database: db/test.sqlite3

production:
  <<: *default
  database: db/production.sqlite3
```

As you are working in Development mode, Rails has created a new SQLite3 database in the file db/development.sqlite3 as a result of rails db:migrate and will save all data there.

Fans of command-line clients can use sqlite3 for viewing this database.

```
$ sqlite3 db/development.sqlite3
SQLite version 3.19.3 2017-06-27 16:48:08
Enter ".help" for usage hints.
sqlite> .tables
ar_internal_metadata   countries              schema_migrations
sqlite> .schema countries
CREATE TABLE "countries" ("id" INTEGER PRIMARY KEY AUTOINCREMENT NOT NULL,
"name" varchar, "population" integer, "created_at" datetime NOT NULL,
"updated_at" datetime NOT NULL);
sqlite> .exit
```

Adding Records

I will show you how to view records, but to display records, you have to create them first. So, here is how you can create a new record with ActiveRecord.

create

The most frequently used method for creating a new record is create.

Let's try creating a country in the console with the command Country.create(name: 'Germany', population: 81831000).

```
$ rails console
Running via Spring preloader in process 23285
Loading development environment (Rails 5.2.0)
>> Country.create(name: 'Germany', population: 81831000)
   (0.1ms)  begin transaction
  SQL (0.4ms)  INSERT INTO "countries" ("name", "population", "created_at",
  "updated_at") VALUES (?, ?, ?, ?)  [["name", "Germany"],
  ["population", 81831000], ["created_at", "2017-03-22 17:10:30.859482"],
  ["updated_at", "2017-03-22 17:10:30.859482"]]
   (2.2ms)  commit transaction
=> #<Country id: 1, name: "Germany", population: 81831000,
created_at: "2017-03-22 17:10:30", updated_at: "2017-03-22 17:10:30">
>> exit
```

ActiveRecord saves the new record and outputs the executed SQL command in the Development environment. But to make absolutely sure it works, let's take a last look with the command-line client sqlite3.

```
$ sqlite3 db/development.sqlite3
SQLite version 3.19.3 2017-06-27 16:48:08
Enter ".help" for usage hints.
sqlite> SELECT * FROM countries;
1|Germany|81831000|2017-03-23 17:10:03.141592|2017-03-22 17:10:03.141592
sqlite> .exit
```

Syntax

The method create can handle a number of different syntax constructs. If you want to create a single record, you can do this with or without brackets ({}) within the parentheses, as shown here:

- `Country.create(name: 'Germany', population: 81831000)`

- `Country.create({name: 'Germany', population: 81831000})`

Similarly, you can describe the attributes differently, as shown here:

- `Country.create(:name ⇒ 'Germany', :population ⇒ 81831000)`

- `Country.create('name' ⇒ 'Germany', 'population' ⇒ 81831000)`

- `Country.create( name: 'Germany', population: 81831000)`

You can also pass an array of hashes to create and use this approach to create several records at once.

```
Country.create([{name: 'Germany'}, {name: 'France'}])
```

new

In addition to create, there is also new. But you have to use the save method to save an object created with new (which has both advantages and disadvantages).

```
$ rails console
Running via Spring preloader in process 23679
Loading development environment (Rails 5.2.0)
>> france = Country.new
=> #<Country id: nil, name: nil, population: nil, created_at: nil,
updated_at: nil>
>> france.name = 'France'
=> "France"
>> france.population = 65447374
=> 65447374
>> france.save
   (0.1ms)  begin transaction
  SQL (0.5ms)  INSERT INTO "countries" ("name", "population", "created_at",
  "updated_at") VALUES (?, ?, ?, ?)  [["name", "France"],
  ["population", 65447374], ["created_at", "2017-03-22 17:15:30.001686"],
  ["updated_at", "2017-03-22 17:15:30.001686"]]
   (2.1ms)  commit transaction
=> true
>> france
=> #<Country id: 2, name: "France", population: 65447374,
created_at: "2017-03-22 17:15:30", updated_at: "2017-03-22 17:15:30">
```

You can also pass parameters for the new record directly to the method new, just as with create.

```
>> belgium = Country.new(name: 'Belgium', population: 10839905)
=> #<Country id: nil, name: "Belgium", population: 10839905,
created_at: nil, updated_at: nil>
>> belgium.save
   (0.1ms)  begin transaction
  SQL (0.5ms)  INSERT INTO "countries" ("name", "population",
  "created_at", "updated_at") VALUES (?, ?, ?, ?)  [["name", "Belgium"],
  ["population", 10839905], ["created_at", "2017-03-22 17:16:31.091853"],
  ["updated_at", "2017-03-22 17:16:31.091853"]]
   (2.5ms)  commit transaction
=> true
>> exit
```

new_record?

With the method new_record?, you can find out whether a record has already been saved. If a new object has been created with new and has not yet been saved, then the result of new_record? is true. After a save, it's false.

Here's an example:

```
$ rails console
Running via Spring preloader in process 23823
Loading development environment (Rails 5.2.0)
>> netherlands = Country.new(name: 'Netherlands')
=> #<Country id: nil, name: "Netherlands", population: nil,
created_at: nil, updated_at: nil>
>> netherlands.new_record?
=> true
>> netherlands.save
   (0.1ms)  begin transaction
  SQL (0.5ms)  INSERT INTO "countries" ("name", "created_at",
  "updated_at") VALUES (?, ?, ?)  [["name", "Netherlands"],
```

```
   ["created_at", "2017-03-22 17:17:34.694389"],
   ["updated_at", "2017-03-22 17:17:34.694389"]]
    (2.1ms)  commit transaction
=> true
>> netherlands.new_record?
=> false
>> exit
```

> 💡 For already existing records, you can also check for changes with the
> method changed? (see the section "changed?"). You can even use netherland.
> population_changed? to check whether just the attribute popluation was
> changed.

first, last, and all

In certain cases, you may need the first record or the last one or perhaps even all records.
Conveniently, there is a ready-made method for each case. Let's start with the easiest
ones: first and last.

```
$ rails console
Running via Spring preloader in process 24090
Loading development environment (Rails 5.2.0)
>> Country.first
  Country Load (0.2ms)  SELECT  "countries".* FROM "countries" ORDER BY
  "countries"."id" ASC LIMIT ?  [["LIMIT", 1]]
=> #<Country id: 1, name: "Germany", population: 81831000, created_at:
"2017-03-22 17:10:30", updated_at: "2017-03-22 17:10:30">
>> Country.last
  Country Load (0.3ms)  SELECT  "countries".* FROM "countries" ORDER BY
  "countries"."id" DESC LIMIT ?  [["LIMIT", 1]]
=> #<Country id: 4, name: "Netherlands", population: nil, created_at:
"2017-03-22 17:17:34", updated_at: "2017-03-22 17:17:34">
```

Here's an example all at once with all:

```
>> Country.all
  Country Load (0.2ms)  SELECT "countries".* FROM "countries"
=> #<ActiveRecord::Relation [#<Country id: 1, name: "Germany",
population: 81831000, created_at: "2017-03-22 17:10:30",
updated_at: "2017-03-22 17:10:30">, #<Country id: 2, name: "France",
population: 65447374, created_at: "2017-03-22 17:15:30",
updated_at: "2017-03-22 17:15:30">, #<Country id: 3, name: "Belgium",
population: 10839905, created_at: "2017-03-22 17:16:31",
updated_at: "2017-03-22 17:16:31">, #<Country id: 4, name: "Netherlands",
population: nil, created_at: "2017-03-22 17:17:34",
updated_at: "2017-03-22 17:17:34">]>
```

But the objects created by first, last, and all are different.

```
>> Country.first.class
  Country Load (0.3ms)  SELECT  "countries".* FROM "countries"
  ORDER BY "countries"."id" ASC LIMIT ?  [["LIMIT", 1]]
=> Country(id: integer, name: string, population: integer,
created_at: datetime, updated_at: datetime)
>> Country.all.class
=> Country::ActiveRecord_Relation
```

So, Country.first is a Country, which makes sense. But Country.all is something you haven't had yet. Let's use the console to get a better idea of it.

```
>> puts Country.all.to_yaml
  Country Load (0.4ms)  SELECT "countries".* FROM "countries"
---
- !ruby/object:Country
  concise_attributes:
  - !ruby/object:ActiveRecord::Attribute::FromDatabase
    name: id
    value_before_type_cast: 1
  - !ruby/object:ActiveRecord::Attribute::FromDatabase
    name: name
    value_before_type_cast: Germany
```

```
  - !ruby/object:ActiveRecord::Attribute::FromDatabase
    name: population
    value_before_type_cast: 81831000
  - !ruby/object:ActiveRecord::Attribute::FromDatabase
    name: created_at
    value_before_type_cast: '2017-03-22 17:10:30.859482'
  - !ruby/object:ActiveRecord::Attribute::FromDatabase
    name: updated_at
    value_before_type_cast: '2017-03-22 17:10:30.859482'
  new_record: false
  active_record_yaml_version: 2
[...]
=> nil
```

By using the to_yaml method, suddenly the database has work to do. The reason for this behavior is optimization. Let's assume you want to chain a couple of methods. Then it might be better for ActiveRecord to wait until the very last second, which it does. It only requests the data from the SQL database when it has to do it (which is called *lazy loading*). Until then, it stores the request in an ActiveRecord::Relation.

The result of Country.all is actually an Array of Country.

If Country.all returns an array, then you should also be able to use iterators and each, right? Yes, of course! That is the beauty of it. Here is a little experiment with each:

```
>> Country.all.each do |country|
?> puts country.name
>> end
  Country Load (0.1ms)  SELECT "countries".* FROM "countries"
Germany
France
Belgium
Netherlands
=> [#<Country id: 1, name: "Germany", [...]]
```

So, can you also use `.all.first` as an alternative for `.first`? Yes, but it does not make much sense. Take a look for yourself.

```
>> Country.first
  Country Load (0.2ms)  SELECT  "countries".* FROM "countries"
  ORDER BY "countries"."id" ASC LIMIT ?  [["LIMIT", 1]]
=> #<Country id: 1, name: "Germany", population: 81831000,
created_at: "2017-03-22 17:10:30", updated_at: "2017-03-22 17:10:30">
>> Country.all.first
  Country Load (0.2ms)  SELECT  "countries".* FROM "countries"
  ORDER BY "countries"."id" ASC LIMIT ?  [["LIMIT", 1]]
=> #<Country id: 1, name: "Germany", population: 81831000,
created_at: "2017-03-22 17:10:30", updated_at: "2017-03-22 17:10:30">
>> exit
```

Country.first and Country.all.first result in the same SQL query because ActiveRecord optimizes it.

ℹ️   ActiveRecord provides not only the `first` method but also `second`, `third`, `fourth`, and `fifth`. It's obvious what they do.

Populating the Database with seeds.rb

With the file `db/seeds.rb`, the Rails gods have given you a way of feeding default values easily and quickly to a fresh installation. This is a normal Ruby program within the Rails environment. You have full access to all classes and methods of your application.

With that, you don't need to enter everything manually with `rails console` to create all the initial records in a new Rails application. You can use the file `db/seeds.rb`, as shown in Listing 3-5.

Listing 3-5. db/seeds.rb

```
Country.create(name: 'Germany', population: 81831000)
Country.create(name: 'France', population: 65447374)
Country.create(name: 'Belgium', population: 10839905)
Country.create(name: 'Netherlands', population: 16680000)
```

You then populate it with data via `rails db:seed`.

If you want to delete the existing database, re-create it, and then populate it with the seeds, you can use `rails db:reset`. That's what you do here:

```
$ rails db:reset
Dropped database 'db/development.sqlite3'
Dropped database 'db/test.sqlite3'
Created database 'db/development.sqlite3'
Created database 'db/test.sqlite3'
-- create_table("countries", {:force=>:cascade})
   -> 0.0050s
-- create_table("countries", {:force=>:cascade})
   -> 0.0032s
```

I use the file db/seeds.rb at this point because it offers a simple mechanism for filling an empty database with useful values. In the course of this book, this will make it easier to set up quick example scenarios.

It's All Just Ruby Code

db/seeds.rb is a Ruby program. Correspondingly, you can also use the approach shown in Listing 3-6 as an alternative.

Listing 3-6. db/seeds.rb

```
country_list = [
  [ "Germany", 81831000 ],
  [ "France", 65447374 ],
  [ "Belgium", 10839905 ],
  [ "Netherlands", 16680000 ]
]

country_list.each do |name, population|
  Country.create( name: name, population: population )
end
```

The result is the same. I am showing you this example to make it clear that you can program normally within db/seeds.rb.

Generating **seeds.rb** from Existing Data

Sometimes it can be useful to export the current data pool of a Rails application into db/seeds.rb. While writing this book, I encountered this problem in almost every chapter. Unfortunately, there is no standard approach for this. I am showing you what you can do in this case. There are other, more complex scenarios that can be derived from my approach.

You can create your own little rake task for that, as shown in Listing 3-7. A rake task is a Ruby program that is stored in the lib/tasks/ directory and that has full access to the Rails environment.

Listing 3-7. lib/tasks/export.rake

```
namespace :export do
  desc "Prints Country.all in a seeds.rb way."
  task :seeds_format => :environment do
    Country.order(:id).all.each do |country|
      bad_keys = ['created_at', 'updated_at', 'id']
      serialized = country.serializable_hash.
                   delete_if{|key,value| bad_keys.include?(key)}
      puts "Country.create(#{serialized})"
    end
  end
end
```

Then you can call the corresponding rake task with the command rails export:seeds_format.

```
$ rails export:seeds_format
Country.create({"name"=>"Germany", "population"=>81831000})
Country.create({"name"=>"France", "population"=>65447374})
Country.create({"name"=>"Belgium", "population"=>10839905})
Country.create({"name"=>"Netherlands", "population"=>16680000})
```

You can either expand this program so that the output is written directly into db/seeds.rb or simply use the shell.

```
$ rails export:seeds_format > db/seeds.rb
```

Searching and Finding with Queries

The methods `first` and `all` are already quite nice, but usually you want to search for something more specific with a query.

For describing queries, you create a new Rails project.

```
$ rails new jukebox
  [...]
$ cd jukebox
$ rails generate model Album name release_year:integer
  [...]
$ rails db:migrate
  [...]
```

For the examples used here, use db/seeds.rb with the content shown in Listing 3-8.

Listing 3-8. db/seeds.rb

```
Album.create(name: "Sgt. Pepper's Lonely Hearts Club Band", release_year: 1967)
Album.create(name: "Pet Sounds", release_year: 1966)
Album.create(name: "Revolver", release_year: 1966)
Album.create(name: "Highway 61 Revisited", release_year: 1965)
Album.create(name: "Rubber Soul", release_year: 1965)
Album.create(name: "What's Going On", release_year: 1971)
Album.create(name: "Exile on Main St.", release_year: 1972)
Album.create(name: "London Calling", release_year: 1979)
Album.create(name: "Blonde on Blonde", release_year: 1966)
Album.create(name: "The Beatles", release_year: 1968)
```

Then, set up the new database with `rails db:reset`.

```
$ rails db:reset
Dropped database 'db/development.sqlite3'
Database 'db/test.sqlite3' does not exist
Created database 'db/development.sqlite3'
Created database 'db/test.sqlite3'
-- create_table("active_storage_attachments", {:force=>:cascade})
   -> 0.0074s
```

```
-- create_table("active_storage_blobs", {:force=>:cascade})
   -> 0.0033s
-- create_table("albums", {:force=>:cascade})
   -> 0.0020s
-- create_table("active_storage_attachments", {:force=>:cascade})
   -> 0.0077s
-- create_table("active_storage_blobs", {:force=>:cascade})
   -> 0.0040s
-- create_table("albums", {:force=>:cascade})
   -> 0.0021s
```

find

The simplest case is searching for a record via a primary key (by default, the id field in the database table). If I know the ID of an object, then I can search for the individual object or several objects at once via the ID.

```
$ rails console
Running via Spring preloader in process 26956
Loading development environment (Rails 5.2.0)
>> Album.find(2)
  Album Load (0.2ms)  SELECT  "albums".* FROM "albums"
  WHERE "albums"."id" = ? LIMIT ?  [["id", 2], ["LIMIT", 1]]
=> #<Album id: 2, name: "Pet Sounds", release_year: 1966,
created_at: "2017-03-22 18:19:06", updated_at: "2017-03-22 18:19:06">
>> Album.find([1,3,7])
  Album Load (0.4ms)  SELECT "albums".* FROM "albums"
  WHERE "albums"."id" IN (1, 3, 7)
=> [#<Album id: 1, name: "Sgt. Pepper's Lonely Hearts Club Band",
release_year: 1967, created_at: "2017-03-22 18:19:06",
updated_at: "2017-03-22 18:19:06">, #<Album id: 3, name: "Revolver",
release_year: 1966, created_at: "2017-03-22 18:19:06",
updated_at: "2017-03-22 18:19:06">, #<Album id: 7,
name: "Exile on Main St.", release_year: 1972,
created_at: "2017-03-22 18:19:06", updated_at: "2017-03-22 18:19:06">]
```

If you always want to have an array as the result, you also always have to pass an array as a parameter.

```
>> Album.find(5).class
  Album Load (0.2ms)  SELECT  "albums".* FROM "albums"
  WHERE "albums"."id" = ? LIMIT ?  [["id", 5], ["LIMIT", 1]]
=> Album(id: integer, name: string, release_year: integer,
created_at: datetime, updated_at: datetime)
>> Album.find([5]).class
  Album Load (0.1ms)  SELECT  "albums".* FROM "albums"
  WHERE "albums"."id" = ? LIMIT ?  [["id", 5], ["LIMIT", 1]]
=> Array
>> exit
```

⚠ The method find generates an exception if the ID you are searching for does not have a record in the database.

where

With the method where, you can search for specific values in the database. Let's search for all albums from the year 1966.

```
$ rails console
Running via Spring preloader in process 27119
Loading development environment (Rails 5.2.0)
>> Album.where(release_year: 1966)
  Album Load (0.2ms)  SELECT "albums".* FROM "albums"
  WHERE "albums"."release_year" = ?  [["release_year", 1966]]
=> #<ActiveRecord::Relation [#<Album id: 2, name: "Pet Sounds",
release_year: 1966, created_at: "2017-03-22 18:19:06",
updated_at: "2017-03-22 18:19:06">, #<Album id: 3,
name: "Revolver", release_year: 1966,
created_at: "2017-03-22 18:19:06", updated_at: "2017-03-22 18:19:06">,
#<Album id: 9, name: "Blonde on Blonde", release_year: 1966,
```

```
created_at: "2017-03-22 18:19:06", updated_at: "2017-03-22 18:19:06">]>
>> Album.where(release_year: 1966).count
   (0.3ms)   SELECT COUNT(*) FROM "albums"
   WHERE "albums"."release_year" = ?  [["release_year", 1966]]
=> 3
```

You can also use where to search for ranges.

```
>> Album.where(release_year: 1960..1966).count
   (0.3ms)   SELECT COUNT(*) FROM "albums"
   WHERE ("albums"."release_year" BETWEEN ? AND ?)
   [["release_year", 1960], ["release_year", 1966]]
=> 5
```

In addition, you can specify several search factors simultaneously, separated by commas.

```
>> Album.where(release_year: 1960..1966, id: 1..5).count
   (0.4ms)   SELECT COUNT(*) FROM "albums"
   WHERE ("albums"."release_year" BETWEEN ? AND ?)
   AND ("albums"."id" BETWEEN ? AND ?)  [["release_year", 1960],
   ["release_year", 1966], ["id", 1], ["id", 5]]
=> 4
```

Or you can specify an array of parameters.

```
>> Album.where(release_year: [1966, 1968]).count
   (0.2ms)   SELECT COUNT(*) FROM "albums"
   WHERE "albums"."release_year" IN (1966, 1968)
=> 4
```

The result of where is always an array, even if it contains only one hit or if no hit is returned (which will result in an empty array). If you are looking for the first hit, you need to combine the method where with the method first.

```
>> Album.where(release_year: [1966, 1968]).first
  Album Load (0.4ms)   SELECT  "albums".* FROM "albums"
  WHERE "albums"."release_year" IN (1966, 1968)
  ORDER BY "albums"."id" ASC LIMIT ?  [["LIMIT", 1]]
```

```
=> #<Album id: 2, name: "Pet Sounds", release_year: 1966,
created_at: "2017-03-22 18:19:06", updated_at: "2017-03-22 18:19:06">
>> exit
```

not

The method not provides a way to search for the exact opposite of a where query. Here's an example:

```
$ rails console
Running via Spring preloader in process 27349
Loading development environment (Rails 5.2.0)
>> Album.where.not(release_year: 1968).count
   (0.2ms)  SELECT COUNT(*) FROM "albums"
   WHERE ("albums"."release_year" != ?)  [["release_year", 1968]]
=> 9
>> exit
```

or

The method or provides a way to combine queries with a logical or. Here's an example:

```
$ rails console
Running via Spring preloader in process 27449
Loading development environment (Rails 5.2.0)
>> Album.where(release_year: 1967).or(Album.where(name: 'The Beatles')).count
   (0.2ms)  SELECT COUNT(*) FROM "albums"
   WHERE ("albums"."release_year" = ? OR "albums"."name" = ?)
   [["release_year", 1967], ["name", "The Beatles"]]
=> 2
>> exit
```

SQL Queries with where

Sometimes there is no other way, and you just have to define and execute your own SQL query. In ActiveRecord, there are two different ways of doing this. One *sanitizes* each query before executing it, and the other passes the query on to the SQL database one to one as it is. Normally, you should always use the sanitized version because otherwise you can easily fall victim to an *SQL injection* attack (see http://en.wikipedia.org/wiki/Sql_injection).

ℹ If you do not know much about SQL, you can safely skip this section. The SQL commands used here are not explained further.

Sanitized Queries

In this variant, all dynamic search parts are replaced with a question mark as a placeholder and only listed as parameters after the SQL string.

In the following example, you are searching for all albums whose name contains the string "on":

```
$ rails console
Running via Spring preloader in process 27553
Loading development environment (Rails 5.2.0)
>> Album.where( 'name like ?', '%on%').count
   (0.1ms)  SELECT COUNT(*) FROM "albums" WHERE (name like '%on%')
=> 5
```

Now you're searching for the number of albums that were published from 1965 onward.

```
>> Album.where( 'release_year > ?', 1964 ).count
   (0.2ms)  SELECT COUNT(*) FROM "albums" WHERE (release_year > 1964)
=> 10
```

Here are the number of albums that are more recent than 1970 and whose name contains the string "on":

```
>> Album.where( 'name like ? AND release_year > ?', '%on%', 1970 ).count
   (0.4ms)  SELECT COUNT(*) FROM "albums" WHERE (name like '%on%'
   AND release_year > 1970)
=> 3
```

If the variable `search_string` contains the desired string, you can search for it as follows:

```
>> search_string = 'ing'
=> "ing"
>> Album.where( 'name like ?', "%#{search_string}%").count
   (0.2ms)  SELECT COUNT(*) FROM "albums" WHERE (name like '%ing%')
=> 2
>> exit
```

Dangerous SQL Queries

If you really know what you are doing, you can of course also define the SQL query completely and forego the *sanitizing* of the query.

Let's count all albums whose name contains the string "on".

```
$ rails console
Running via Spring preloader in process 27699
Loading development environment (Rails 5.2.0)
>> Album.where( "name like '%on%'" ).count
   (0.2ms)  SELECT COUNT(*) FROM "albums" WHERE (name like '%on%')
=> 5
>> exit
```

Please use this variation only if you know exactly what you are doing and after you have familiarized yourself with the topic SQL injections (see http://en.wikipedia.org/wiki/Sql_injection).

Lazy Loading

Lazy loading is a mechanism that carries out a database query only if the program flow cannot be realized without the result of this query. Until then, the query is saved as `ActiveRecord::Relation`.

  Incidentally, the opposite of lazy loading is referred to as *eager loading*.

Does it make sense in principle but you aren't sure what the point of it all is? Then let's cobble together a query where you nest several methods. In the following example, `a` is defined more and more closely, and only at the end (when calling the method `all`) the database query would really be executed in a production system. With the `ActiveRecord` methods `to_sql`, you can display the current SQL query.

```
$ rails console
Running via Spring preloader in process 27764
Loading development environment (Rails 5.2.0)
>> a = Album.where(release_year: 1965..1968)
  Album Load (0.2ms)  SELECT "albums".* FROM "albums" WHERE
  ("albums"."release_year" BETWEEN 1965 AND 1968)
=> #<ActiveRecord::Relation [#<Album id: 1, [...]]>
>> a.class
=> Album::ActiveRecord_Relation
>> a = a.order(:release_year)
  Album Load (0.3ms)  SELECT "albums".* FROM "albums" WHERE
  ("albums"."release_year" BETWEEN 1965 AND 1968)  ORDER BY
  "albums"."release_year" ASC
=> #<ActiveRecord::Relation [#<Album id: 4, [...]]>
>> a = a.limit(3)
  Album Load (0.4ms)  SELECT  "albums".* FROM "albums" WHERE
  ("albums"."release_year" BETWEEN 1965 AND 1968)  ORDER BY
  "albums"."release_year" ASC LIMIT 3
=> #<ActiveRecord::Relation [#<Album id: 4, [...]]>
>> exit
```

The console can be a bit tricky about this. It tries to help the developer by actually showing the result, but in a nonconsole environment, this would only happen the last time.

Automatic Optimization

One of the great advantages of lazy loading is the automatic optimization of the SQL query through `ActiveRecord`.

Let's take the sum of all the release years of the albums that came out in the 1970s. Then you sort the albums alphabetically and calculate the sum.

```
$ rails console
Running via Spring preloader in process 27764
Loading development environment (Rails 5.2.0)
>> Album.where(release_year: 1970..1979).sum(:release_year)
   (1.5ms)  SELECT SUM("albums"."release_year") FROM "albums" WHERE
   ("albums"."release_year" BETWEEN 1970 AND 1979)
=> 5922
>> Album.where(release_year: 1970..1979).order(:name).sum(:release_year)
   (0.3ms)  SELECT SUM("albums"."release_year") FROM "albums" WHERE
   ("albums"."release_year" BETWEEN 1970 AND 1979)
=> 5922
>> exit
```

Logically, the result is the same for both queries. But the interesting thing is that ActiveRecord uses the same SQL code for both queries. It has detected that order is completely irrelevant for sum and therefore took it out altogether.

ⓘ   If you are asking yourself why the first query took 1.5ms and the second 0.3ms, ActiveRecord cached the results of the first SQL request.

---

order and reverse_order

To sort a database query, you can use the method order.

Here's an example of all albums from the 1960s, sorted by name:

```
$ rails console
Running via Spring preloader in process 27764
Loading development environment (Rails 5.2.0)
>> Album.where(release_year: 1960..1969).order(:name)
  Album Load (0.2ms)  SELECT "albums".* FROM "albums" WHERE
  ("albums"."release_year" BETWEEN 1960 AND 1969)  ORDER BY "albums"."name"
  ASC
=> #<ActiveRecord::Relation [#<Album id: 9, name: "Blonde on Blonde" [...]]>
```

With the method reverse_order, you can reverse an order previously defined via order.

```
>> Album.where(release_year: 1960..1969).order(:name).reverse_order
   Album Load (0.3ms)  SELECT "albums".* FROM "albums" WHERE
   ("albums"."release_year" BETWEEN 1960 AND 1969)  ORDER BY "albums"."name"
   DESC
=> #<ActiveRecord::Relation [#<Album id: 10, name: "The Beatles" [...]]>
```

limit

The result of any search can be limited to a certain range via the method limit.

Here are the first five albums from the 1960s:

```
>> Album.where(release_year: 1960..1969).limit(5)
   Album Load (0.3ms)  SELECT  "albums".* FROM "albums" WHERE
   ("albums"."release_year" BETWEEN 1960 AND 1969) LIMIT 5
=> #<ActiveRecord::Relation [#<Album id: 1, [...]]>
```

Here are all albums sorted by name and then the first five of those:

```
>> Album.order(:name).limit(5)
   Album Load (0.4ms)  SELECT  "albums".* FROM "albums"  ORDER BY
   "albums"."name" ASC LIMIT 5
=> #<ActiveRecord::Relation [#<Album id: 9, name: "Blonde [...]]>
```

offset

With the method offset, you can define the starting position of the method limit.

First, you return the first two records and then the first two records with an offset of 5.

```
>> Album.limit(2)
   Album Load (1.0ms)  SELECT  "albums".* FROM "albums" LIMIT 2
=> #<ActiveRecord::Relation [#<Album id: 1, [...]>, #<Album id: 2, [...]]>
>> Album.limit(2).offset(5)
   Album Load (0.3ms)  SELECT  "albums".* FROM "albums" LIMIT 2 OFFSET 5
=> #<ActiveRecord::Relation [#<Album id: 6, [...]>, #<Album id: 7, [...]>]>
```

group

With the method group, you can return the result of a query in grouped form.

Let's return all albums, grouped by their release_year.

```
$ rails console
Running via Spring preloader in process 27764
Loading development environment (Rails 5.2.0)
>> Album.group(:release_year)
  Album Load (0.3ms)  SELECT "albums".* FROM "albums" GROUP BY
  "albums"."release_year"
=> #<ActiveRecord::Relation [#<Album id: 5, name: "Rubber Soul",
release_year: 1965, created_at: "2015-12-16 17:45:34", updated_at: "2015-
12-16 17:45:34">, #<Album id: 9, name: "Blonde on Blonde", release_year:
1966, created_at:"2015-12-16 17:45:34", updated_at: "2015-12-16 17:45:34">,
#<Album id: 1,name: "Sgt. Pepper's Lonely Hearts Club Band", release_year:
1967, created_at:"2015-12-16 17:45:34", updated_at: "2015-12-16 17:45:34">,
#<Album id: 10,name: "The Beatles", release_year: 1968, created_at: "2015-
12-16 17:45:34",updated_at: "2015-12-16 17:45:34">, #<Album id: 6, name:
"What's Going On",release_year: 1971, created_at: "2015-12-16 17:45:34",
updated_at: "2015-12-16 17:45:34">, #<Album id: 7, name: "Exile on Main
St.", release_year: 1972,created_at: "2015-12-16 17:45:34", updated_at:
"2015-12-16 17:45:34">, #<Albumid: 8, name: "London Calling", release_
year: 1979, created_at: "2015-12-16 17:45:34", updated_at: "2015-12-16
17:45:34">]>>> exit
```

pluck

Normally, ActiveRecord pulls all table columns from the database and leaves it up to programmers to later pick out the components they are interested in. But when you have a large amount of data, it can be useful and, above all, much quicker to define a specific database field directly for the query. You can do this via the method pluck.

```
$ rails console
Running via Spring preloader in process 27927
Loading development environment (Rails 5.2.0)
>> Album.where(release_year: 1960..1969).pluck(:name)
   (0.2ms)  SELECT "albums"."name" FROM "albums"
   WHERE ("albums"."release_year" BETWEEN ? AND ?)
   [["release_year", 1960], ["release_year", 1969]]
=> ["Sgt. Pepper's Lonely Hearts Club Band", "Pet Sounds", "Revolver",
"Highway 61 Revisited", "Rubber Soul", "Blonde on Blonde", "The Beatles"]
```

As a result, pluck returns an array. You can pluck more than one field too.

```
>> Album.where(release_year: 1960..1969).pluck(:name, :release_year)
   (0.3ms)  SELECT "albums"."name", "albums"."release_year"
   FROM "albums" WHERE ("albums"."release_year" BETWEEN ? AND ?)
   [["release_year", 1960], ["release_year", 1969]]
=> [["Sgt. Pepper's Lonely Hearts Club Band", 1967],
["Pet Sounds", 1966], ["Revolver", 1966], ["Highway 61 Revisited", 1965],
["Rubber Soul", 1965], ["Blonde on Blonde", 1966], ["The Beatles", 1968]]
```

select

select works like pluck but returns an ActiveRecord::Relation.

```
>> Album.where(release_year: 1960..1969).select(:name)
  Album Load (0.2ms)  SELECT "albums"."name" FROM "albums"
  WHERE ("albums"."release_year" BETWEEN 1960 AND 1969)
=> #<ActiveRecord::Relation [#<Album id: nil,
name: "Sgt. Pepper's Lonely Hearts Club Band">,
#<Album id: nil, name: "Pet Sounds">,
#<Album id: nil, name: "Revolver">,
#<Album id: nil, name: "Highway 61 Revisited">,
#<Album id: nil, name: "Rubber Soul">,
#<Album id: nil, name: "Blonde on Blonde">,
#<Album id: nil, name: "The Beatles">]>
```

first_or_create and first_or_initialize

The methods first_or_create and first_or_initialize are ways to search for a specific entry in your database or create one if the entry doesn't exist already. Both have to be chained to a where search.

```
>> Album.where(name: 'Test')
  Album Load (0.2ms)  SELECT "albums".* FROM "albums"
  WHERE "albums"."name" = ?  [["name", "Test"]]
=> #<ActiveRecord::Relation []>
>> test = Album.where(name: 'Test').first_or_create
  Album Load (0.3ms)  SELECT  "albums".* FROM "albums"
  WHERE "albums"."name" = ?  ORDER BY "albums"."id" ASC LIMIT 1
  [["name", "Test"]]
   (0.1ms)  begin transaction
  SQL (0.4ms)  INSERT INTO "albums" ("name", "created_at", "updated_at")
  VALUES (?, ?, ?)  [["name", "Test"],
  ["created_at", "2015-12-16 18:34:35.775645"],
  ["updated_at", "2015-12-16 18:34:35.775645"]]
   (9.2ms)  commit transaction
=> #<Album id: 11, name: "Test", release_year: nil,
created_at: "2015-12-16 18:34:35", updated_at: "2015-12-16 18:34:35">
```

Calculations

Here are some examples of calculations.

average

With the method average, you can calculate the average of the values in a particular column of the table. The data material is of course not really suited to this. But as an example, let's calculate the average release year of all albums and then do the same for albums from the 1960s.

```
>> Album.average(:release_year)
   (0.3ms)  SELECT AVG("albums"."release_year") FROM "albums"
=> #<BigDecimal:7fd76fd027a0,'0.19685E4',18(36)>
>> Album.average(:release_year).to_s
   (0.2ms)  SELECT AVG("albums"."release_year") FROM "albums"
=> "1968.5"
>> Album.where( :release_year => 1960..1969 ).average(:release_year)
   (0.1ms)  SELECT AVG("albums"."release_year") FROM "albums" WHERE
   ("albums"."release_year" BETWEEN 1960 AND 1969)
=> #<BigDecimal:7fd76fc908d0,'0.1966142857 14286E4',27(36)>
>> Album.where( :release_year => 1960..1969 ).average(:release_year).to_s
   (0.3ms)  SELECT AVG("albums"."release_year") FROM "albums" WHERE
   ("albums"."release_year" BETWEEN 1960 AND 1969)
=> "1966.14285714286"
```

count

The name says it all: the method count counts the number of records.

First, you return the number of all albums in the database and then the number of albums from the 1960s.

```
>> Album.count
   (0.1ms)  SELECT COUNT(*) FROM "albums"
=> 11
```

maximum

With the method maximum, you can output the item with the highest value within a query.

Let's look for the highest release year.

```
>> Album.maximum(:release_year)
   (0.2ms)  SELECT MAX("albums"."release_year") FROM "albums"
=> 1979
```

minimum

With the method minimum, you can output the item with the lowest value within a query.

Let's find the lowest release year.

```
>> Album.minimum(:release_year)
   (0.2ms)  SELECT MIN("albums"."release_year") FROM "albums"
=> 1965
```

sum

With the method sum, you can calculate the sum of all items in a specific column of the database query.

Let's find the sum of all release years.

```
>> Album.sum(:release_year)
   (0.2ms)  SELECT SUM("albums"."release_year") FROM "albums"
=> 19685
```

SQL EXPLAIN

Most SQL databases can provide detailed information on a SQL query with the command EXPLAIN. This does not make much sense for your mini application, but if you are working with a large database one day, then EXPLAIN is a good debugging method, for example to find out where to place an index. SQL EXPLAIN can be called with the method explain (it will be displayed in prettier form if you add puts).

```
>> Album.where(release_year: 1960..1969)
  Album Load (0.2ms)  SELECT "albums".* FROM "albums" WHERE
  ("albums"."release_year" BETWEEN 1960 AND 1969)
=> #<ActiveRecord::Relation [#<Album id: 1, [...]>]>
>> Album.where(release_year: 1960..1969).explain
  Album Load (0.3ms)  SELECT "albums".* FROM "albums" WHERE
  ("albums"."release_year" BETWEEN 1960 AND 1969)
=> EXPLAIN for: SELECT "albums".* FROM "albums" WHERE ("albums"."release_year"
BETWEEN 1960 AND 1969)
0|0|0|SCAN TABLE albums
```

Batches

`ActiveRecord` stores the results of a query in memory, with very large tables and results that can become a performance issue. To address this, you can use the `find_each` method that splits up the query into batches with the default size of 1,000 (can be configured with the `:batch_size` option). The example `Album` table is too small to show the effect, but the method would be used like this:

```
>> Album.where(release_year: 1960..1969).find_each do |album|
?>    puts album.name.upcase
>> end
  Album Load (0.2ms)  SELECT  "albums".* FROM "albums" WHERE
  ("albums"."release_year" BETWEEN 1960 AND 1969)  ORDER BY "albums"."id" ASC
  LIMIT 1000
SGT. PEPPER'S LONELY HEARTS CLUB BAND
PET SOUNDS
REVOLVER
HIGHWAY 61 REVISITED
RUBBER SOUL
BLONDE ON BLONDE
THE BEATLES
=> nil
```

Editing a Record

Adding and searching data is quite nice, but often you want to edit a record. To show how that's done, I use the `album` database covered in the section "Searching and Finding with Queries."

Simple Editing

You can edit record with the following steps:

1. Find the record and create a corresponding instance.

2. Change the attribute.

3. Save the record via the `ActiveRecord` method's `save` method.

Here you are searching for the album *The Beatles* and changing its name to *A Test*:

```
$ rails console
Running via Spring preloader in process 27927
Loading development environment (Rails 5.2.0)
>> beatles_album = Album.where(name: 'The Beatles').first
  Album Load (0.2ms)  SELECT  "albums".* FROM "albums"
  WHERE "albums"."name" = ?  ORDER BY "albums"."id" ASC LIMIT 1
  [["name", "The Beatles"]]
=> #<Album id: 10, name: "The Beatles", release_year: 1968,
created_at: "2015-12-16 17:45:34", updated_at: "2015-12-16 17:45:34">
>> beatles_album.name
=> "The Beatles"
>> beatles_album.name = 'A Test'
=> "A Test"
>> beatles_album.save
  (0.1ms)  begin transaction
  SQL (0.6ms)  UPDATE "albums" SET "name" = ?, "updated_at" = ?
  WHERE "albums"."id" = ?  [["name", "A Test"],
  ["updated_at", "2015-12-16 18:46:03.851575"], ["id", 10]]
  (9.2ms)  commit transaction
=> true
>> exit
```

Active Model Dirty

ActiveModel::Dirty provides simple mechanisms to track the changes of an
ActiveRecord model.

changed?

If you are not sure whether a record has been changed or saved yet, you can check via
the method changed?.

```
>> beatles_album = Album.where(id: 10).first
  Album Load (0.4ms)  SELECT  "albums".* FROM "albums" WHERE "albums"."id" = ?
  ORDER BY "albums"."id" ASC LIMIT 1  [["id", 10]]
```

```
=> #<Album id: 10, name: "A Test", release_year: 1968, created_at:
"2015-12-16
17:45:34", updated_at: "2015-12-16 18:46:03">
>> beatles_album.changed?
=> false
>> beatles_album.name = 'The Beatles'
=> "The Beatles"
>> beatles_album.changed?
=> true
>> beatles_album.save
   (0.1ms)  begin transaction SQL (0.6ms)  UPDATE "albums" SET "name" = ?,
   "updated_at" = ? WHERE "albums"."id" = ?  [["name", "The Beatles"],
   ["updated_at", "2015-12-16 18:47:26.794527"], ["id", 10]] (9.2ms)  commit
   transaction
=> true
>> beatles_album.changed?
=> false
```

_changed?

An attribute name followed by _changed? tracks changes to a specific attribute.

```
>> beatles_album = Album.where(id: 10).first
  Album Load (0.5ms)   SELECT  "albums".* FROM "albums" WHERE "albums"."id"
= ? ORDER BY "albums"."id" ASC LIMIT ?  [["id", 10], ["LIMIT", 1]]
=> #<Album id: 10, name: "The Beatles", release_year: 1968, created_at:
"2016-01-21 10:15:51", updated_at: "2016-01-21 10:15:51">
>> beatles_album.release_year_changed?
=> false
>> beatles_album.release_year = 1900
=> 1900
>> beatles_album.release_year_changed?
=> true
```

update

With the method update, you can change several attributes of an object in one go and then immediately save them automatically.

Let's use this method within the example from the section "Simple Editing."

```
>> first_album = Album.first
  Album Load (0.1ms)  SELECT  "albums".* FROM "albums" ORDER BY
"albums"."id" ASC LIMIT ?  [["LIMIT", 1]]
=> #<Album id: 1, name: "Sgt. Pepper's Lonely Hearts Club Band", release_
year: 1967, created_at: "2016-01-21 10:15:51", updated_at: "2016-01-21
10:15:51">
>> first_album.changed?
=> false
>> first_album.update(name: 'Another Test')
  (0.1ms)  begin transaction
  SQL (0.4ms)  UPDATE "albums" SET "name" = ?, "updated_at" = ? WHERE
  "albums"."id" = ?  [["name", "Another Test"], ["updated_at", 2016-01-21
  12:11:27 UTC], ["id", 1]]
  (0.9ms)  commit transaction
=> true
>> first_album.changed?
=> false
>> first_album
=> #<Album id: 1, name: "Another Test", release_year: 1967, created_at:
"2016-01-21 10:15:51", updated_at: "2016-01-21 12:11:27">
```

Locking

There are many ways to lock a database. By default, Rails uses the *optimistic locking* of records. To activate locking, a model needs to have an attribute with the name lock_version, which has to be an integer. To show how it works, I'll create a new Rails project with a Product model. Then I'll try to change the price of the first Product on two different instances. The second change will raise an ActiveRecord::StaleObjectError.

Here's an example setup:

```
$ rails new shop
  [...]
$ cd shop
$ rails generate model Product name 'price:decimal{8,2}'
  lock_version:integer
  [...]
$ rails db:migrate
  [...]
$
```

Here's an example of raising an ActiveRecord::StaleObjectError:

```
$ rails console
Running via Spring preloader in process 27927
Loading development environment (Rails 5.2.0)
>> Product.create(name: 'Orange', price: 0.5)
   (0.1ms)  begin transaction SQL (0.7ms)  INSERT INTO "products" ("name",
   "price", "created_at", "updated_at", "lock_version")
   VALUES (?, ?, ?, ?, ?) [["name", "Orange"], ["price", 0.5],
   ["created_at", "2015-12-16 19:02:17.338531"],
   ["updated_at", "2015-12-16 19:02:17.338531"],
   ["lock_version", 0]]
   (1.0ms)  commit transaction
=> #<Product id: 1, name: "Orange", price:
#<BigDecimal:7feb59231198,'0.5E0',9(27)>, lock_version: 0, created_at:
"2015-12-16 19:02:17", updated_at: "2015-12-16 19:02:17">
>> a = Product.first
  Product Load (0.4ms)  SELECT  "products".* FROM "products"  ORDER BY
  "products"."id" ASC LIMIT 1
=> #<Product id: 1, name: "Orange", price:
#<BigDecimal:7feb5918a870,'0.5E0',9(27)>, lock_version: 0, created_at:
"2015-12-16 19:02:17", updated_at: "2015-12-16 19:02:17">
>> b = Product.first
  Product Load (0.3ms)  SELECT  "products".* FROM "products"  ORDER BY
  "products"."id" ASC LIMIT 1 => #<Product id: 1, name: "Orange", price:
```

```
  #<BigDecimal:7feb59172d60,'0.5E0',9(27)>, lock_version: 0, created_at:
  "2015-12-16 19:02:17", updated_at: "2015-12-16 19:02:17">
>> a.price = 0.6
=> 0.6
>> a.save
   (0.1ms)   begin transaction
  SQL (0.4ms)   UPDATE "products" SET "price" = 0.6, "updated_at" =
  '2015-12-16 19:02:59.514736', "lock_version" = 1 WHERE "products"."id" = ? AND
  "products"."lock_version" = ?   [["id", 1], ["lock_version", 0]]
   (9.1ms)   commit transaction
=> true
>> b.price = 0.7
=> 0.7
>> b.save
   (0.1ms)   begin transaction
  SQL (0.3ms)   UPDATE "products" SET "price" = 0.7, "updated_at" =
  '2015-12-16 19:03:08.408511', "lock_version" = 1 WHERE "products"."id" = ? AND
  "products"."lock_version" = ?   [["id", 1], ["lock_version", 0]]
   (0.1ms)   rollback transaction
ActiveRecord::StaleObjectError: Attempted to update a stale object: Product
[...]
>> exit
```

You have to deal with the conflict by rescuing the exception and then fix the conflict depending on your business logic.

> ❗   Please make sure to add a `lock_version` hidden field in your forms when using this mechanism with a WebGUI.

has_many, a 1:n Association

To explain has_many, let's create a food store application. Create a Category model and a Product model. A Product belongs to a Category. It's a 1:n association (called a *one-to-many association*).

 Associations are also sometimes referred to as *relations* or *relationships*.

First, you create a Rails application.

```
$ rails new food_store
  [...]
$ cd food_store
```

Now you create the model for the categories.

```
$ rails generate model Category name
  [...]
$
```

Finally, you create the database table for the Product. In this, you need an assignment field to the category table. This *foreign key* is always set by default as the name of the referenced object (here: category) with an attached _id. You could run the command rails generate model product name price:integer category_id:integer, but there is a better way of doing it, shown here:

```
$ rails generate model product name price:integer category:references
Running via Spring preloader in process 35988
      invoke  active_record
      create    db/migrate/20170323074157_create_products.rb
      create    app/models/product.rb
      invoke    test_unit
      create      test/models/product_test.rb
      create      test/fixtures/products.yml
```

Why is it better? It creates a different kind of migration that includes a foreign key optimization, as shown in Listing 3-9.

Listing 3-9. db/migrate/20170323074157_create_products.rb

```ruby
class CreateProducts < ActiveRecord::Migration[5.1]
  def change
    create_table :products do |t|
      t.string :name
      t.integer :price
      t.references :category, foreign_key: true

      t.timestamps
    end
  end
end
```

Then execute `rails db:migrate` so that the database tables are actually created.

```
$ rails db:migrate
```

Let's take a look at this on the console:

```
$ rails console
Running via Spring preloader in process 36245
Loading development environment (Rails 5.2.0)
>> Category.column_names
=> ["id", "name", "created_at", "updated_at"]
>> Product.column_names
=> ["id", "name", "price", "category_id", "created_at", "updated_at"]
>> exit
```

The two database tables are set up and can be used with `ActiveRecord`. And because you used `category:references`, it automatically inserted the `belongs_to` relationship into the `Product` model, as shown in Listing 3-10.

Listing 3-10. app/models/product.rb

```ruby
class Product < ApplicationRecord
  belongs_to :category
end
```

But you have to add the has_many part manually in the Category model, as shown in Listing 3-11.

Listing 3-11. app/models/category.rb

```
class Category < ApplicationRecord
  has_many :products
end
```

That's all you need to do to tell ActiveRecord about the 1:n relation. These two simple definitions form the basis for a good deal of ActiveRecord magic. It will generate a bunch of cool new methods for you to link both models.

Creating Records

In this example, you want to save a record for the product Apple, which belongs to the category Fruits. Fire up your console and follow my lead.

create

First create a new category for the fruits.

```
$ rails console
Running via Spring preloader in process 37142
Loading development environment (Rails 5.2.0)
>> fruits = Category.create(name: "Fruits")
   (0.1ms)  begin transaction
  SQL (0.5ms)  INSERT INTO "categories"
  ("name", "created_at", "updated_at") VALUES (?, ?, ?)
  [["name", "Fruits"], ["created_at", "2017-03-23 07:55:13.482884"],
  ["updated_at", "2017-03-23 07:55:13.482884"]]
   (2.3ms)  commit transaction
=> #<Category id: 1, name: "Fruits",
created_at: "2017-03-23 07:55:13",
updated_at: "2017-03-23 07:55:13">
```

Because the `Category` model has a `has_many :products` definition, it provides a `products` method, which you can use to get all the products of a given category.

```
>> fruits.products
  Product Load (0.2ms)  SELECT "products".* FROM "products" WHERE
"products"."category_id" = ?  [["category_id", 1]]
=> #<ActiveRecord::Associations::CollectionProxy []>
```

But it gets even better. You can chain the `create` method after `fruits.products` to actually create a new product, which has the correct `category_id`.

```
>> apple = fruits.products.create(name: "Apple", price: 1)
  (0.1ms)  begin transaction
  SQL (0.4ms)  INSERT INTO "products"
  ("name", "price", "category_id", "created_at", "updated_at")
  VALUES (?, ?, ?, ?, ?)  [["name", "Apple"], ["price", 1],
  ["category_id", 1], ["created_at", "2017-03-23 08:00:39.595699"],
  ["updated_at", "2017-03-23 08:00:39.595699"]]
  (3.4ms)  commit transaction
=> #<Product id: 1, name: "Apple", price: 1, category_id: 1,
created_at: "2017-03-23 08:00:39", updated_at: "2017-03-23 08:00:39">
```

Of course, this can be done manually too.

```
>> pineapple = Product.create(name: "Pineapple", price: 2, category_id: 1)
  (0.1ms)  begin transaction
  Category Load (0.3ms)  SELECT  "categories".* FROM "categories"
  WHERE "categories"."id" = ? LIMIT ?  [["id", 1], ["LIMIT", 1]]
  SQL (0.4ms)  INSERT INTO "products"
  ("name", "price", "category_id", "created_at", "updated_at")
  VALUES (?, ?, ?, ?, ?)  [["name", "Pineapple"], ["price", 2],
  ["category_id", 1], ["created_at", "2017-03-23 08:04:16.382548"],
  ["updated_at", "2017-03-23 08:04:16.382548"]]
  (2.5ms)  commit transaction
=> #<Product id: 2, name: "Pineapple", price: 2, category_id: 1,
created_at: "2017-03-23 08:04:16", updated_at: "2017-03-23 08:04:16">
```

If you don't want to chain create after fruits.products, you can create a new Product and fill in the category_id like this:

```
>> orange = Product.create(name: "Orange", price: 1, category: fruits)
   (0.1ms)  begin transaction
  SQL (1.3ms)  INSERT INTO "products"
  ("name", "price", "category_id", "created_at", "updated_at")
  VALUES (?, ?, ?, ?, ?)  [["name", "Orange"], ["price", 1],
  ["category_id", 1], ["created_at", "2017-03-23 08:15:37.575534"],
  ["updated_at", "2017-03-23 08:15:37.575534"]]
   (2.4ms)  commit transaction
=> #<Product id: 3, name: "Orange", price: 1, category_id: 1,
created_at: "2017-03-23 08:15:37", updated_at: "2017-03-23 08:15:37">
```

I think the chained version is the best, but who am I to judge?

Now you have three products that belong to fruits.

```
>> fruits.products.count
   (0.2ms)  SELECT COUNT(*) FROM "products"
   WHERE "products"."category_id" = ?  [["category_id", 1]]
=> 3
>> exit
```

build

The method build resembles create. But the record is not saved. This happens only after a save.

```
$ rails console
Running via Spring preloader in process 40092
Loading development environment (Rails 5.2.0)
>> fruits = Category.where(name: "Fruits").first
  Category Load (0.1ms)  SELECT "categories".* FROM "categories"
  WHERE "categories"."name" = ? ORDER BY "categories"."id" ASC LIMIT ?
  [["name", "Fruits"], ["LIMIT", 1]]
=> #<Category id: 1, name: "Fruits", created_at: "2017-03-23 07:55:13",
updated_at: "2017-03-23 07:55:13">
>> cherry = fruits.products.build(name: "Cherry", price: 1)
```

```
=> #<Product id: nil, name: "Cherry", price: 1, category_id: 1,
created_at: nil, updated_at: nil>
>> cherry.save
   (0.1ms)  begin transaction
  SQL (1.9ms)  INSERT INTO "products" ("name", "price", "category_id",
  "created_at", "updated_at") VALUES (?, ?, ?, ?, ?)  [["name", "Cherry"],
  ["price", 1], ["category_id", 1],
  ["created_at", "2017-03-23 08:22:48.044002"],
  ["updated_at", "2017-03-23 08:22:48.044002"]]
   (2.6ms)  commit transaction
=> true
>> exit
```

⚠   When using `create` and `build`, you of course have to observe logical dependencies or there will be an error. For example, you cannot chain two `build` methods. Here's an example:

```
>> Category.build(name: "Vegetable").products.build(name: "Potato")
NoMethodError: undefined method `build' for #
<Class:0x007f8d7c72c020>
    from (irb):3
```

Accessing Records

To access records, first you need example data. Please populate the file db/seeds.rb with the content shown in Listing 3-12.

Listing 3-12. db/seeds.rb

```
fruits = Category.create(name: "Fruits")
vegetables = Category.create(name: "Vegetables")
jams = Category.create(name: "Jams")

fruits.products.create(name: "Apple", price: 1)
fruits.products.create(name: "Banana", price: 2)
```

```
fruits.products.create(name: "Pineapple", price: 3)
fruits.products.create(name: "Raspberry", price: 1)
fruits.products.create(name: "Strawberry", price: 1)

vegetables.products.create(name: "Potato", price: 2)
vegetables.products.create(name: "Carrot", price: 1)
vegetables.products.create(name: "Broccoli", price: 2)
vegetables.products.create(name: "Cauliflower", price: 1)

jams.products.create(name: "Strawberry", price: 1)
jams.products.create(name: "Raspberry", price: 1)
```

Now drop the database and refill it with db/seeds.rb.

```
$ rails db:reset
```

You already know how to access the products of a given category.

```
$ rails console
Running via Spring preloader in process 45107
Loading development environment (Rails 5.2.0)
>> Category.first.products.count
  Category Load (0.1ms)  SELECT  "categories".* FROM "categories"
  ORDER BY "categories"."id" ASC LIMIT ?  [["LIMIT", 1]]
   (0.1ms)  SELECT COUNT(*) FROM "products"
   WHERE "products"."category_id" = ?  [["category_id", 1]]
=> 5
```

You can access the records simply via the plural form of the n model. Hm, do you think it also works the other way around? Let's try the singular of the 1 model.

```
>> Product.first.category
  Product Load (0.3ms)  SELECT  "products".* FROM "products"
  ORDER BY "products"."id" ASC LIMIT ?  [["LIMIT", 1]]
  Category Load (0.2ms)  SELECT  "categories".* FROM "categories"
  WHERE "categories"."id" = ? LIMIT ?  [["id", 1], ["LIMIT", 1]]
=> #<Category id: 1, name: "Fruits", created_at: "2017-03-23 14:23:16",
updated_at: "2017-03-23 14:23:16">
>> exit
```

Bingo! Accessing the associated Category class is also easy. And as it's only a single record (belongs_to), the singular form is used in this case.

ℹ   If there is no product for a category, the result will be an empty array. If no category is associated with an product, then ActiveRecord outputs the value nil as Category.

Searching for Records

To search for records, first you check how many products are in the database.

```
$ rails console
Running via Spring preloader in process 45328
Loading development environment (Rails 5.2.0)
>> Product.count
   (0.1ms)  SELECT COUNT(*) FROM "products"
=> 11
```

And you check how many categories there are.

```
>> Category.count
   (0.1ms)  SELECT COUNT(*) FROM "categories"
=> 3
```

joins method

To find all categories that have at least one product with the name Strawberry, you use a joins method.

```
>> Category.joins(:products).where(:products => {name: "Strawberry"})
   Category Load (0.2ms)  SELECT "categories".* FROM "categories"
   INNER JOIN "products" ON "products"."category_id" = "categories"."id"
   WHERE "products"."name" = ?  [["name", "Strawberry"]]
=> #<ActiveRecord::Relation [#<Category id: 1, name: "Fruits",
created_at: "2017-03-23 14:33:14", updated_at: "2017-03-23 14:33:14">,
```

```
#<Category id: 3, name: "Jams", created_at: "2017-03-23 14:33:14",
updated_at: "2017-03-23 14:33:14">]>
>>
```

The database contains two categories with a product Strawberry. In the SQL, you can see that the method joins executes an INNER JOIN.

Of course, you can also do it the other way around. You could search for the products with the category Jams.

```
>> Product.joins(:category).where(:categories => {name: "Jams"})
  Product Load (0.4ms)  SELECT "products".* FROM "products"
  INNER JOIN "categories" ON "categories"."id" = "products"."category_id"
  WHERE "categories"."name" = ?  [["name", "Jams"]]
=> #<ActiveRecord::Relation [#<Product id: 10, name: "Strawberry",
price: 1, category_id: 3, created_at: "2017-03-23 14:33:15",
updated_at: "2017-03-23 14:33:15">, #<Product id: 11, name: "Raspberry",
price: 1, category_id: 3, created_at: "2017-03-23 14:33:15",
updated_at: "2017-03-23 14:33:15">]>
```

includes

includes is similar to the method joins (see the section "joins"). Again, you can use it to search within a 1:n association. Let's repeat the searches you just did with includes instead of joins.

```
>> Category.includes(:products).where(:products => {name: "Strawberry"})
  SQL (0.4ms)  SELECT "categories"."id" AS t0_r0, "categories"."name"
  AS t0_r1, "categories"."created_at" AS t0_r2, "categories"."updated_at"
  AS t0_r3, "products"."id" AS t1_r0, "products"."name" AS t1_r1,
  "products"."price" AS t1_r2, "products"."category_id" AS t1_r3,
  "products"."created_at" AS t1_r4, "products"."updated_at" AS t1_r5
  FROM "categories" LEFT OUTER JOIN "products" ON
  "products"."category_id" = "categories"."id" WHERE
  "products"."name" = ?  [["name", "Strawberry"]]
=> #<ActiveRecord::Relation [#<Category id: 1, name: "Fruits",
created_at: "2017-03-23 14:33:14", updated_at: "2017-03-23 14:33:14">,
```

```
#<Category id: 3, name: "Jams", created_at: "2017-03-23 14:33:14",
updated_at: "2017-03-23 14:33:14">]>
>> exit
```

In the console output, you can see that the SQL code is different from the `joins` query. `joins` only reads in the `Category` records; `includes` reads the associated `Product` records.

joins vs. includes

Why would you want to use `includes` at all? Well, if you already know before the query that you will later need all the product data, then it makes sense to use `includes`, because then you need only one database query. That is a lot faster than starting a separate query for each one.

In that case, would it not be better to always work with `includes`? No, it depends on the specific case. When you are using `includes`, a lot more data is transported initially. This has to be cached and processed by ActiveRecord, which takes longer and requires more resources.

delete and destroy

With the methods `destroy`, `destroy_all`, `delete`, and `delete_all`, you can delete records, as described in the section called "Deleting/Destroying a Record." In the context of `has_many`, this means you can delete the `Product` records associated with a `Category` in one go.

```
$ rails console
Running via Spring preloader in process 46835
Loading development environment (Rails 5.2.0)
>> Category.first.products.destroy_all
  Category Load (0.3ms)  SELECT  "categories".* FROM "categories"
  ORDER BY "categories"."id" ASC LIMIT ?  [["LIMIT", 1]]
  Product Load (0.2ms)  SELECT "products".* FROM "products"
  WHERE "products"."category_id" = ?  [["category_id", 1]]
   (0.1ms)  begin transaction
```

```
SQL (0.4ms)  DELETE FROM "products" WHERE "products"."id" = ?  [["id", 1]]
SQL (0.1ms)  DELETE FROM "products" WHERE "products"."id" = ?  [["id", 2]]
SQL (0.1ms)  DELETE FROM "products" WHERE "products"."id" = ?  [["id", 3]]
SQL (0.1ms)  DELETE FROM "products" WHERE "products"."id" = ?  [["id", 4]]
SQL (0.1ms)  DELETE FROM "products" WHERE "products"."id" = ?  [["id", 5]]
  (2.8ms)  commit transaction
=> [#<Product id: 1, name: "Apple", price: 1, category_id: 1,
created_at: "2017-03-23 14:33:15", updated_at: "2017-03-23 14:33:15">,
#<Product id: 2, name: "Banana", price: 2, category_id: 1,
created_at: "2017-03-23 14:33:15", updated_at: "2017-03-23 14:33:15">,
#<Product id: 3, name: "Pineapple", price: 3, category_id: 1,
created_at: "2017-03-23 14:33:15", updated_at: "2017-03-23 14:33:15">,
#<Product id: 4, name: "Raspberry", price: 1, category_id: 1,
created_at: "2017-03-23 14:33:15", updated_at: "2017-03-23 14:33:15">,
#<Product id: 5, name: "Strawberry", price: 1, category_id: 1,
created_at: "2017-03-23 14:33:15", updated_at: "2017-03-23 14:33:15">]
>> Category.first.products.count
  Category Load (0.2ms)  SELECT  "categories".* FROM "categories"
  ORDER BY "categories"."id" ASC LIMIT ?  [["LIMIT", 1]]
  (0.3ms)  SELECT COUNT(*) FROM "products"
  WHERE "products"."category_id" = ?  [["category_id", 1]]
=> 0
>> exit
```

Options

I can't comment on all possible options at this point. But I'd like to show you the most often used ones. For all others, please refer to the Ruby on Rails documentation that you can find on the Internet at http://rails.rubyonrails.org/classes/ActiveRecord/Associations/ClassMethods.html.

belongs_to

The most important option for belongs_to is this:

```
touch: true
```

It automatically sets the field updated_at of the entry in the table Category to the current time when a Product is edited. In app/models/product.rb, it would look like Listing 3-13.

Listing 3-13. app/models/product.rb

```
class Product < ApplicationRecord
  belongs_to :category, touch: true
end
```

has_many

The most important option for has_many is as follows:

dependent: :destroy

If a category is removed, then it usually makes sense to also automatically remove all products dependent on this category. This can be done via :dependent ⇒ :destroy in app/models/category.rb, as shown in Listing 3-14.

Listing 3-14. app/models/category.rb

```
class Category < ApplicationRecord
  has_many :products, dependent: :destroy
end
```

In the following example, you destroy the last category in the database table. All products of this category are also automatically destroyed.

```
$ rails console
Running via Spring preloader in process 47105
Loading development environment (Rails 5.2.0)
>> Product.count
   (0.1ms)  SELECT COUNT(*) FROM "products"
=> 6
>> Category.last.destroy
  Category Load (0.1ms)  SELECT  "categories".* FROM "categories"
  ORDER BY "categories"."id" DESC LIMIT ?  [["LIMIT", 1]]
   (0.1ms)  begin transaction
```

```
Product Load (0.2ms)  SELECT "products".* FROM "products"
WHERE "products"."category_id" = ?  [["category_id", 3]]
SQL (0.6ms)  DELETE FROM "products" WHERE "products"."id" = ?  [["id", 10]]
SQL (0.1ms)  DELETE FROM "products" WHERE "products"."id" = ?  [["id", 11]]
SQL (0.1ms)  DELETE FROM "categories" WHERE "categories"."id" = ?  [["id", 3]]
  (4.7ms)  commit transaction
=> #<Category id: 3, name: "Jams", created_at: "2017-03-23 14:33:14",
updated_at: "2017-03-23 15:02:08">
>> Product.count
  (0.2ms)  SELECT COUNT(*) FROM "products"
=> 4
>> exit
```

❗ Please always remember the difference between the methods `destroy` (see the section "destroy") and `delete` (see the section "delete"). This association works only with the method `destroy`.

Many-to-Many, an n:n Association

Up to now, you have always associated a database table directly with another table. For many-to-many, you will associate two tables via a third table. As an example for this kind of relation, let's use an order in an online shop. In this type of shop system, a `Product` can appear in several orders (`Order`), and at the same time an order can contain several products. This is referred to as *many-to-many*. Let's re-create this scenario with code.

Preparation

Create the shop application.

```
$ rails new online_shop
  [...]
$ cd online_shop
```

Here's a model for the products:

```
$ rails generate model product name 'price:decimal{7,2}'
```

Here's a model for an order:

```
$ rails generate model order delivery_address
```

Here's a model for individual items of an order:

```
$ rails generate model line_item order:references \
product:references quantity:integer
```

Then, create the database.

```
$ rails db:migrate
```

Finally, set up some example data, as shown in Listing 3-15.

Listing 3-15. db/seeds.rb

```
Product.create(name: 'Milk', price: 0.45)
Product.create(name: 'Butter', price: 0.75)
Product.create(name: 'Flour', price: 0.45)
Product.create(name: 'Eggs', price: 1.45)

$ rails db:seed
```

The Association

An order (Order) consists of one or several items (LineItem). This LineItem consists of the order_id, a product_id, and the number of items ordered (quantity). The individual product is defined in the product database (Product).

Associating the models happens as always in the directory app/models. First, Listing 3-16 shows the file app/models/order.rb.

Listing 3-16. app/models/order.rb

```
class Order < ApplicationRecord
  has_many :line_items
  has_many :products, through: :line_items
end
```

Then Listing 3-17 shows the counterpart in the file app/models/product.rb.

Listing 3-17. app/models/product.rb

```ruby
class Product < ApplicationRecord
  has_many :line_items
  has_many :orders, through: :line_items
end
```

The file app/models/line_item.rb has been filled by the generator, as shown in Listing 3-18.

Listing 3-18. app/models/line_item.rb

```ruby
class LineItem < ApplicationRecord
  belongs_to :order
  belongs_to :product
end
```

The Association Works Transparently

As you implement the associations via has_many, most things will already be familiar to you from the section "has_many, a 1:n Association." I am going to show a few examples.

First create a new Order object.

```
$ rails console
Running via Spring preloader in process 48290
Loading development environment (Rails 5.2.0)
>> order = Order.new(delivery_address: '123 Acme Street')
=> #<Order id: nil, delivery_address: "123 Acme Street",
created_at: nil, updated_at: nil>
```

Logically, this new order does not yet contain any products.

```
>> order.products.count
=> 0
```

Usually, there are several ways of adding products to the order. The simplest way is that the products are integrated as an array, and you can simply insert them as elements of an array.

```
>> order.products << Product.first
  Product Load (0.5ms)  SELECT  "products".* FROM "products"
  ORDER BY "products"."id" ASC LIMIT ?  [["LIMIT", 1]]
=> #<ActiveRecord::Associations::CollectionProxy
[#<Product id: 1, name: "Milk", price: 0.45e0,
created_at: "2017-03-23 15:14:22",
updated_at: "2017-03-23 15:14:22">]>
```

But if the customer wants to buy three times the milk, you need to enter it in the LineItem (in the linking element) table. ActiveRecord already built an object for you.

```
>> order.line_items
=> #<ActiveRecord::Associations::CollectionProxy
[#<LineItem id: nil, order_id: nil, product_id: 1, quantity: nil,
created_at: nil, updated_at: nil>]>
```

And you have access to it. So, you can change the quantity like so:

```
>> order.line_items.first.quantity = 3
=> 3
```

But neither the order nor any other object has been saved in the database yet. You have to call the save method to do this.

```
>> order.save
  (0.1ms)  begin transaction
  SQL (0.6ms)  INSERT INTO "orders" ("delivery_address", "created_at",
  "updated_at") VALUES (?, ?, ?)  [["delivery_address", "123 Acme Street"],
  ["created_at", "2017-03-23 15:22:48.536239"],
  ["updated_at", "2017-03-23 15:22:48.536239"]]
  SQL (0.2ms)  INSERT INTO "line_items" ("order_id", "product_id",
  "quantity", "created_at", "updated_at") VALUES (?, ?, ?, ?, ?)
  [["order_id", 2], ["product_id", 1], ["quantity", 3],
```

```
    ["created_at", "2017-03-23 15:22:48.539047"],
    ["updated_at", "2017-03-23 15:22:48.539047"]]
     (2.1ms)  commit transaction
 => true
```

Alternatively, you can also buy butter twice directly by adding a LineItem.

```
>> order.line_items.create(product: Product.second, quantity: 2)
  Product Load (0.2ms)  SELECT  "products".* FROM "products"
  ORDER BY "products"."id" ASC LIMIT ? OFFSET ?  [["LIMIT", 1],
  ["OFFSET", 1]]
   (0.1ms)  begin transaction
  SQL (2.1ms)  INSERT INTO "line_items" ("order_id", "product_id",
  "quantity", "created_at", "updated_at") VALUES (?, ?, ?, ?, ?)
  [["order_id", 2], ["product_id", 2], ["quantity", 2],
  ["created_at", "2017-03-23 15:25:32.991756"],
  ["updated_at", "2017-03-23 15:25:32.991756"]]
   (2.2ms)  commit transaction
 => #<LineItem id: 3, order_id: 2, product_id: 2, quantity: 2,
created_at: "2017-03-23 15:25:32", updated_at: "2017-03-23 15:25:32">
```

All searches and queries (including via joins and includes) work for you as a Rails programmer the same as without the has_many. ActiveRecord takes care of the details.

Polymorphic Associations

The word *polymorphic* probably makes you tense up. What can it mean? Here is what the web site http://api.rubyonrails.org/classes/ActiveRecord/Associations/ ClassMethods.html tells us: "Polymorphic associations on models are not restricted on what types of models they can be associated with." Well, there you go—as clear as mud!

I will show you an example in which you create a Car model and a Bike model. To describe a car or bike, you use a Tag model. A car and a bike can have any number of tags.

Here's the application:

```
$ rails new bike_car_example
  [...]
$ cd bike_car_example
```

Here are the three required models:

```
$ rails generate model Car name
  [...]
$ rails generate model Bike name
  [...]
$ rails generate model Tag name taggable:references{polymorphic}
  [...]
$ rails db:migrate
  [...]
```

Car and Bike are clear. For Tag you use the migration shortcut taggable:refer ences{polymorphic} to generate the fields taggable_type and taggable_id to give ActiveRecord an opportunity to save the assignment for the polymorphic association. You have to enter it accordingly in the model.

The model generator already filled the app/models/tag.rb file with the configuration for the polymorphic association, as shown in Listing 3-19.

Listing 3-19. app/models/tag.rb

```
class Tag < ApplicationRecord
  belongs_to :taggable, polymorphic: true
end
```

For the other models, you have to add the polymorphic association manually, as shown in Listing 3-20 and Listing 3-21.

Listing 3-20. app/models/car.rb

```
class Car < ApplicationRecord
  has_many :tags, as: :taggable
end
```

Listing 3-21. app/models/bike.rb

```
class Bike < ApplicationRecord
  has_many :tags, as: :taggable
end
```

For Car and Bike you use an additional :as: :taggable when defining has_many. For Tag, you use belongs_to :taggable, polymorphic: true to indicate the polymorphic association to ActiveRecord.

> 💡 The suffix *able* in the name *taggable* is commonly used in Rails, but not obligatory. For creating the association you not only need the ID of the entry but also need to know which *model* it actually is. So, the term taggable_type makes sense.

Let's go into the console and create a car and a bike.

```
$ rails console
Running via Spring preloader in process 27927
Loading development environment (Rails 5.2.0)
>> beetle = Car.create(name: 'Beetle')
   (0.1ms)  begin transaction
  SQL (0.8ms)  INSERT INTO "cars" ("name", "created_at", "updated_at") VALUES
  (?, ?, ?)  [["name", "Beetle"], ["created_at", "2015-12-17
  13:39:54.793336"], ["updated_at", "2015-12-17 13:39:54.793336"]]
   (0.8ms)  commit transaction
=> #<Car id: 1, name: "Beetle", created_at: "2015-12-17 13:39:54", updated_at:
"2015-12-17 13:39:54">
>> mountainbike = Bike.create(name: 'Mountainbike')
   (0.1ms)  begin transaction
  SQL (0.3ms)  INSERT INTO "bikes" ("name", "created_at", "updated_at") VALUES
  (?, ?, ?)  [["name", "Mountainbike"], ["created_at", "2015-12-17
  13:39:55.896512"], ["updated_at", "2015-12-17 13:39:55.896512"]]
   (9.0ms)  commit transaction
=> #<Bike id: 1, name: "Mountainbike", created_at: "2015-12-17 13:39:55",
updated_at: "2015-12-17 13:39:55">
```

Now you define for each a tag with the color of the corresponding object.

```
>> beetle.tags.create(name: 'blue')
   (0.1ms)  begin transaction
  SQL (1.0ms)  INSERT INTO "tags" ("name", "taggable_id", "taggable_type",
  "created_at", "updated_at") VALUES (?, ?, ?, ?, ?)  [["name", "blue"],
  ["taggable_id", 1], ["taggable_type", "Car"], ["created_at", "2015-12-17
  13:41:04.984444"], ["updated_at", "2015-12-17 13:41:04.984444"]]
   (0.9ms)  commit transaction
=> #<Tag id: 1, name: "blue", taggable_id: 1, taggable_type: "Car",
created_at: "2015-12-17 13:41:04", updated_at: "2015-12-17 13:41:04">
>> mountainbike.tags.create(name: 'black')
   (0.1ms)  begin transaction
  SQL (0.7ms)  INSERT INTO "tags" ("name", "taggable_id", "taggable_type",
  "created_at", "updated_at") VALUES (?, ?, ?, ?, ?)  [["name", "black"],
  ["taggable_id", 1], ["taggable_type", "Bike"], ["created_at", "2015-12-17
  13:41:17.315318"], ["updated_at", "2015-12-17 13:41:17.315318"]]
   (8.2ms)  commit transaction
=> #<Tag id: 2, name: "black", taggable_id: 1, taggable_type: "Bike",
created_at: "2015-12-17 13:41:17", updated_at: "2015-12-17 13:41:17">
```

For the beetle, you add another Tag.

```
>> beetle.tags.create(name: 'Automatic')
   (0.1ms)  begin transaction
  SQL (0.4ms)  INSERT INTO "tags" ("name", "taggable_id", "taggable_type",
  "created_at", "updated_at") VALUES (?, ?, ?, ?, ?)  [["name", "Automatic"],
  ["taggable_id", 1], ["taggable_type", "Car"], ["created_at", "2015-12-17
  13:41:51.042746"], ["updated_at", "2015-12-17 13:41:51.042746"]]
   (9.2ms)  commit transaction
=> #<Tag id: 3, name: "Automatic", taggable_id: 1, taggable_type: "Car",
created_at: "2015-12-17 13:41:51", updated_at: "2015-12-17 13:41:51">
```

Let's take a look at all the Tag items.

```
>> Tag.all
  Tag Load (0.3ms)  SELECT "tags".* FROM "tags"
=> #<ActiveRecord::Relation [#<Tag id: 1, name: "blue", taggable_id: 1,
taggable_type: "Car", created_at: "2015-12-17 13:41:04", updated_at:
"2015-12-17 13:41:04">, #<Tag id: 2, name: "black", taggable_id: 1,
taggable_type: "Bike", created_at: "2015-12-17 13:41:17", updated_at:
"2015-12-17 13:41:17">, #<Tag id: 3, name: "Automatic", taggable_id: 1,
taggable_type: "Car", created_at: "2015-12-17 13:41:51", updated_at:
"2015-12-17 13:41:51">]>
```

Here are all the tags of the beetle.

```
>> beetle.tags
  Tag Load (0.3ms)  SELECT "tags".* FROM "tags" WHERE "tags"."taggable_id" = ?
  AND "tags"."taggable_type" = ?  [["taggable_id", 1], ["taggable_type",
  "Car"]]
=> #<ActiveRecord::Associations::CollectionProxy [#<Tag id: 1, name: "blue",
taggable_id: 1, taggable_type: "Car", created_at: "2015-12-17 13:41:04",
updated_at: "2015-12-17 13:41:04">, #<Tag id: 3, name: "Automatic",
taggable_id: 1, taggable_type: "Car", created_at: "2015-12-17 13:41:51",
updated_at: "2015-12-17 13:41:51">]>
```

Of course, you can also check which object the last Tag belongs to.

```
>> Tag.last.taggable
  Tag Load (0.3ms)  SELECT  "tags".* FROM "tags"  ORDER BY "tags"."id" DESC
  LIMIT 1
  Car Load (0.4ms)  SELECT  "cars".* FROM "cars" WHERE "cars"."id" = ? LIMIT 1
  [["id", 1]]
=> #<Car id: 1, name: "Beetle", created_at: "2015-12-17 13:39:54", updated_at:
"2015-12-17 13:39:54">
>> exit
```

Polymorphic associations are always useful if you want to normalize the database structure. In this example, you could also have defined models called CarTag and BikeTag, but as Tag is the same for both, a polymorphic association makes more sense in this case.

Options

Polymorphic associations can be configured with the same options as a normal has_many association.

Deleting/Destroying a Record

To remove a database record, you can use the methods destroy and delete. It's quite easy to confuse these two terms, but they are different, and after a while you get used to them.

As an example, = use the following Rails application:

```
$ rails new bookshelf
  [...]
$ cd bookshelf
$ rails generate model book title
  [...]
$ rails generate model author book:references first_name last_name
  [...]
$ rails db:migrate
  [...]
$
```

Listing 3-22 and Listing 3-23 show the models.

Listing 3-22. app/models/book.rb

```ruby
class Book < ApplicationRecord
  has_many :authors, dependent: :destroy
end
```

Listing 3-23. app/models/author.rb

```ruby
class Author < ApplicationRecord
  belongs_to :book
end
```

destroy

With destroy you can remove a record, and any existing dependencies are also taken into account (see, for example, :dependent ⇒ :destroy). Simply put, to be on the safe side, it's better to use destroy because then the Rails system does more for you.

Let's create a record and then destroy it again.

```
$ rails console
Running via Spring preloader in process 27927
Loading development environment (Rails 5.2.0)
>> book = Book.create(title: 'Homo faber')
   (0.1ms)  begin transaction
  SQL (0.7ms)  INSERT INTO "books" ("title", "created_at", "updated_at")
  VALUES (?, ?, ?)  [["title", "Homo faber"], ["created_at", "2015-12-17
  13:49:58.092997"], ["updated_at", "2015-12-17 13:49:58.092997"]]
   (9.0ms)  commit transaction
=> #<Book id: 1, title: "Homo faber", created_at: "2015-12-17 13:49:58",
updated_at: "2015-12-17 13:49:58">
>> Book.count
   (0.3ms)  SELECT COUNT(*) FROM "books"
=> 1
>> book.destroy
   (0.1ms)  begin transaction
  Author Load (0.1ms)  SELECT "authors".* FROM "authors" WHERE
  "authors"."book_id" = ?  [["book_id", 1]]
  SQL (0.3ms)  DELETE FROM "books" WHERE "books"."id" = ?  [["id", 1]]
   (9.0ms)  commit transaction
=> #<Book id: 1, title: "Homo faber", created_at: "2015-12-17 13:49:58",
updated_at: "2015-12-17 13:49:58">
>> Book.count
   (0.5ms)  SELECT COUNT(*) FROM "books"
=> 0
```

As you are using the option dependent: :destroy in the Book model, you can also automatically remove all the authors.

```
>> Book.create(title: 'Homo faber').authors.create(first_name: 'Max',
   last_name: 'Frisch')
   (0.1ms)  begin transaction
  SQL (0.4ms)  INSERT INTO "books" ("title", "created_at", "updated_at")
  VALUES (?, ?, ?)  [["title", "Homo faber"], ["created_at", "2015-12-17
  13:50:43.062148"], ["updated_at", "2015-12-17 13:50:43.062148"]]
   (9.1ms)  commit transaction
   (0.1ms)  begin transaction
  SQL (0.3ms)  INSERT INTO "authors" ("first_name", "last_name", "book_id",
  "created_at", "updated_at") VALUES (?, ?, ?, ?, ?)  [["first_name", "Max"],
  ["last_name", "Frisch"], ["book_id", 2], ["created_at", "2015-12-17
  13:50:43.083211"], ["updated_at", "2015-12-17 13:50:43.083211"]]
   (0.9ms)  commit transaction
=> #<Author id: 1, book_id: 2, first_name: "Max", last_name: "Frisch",
created_at: "2015-12-17 13:50:43", updated_at: "2015-12-17 13:50:43">
>> Author.count
   (0.2ms)  SELECT COUNT(*) FROM "authors"
=> 1
>> Book.first.destroy
  Book Load (0.3ms)  SELECT  "books".* FROM "books"  ORDER BY "books"."id" ASC
  LIMIT 1
   (0.1ms)  begin transaction
  Author Load (0.1ms)  SELECT "authors".* FROM "authors" WHERE
  "authors"."book_id" = ?  [["book_id", 2]]
  SQL (0.3ms)  DELETE FROM "authors" WHERE "authors"."id" = ?  [["id", 1]]
  SQL (0.1ms)  DELETE FROM "books" WHERE "books"."id" = ?  [["id", 2]]
   (9.1ms)  commit transaction
=> #<Book id: 2, title: "Homo faber", created_at: "2015-12-17 13:50:43",
updated_at: "2015-12-17 13:50:43">
>> Author.count
   (0.2ms)  SELECT COUNT(*) FROM "authors"
=> 0
```

When removing records, please always consider the difference between the content of the database table and the value of the currently removed object. The instance is *frozen* after removing the database field. So, it is no longer in the database but still present in the program, yet it can no longer be modified there. It is read-only. To check, you can use the method frozen?.

```
>> book = Book.create(title: 'Homo faber')
   (0.2ms)  begin transaction
  SQL (0.5ms)  INSERT INTO "books" ("title", "created_at", "updated_at")
  VALUES (?, ?, ?)  [["title", "Homo faber"], ["created_at", "2015-12-17
  13:51:41.460050"], ["updated_at", "2015-12-17 13:51:41.460050"]]
   (8.9ms)  commit transaction
=> #<Book id: 3, title: "Homo faber", created_at: "2015-12-17 13:51:41",
updated_at: "2015-12-17 13:51:41">
>> book.destroy
   (0.1ms)  begin transaction
  Author Load (0.2ms)  SELECT "authors".* FROM "authors" WHERE
  "authors"."book_id" = ?  [["book_id", 3]]
  SQL (0.5ms)  DELETE FROM "books" WHERE "books"."id" = ?  [["id", 3]]
   (9.2ms)  commit transaction
=> #<Book id: 3, title: "Homo faber", created_at: "2015-12-17 13:51:41",
updated_at: "2015-12-17 13:51:41">
>> Book.count
   (0.2ms)  SELECT COUNT(*) FROM "books"
=> 0
>> book
=> #<Book id: 3, title: "Homo faber", created_at: "2015-12-17 13:51:41",
updated_at: "2015-12-17 13:51:41">
>> book.frozen?
=> true
```

The record has been removed from the database, but the object with all its data is still present in the running Ruby program. So, could you then revive the entire record? The answer is yes, but it will then be a new record.

```
>> Book.create(title: book.title)
   (0.1ms)  begin transaction
  SQL (0.3ms)  INSERT INTO "books" ("title", "created_at", "updated_at")
  VALUES (?, ?, ?)  [["title", "Homo faber"], ["created_at", "2015-12-17
  13:52:51.438501"], ["updated_at", "2015-12-17 13:52:51.438501"]]
   (8.7ms)  commit transaction
=> #<Book id: 4, title: "Homo faber", created_at: "2015-12-17 13:52:51",
updated_at: "2015-12-17 13:52:51">
>> exit
```

delete

With delete you can remove a record directly from the database. Any dependencies to
other records in the model are not taken into account. The method delete deletes only
that one row in the database and nothing else.

Let's create a book with one author and then remove the book with delete.

```
$ rails db:reset
  [...]
$ rails console
Running via Spring preloader in process 27927
Loading development environment (Rails 5.2.0)
>> Book.create(title: 'Homo faber').authors.create(first_name: 'Max',
   last_name: 'Frisch')
   (0.5ms)  begin transaction
   [...]
   (0.8ms)  commit transaction
=> #<Author id: 1, book_id: 1, first_name: "Max", last_name: "Frisch",
created_at: "2015-12-17 13:54:46", updated_at: "2015-12-17 13:54:46">
>> Author.count
   (0.2ms)  SELECT COUNT(*) FROM "authors"
=> 1
>> Book.last.delete
  Book Load (0.2ms)  SELECT  "books".* FROM "books"  ORDER BY "books"."id"
  DESC LIMIT 1
  SQL (1.5ms)  DELETE FROM "books" WHERE "books"."id" = ?  [["id", 1]]
```

```
=> #<Book id: 1, title: "Homo faber", created_at: "2015-12-17 13:54:46",
updated_at: "2015-12-17 13:54:46">
>> Author.count
    (0.2ms)  SELECT COUNT(*) FROM "authors"
=> 1
>> Book.count
    (0.2ms)  SELECT COUNT(*) FROM "books"
=> 0
>> exit
```

The record of the book *Homo faber* is deleted, but the author is still in the database.

As with `destroy`, an object also gets frozen when you use `delete` (see the section "destroy"). The record is already removed from the database, but the object itself is still there.

Transactions

In the world of databases, the term *transaction* refers to a block of SQL statements that must be executed together and without interruption. If an error should occur within the transaction, the database is reset to the state before the start of the transaction.

Now and again, there are areas of application where you need to carry out a database transaction. The classic example is transferring money from one account to another. That makes sense only if both actions (debiting one account and crediting the recipient's account) are executed.

A transaction follows this pattern:

```
ApplicationRecord.transaction do
  Book.create(:title => 'A')
  Book.create(:title => 'B')
  Book.create(:title => 'C').authors.create(:last_name => 'Z')
end
```

Transactions are a complex topic. If you want to find out more, you can consult the `ri` help on the shell via `ri ActiveRecord::Transactions::ClassMethods`.

> **❗** The methods `save` and `destroy` are automatically executed within the transaction *wrapper*. That way, Rails ensures that no undefined state can arise for these two methods.

> **⚠** Transactions are not natively supported by all databases. In that case, the code will still work, but you no longer have the security of the transaction.

Scopes

When programming Rails applications, it is sometimes clearer and simpler to define frequent searches as separate methods. In Rails speak, these are referred to as *NamedScope*. These NamedScopes can be chained, just like other methods.

Preparation

Let's build a little online shop.

```
$ rails new shop
  [...]
$ cd shop
$ rails generate model product name 'price:decimal{7,2}' \
weight:integer in_stock:boolean expiration_date:date
  [...]
$ rails db:migrate
  [...]
$
```

Please populate the file `db/seeds.rb` with the content shown in Listing 3-24.

Listing 3-24. db/seeds.rb

```
Product.create(name: 'Milk (1 liter)', weight: 1000, in_stock: true, price:
0.45, expiration_date: Date.today + 14.days)
Product.create(name: 'Butter (250 g)', weight: 250, in_stock: true, price:
0.75, expiration_date: Date.today + 14.days)
```

```
Product.create(name: 'Flour (1 kg)', weight: 1000, in_stock: false, price:
0.45, expiration_date: Date.today + 100.days)
Product.create(name: 'Jelly Babies (6 x 300 g)', weight: 1500, in_stock: true,
price: 4.96, expiration_date: Date.today + 1.year)
Product.create(name: 'Super-Duper Cake Mix', in_stock: true, price: 11.12,
expiration_date: Date.today + 1.year)
Product.create(name: 'Eggs (12)', in_stock: true, price: 2, expiration_date:
Date.today + 7.days)
Product.create(name: 'Peanuts (8 x 200 g bag)', in_stock: false, weight: 1600,
price: 17.49, expiration_date: Date.today + 1.year)
```

Now populate it with db/seeds.rb.

```
$ rails db:seed
  [...]
$
```

Defining a Scope

If you want to count products that are in stock in your online shop, then you can use the following query each time:

```
$ rails console
Running via Spring preloader in process 27927
Loading development environment (Rails 5.2.0)
>> Product.where(in_stock: true).count
   (0.1ms)  SELECT COUNT(*) FROM "products" WHERE "products"."in_stock" = 't'
=> 5
>> exit
```

But you could also define a NamedScope called available in app/models/product.rb, as shown in Listing 3-25.

Listing 3-25. app/models/product.rb

```
class Product < ApplicationRecord
  scope :available, -> { where(in_stock: true) }
end
```

And then use it like so:

```
$ rails console
Running via Spring preloader in process 27927
Loading development environment (Rails 5.2.0)
>> Product.available.count
   (0.1ms)  SELECT COUNT(*) FROM "products" WHERE "products"."in_stock" = 't'
=> 5
>> exit
```

Let's define a second NamedScope for this example in app/models/product.rb, as shown in Listing 3-26.

Listing 3-26. app/models/product.rb

```
class Product < ApplicationRecord
  scope :available, -> { where(in_stock: true) }
  scope :cheap, -> { where(price: 0..1) }
end
```

Now you can chain both named scopes to output all cheap products that are in stock.

```
$ rails console
Running via Spring preloader in process 27927
Loading development environment (Rails 5.2.0)
>> Product.cheap.count
   (0.3ms)  SELECT COUNT(*) FROM "products" WHERE ("products"."price"
   BETWEEN 0 AND 1)
=> 3
>> Product.cheap.available.count
   (0.3ms)  SELECT COUNT(*) FROM "products" WHERE ("products"."price"
   BETWEEN 0 AND 1) AND "products"."in_stock" = 't'
=> 2
>> exit
```

Passing In Arguments

If you need a NamedScope that can also process parameters, then that is no problem either. The following example outputs products that are cheaper than the specified value. The file app/models/product.rb looks like Listing 3-27.

Listing 3-27. app/models/product.rb

```
class Product < ApplicationRecord
  scope :cheaper_than, ->(price) { where("price < ?", price) }
end
```

Now you can count all products that cost less than 50 cent.

```
$ rails console
Running via Spring preloader in process 27927
Loading development environment (Rails 5.2.0)
>> Product.cheaper_than(0.5).count
   (0.2ms)  SELECT COUNT(*) FROM "products" WHERE (price < 0.5)
=> 2
>> exit
```

Creating New Records with Scopes

Let's use app/models/product.rb, as shown in Listing 3-28.

Listing 3-28. app/models/product.rb

```
class Product < ApplicationRecord
  scope :available, -> { where(in_stock: true) }
end
```

With this NamedScope, not only can you find all products that are in stock, but you can also create new products that contain the value true in the field in_stock.

```
$ rails console
Running via Spring preloader in process 27927
Loading development environment (Rails 5.2.0)
>> product = Product.available.build
```

151

```
=> #<Product id: nil, name: nil, price: nil, weight: nil, in_stock: true,
expiration_date: nil, created_at: nil, updated_at: nil>
>> product.in_stock
=> true
>> exit
```

This works with the method build (see the section "build") and create (see the section "create").

Validation

Nonvalid records are frequently a source of errors in programs. With validates, Rails offers a quick and easy way of validating them. That way you can be sure that only meaningful records will find their way into your database.

Preparation

Let's create a new application for this chapter.

```
$ rails new shop
  [...]
$ cd shop
$ rails generate model product name 'price:decimal{7,2}' \
weight:integer in_stock:boolean expiration_date:date
  [...]
$ rails db:migrate
  [...]
$
```

The Basic Idea

For each model, there is a matching model file in the directory app/models/. In this Ruby code, you can define database dependencies as well as implement all validations. The advantage is that every programmer knows where to find it.

Without any validation, you can create an empty record in a model without a problem.

```
$ rails console
Running via Spring preloader in process 27927
Loading development environment (Rails 5.2.0)
>> product = Product.create
[...]
=> #<Product id: 1, name: nil, price: nil, weight: nil,
in_stock: nil, expiration_date: nil, created_at: "2016-01-21 13:18:31",
updated_at: "2016-01-21 13:18:31">
>> exit
```

But in practice, this record with no content doesn't make any sense. A Product needs to have a name and a price. That's why you can define validations in ActiveRecord. Then you can ensure as a programmer that only records that are valid for you are saved in your database.

To make the mechanism easier to understand, I am going to jump ahead a bit and use the presence helper. Please fill your app/models/product.rb file with the content shown in Listing 3-29.

Listing 3-29. app/models/product.rb

```
class Product < ApplicationRecord
  validates :name,
            presence: true

  validates :price,
            presence: true
end
```

Now you try again to create an empty record in the console.

```
$ rails console
Running via Spring preloader in process 27927
Loading development environment (Rails 5.2.0)
>> product = Product.create
   (0.1ms)  begin transaction
   (0.1ms)  rollback transaction
=> #<Product id: nil, name: nil, price: nil, weight: nil, in_stock: nil,
expiration_date: nil, created_at: nil, updated_at: nil>
```

Watch out for the `rollback transaction` part and the missing `id` of the `Product` object! Rails began the transaction of creating a new record, but for some reason it couldn't do it. So, it had to roll back the transaction. The validation method intervened before the record was saved. So, validating happens before saving.

Can you access the errors? Yes, via the method `errors` or with `errors.messages`, you can look at the errors that occurred.

```
>> product.errors
=> #<ActiveModel::Errors:0x007ff515a71680 @base=#<Product id: nil, name: nil,
price: nil, weight: nil, in_stock: nil, expiration_date: nil, created_at: nil,
updated_at: nil>, @messages={:name=>["can't be blank"], :price=>["can't be
blank"]}>
>> product.errors.messages
=> {:name=>["can't be blank"], :price=>["can't be blank"]}
```

This error message was defined for an English-speaking human user.

Only once you assign a value to the attributes `name` and `price` can you save the object.

```
>> product.name = 'Milk (1 liter)'
=> "Milk (1 liter)"
>> product.price = 0.45
=> 0.45
>> product.save
   (0.1ms)  begin transaction
  SQL (0.5ms)  INSERT INTO "products" ("name", "price", "created_at",
  "updated_at") VALUES (?, ?, ?, ?)  [["name", "Milk (1 liter)"], ["price",
  0.45], ["created_at", "2015-12-17 17:59:09.293831"], ["updated_at",
  "2015-12-17 17:59:09.293831"]]
   (9.0ms)  commit transaction
=> true
```

valid?

The method `valid?` indicates in Boolean form if an object is valid. So, you can check the validity already before you save.

```
>> product = Product.new
=> #<Product id: nil, name: nil, price: nil, weight: nil, in_stock: nil,
expiration_date: nil, created_at: nil, updated_at: nil>
>> product.valid?
=> false
```

save(validate: false)

As so often in life, you can find a way around everything. If you pass the parameter :validate ⇒ false to the method save, the data of Validation is saved.

```
>> product = Product.new
=> #<Product id: nil, name: nil, price: nil, weight: nil, in_stock: nil,
expiration_date: nil, created_at: nil, updated_at: nil>
>> product.valid?
=> false
>> product.save
   (0.1ms)  begin transaction
   (0.1ms)  rollback transaction
=> false
>> product.save(validate: false)
   (0.1ms)  begin transaction
  SQL (0.5ms)  INSERT INTO "products" ("created_at", "updated_at") VALUES (?,
  ?)  [["created_at", "2015-12-17 18:01:46.173590"], ["updated_at",
  "2015-12-17 18:01:46.173590"]]
   (9.1ms)  commit transaction
=> true
>> exit
```

> ⚠️ I assume that you understand the problems involved here. Please use this option only if there is a really good reason to do so.

presence

In your model product, there are a few fields that must be filled in every time. You can achieve this via presence, as shown in Listing 3-30.

ℹ   Please excuse the duplication. I'm aware that I just used the very same code to give you an idea of what validation does.

Listing 3-30. app/models/product.rb

```
class Product < ApplicationRecord
  validates :name,
            presence: true

  validates :price,
            presence: true
end
```

If you try to create an empty user record with this, you get lots of validation errors.

```
$ rails console
Running via Spring preloader in process 27927
Loading development environment (Rails 5.2.0)
>> product = Product.create
   (0.1ms)  begin transaction
   (0.1ms)  rollback transaction
=> #<Product id: nil, name: nil, price: nil, weight: nil, in_stock: nil,
expiration_date: nil, created_at: nil, updated_at: nil>
>> product.errors.messages
=> {:name=>["can't be blank"], :price=>["can't be blank"]}
```

Only once you have entered all the data can the record be saved.

```
>> product.name = 'Milk (1 liter)'
=> "Milk (1 liter)"
>> product.price = 0.45
=> 0.45
```

```
>> product.save
   (0.1ms)  begin transaction
  SQL (0.6ms)  INSERT INTO "products" ("name", "price", "created_at",
  "updated_at") VALUES (?, ?, ?, ?)  [["name", "Milk (1 liter)"], ["price",
  0.45], ["created_at", "2015-12-17 18:04:26.587946"], ["updated_at",
  "2015-12-17 18:04:26.587946"]]
   (9.2ms)  commit transaction
=> true
>> exit
```

length

With length you can limit the length of a specific attribute. It's easiest to explain using an example. Let's limit the maximum length of the name to 20 and the minimum to 2, as shown in Listing 3-31.

Listing 3-31. app/models/product.rb

```ruby
class Product < ApplicationRecord
  validates :name,
            presence: true,
            length: { in: 2..20 }

  validates :price,
            :presence => true
end
```

If you now try to save a product with a name that consists of one letter, you get an error message.

```
$ rails console
Running via Spring preloader in process 27927
Loading development environment (Rails 5.2.0)
>> product = Product.create(:name => 'M', :price => 0.45)
   (0.1ms)  begin transaction
   (0.1ms)  rollback transaction
```

```
=> #<Product id: nil, name: "M", price:
#<BigDecimal:7ff735513400,'0.45E0',9(27)>, weight: nil, in_stock: nil,
expiration_date: nil, created_at: nil, updated_at: nil>
>> product.errors.messages
=> {:name=>["is too short (minimum is 2 characters)"]}
```

Options

`length` can be called with the following options.

`minimum` sets the minimum length of an attribute. Here's an example:

```
validates :name,
          presence: true,
          length: { minimum: 2 }
```

`too_short` defines the error message of `:minimum`. The default is `"is too short (min is %d characters)"`. Here's an example:

```
validates :name,
          presence: true,
          length: { minimum: 5 ,
          too_short: "must have at least %{count} characters"}
```

`maximum` is the maximum length of an attribute. Here's an example:

```
validates :name,
          presence: true,
          length: { maximum: 20 }
```

`too_long` defines the error message of `:maximum`. The default `"is too long (maximum is %d characters)"`. Here's an example:

```
validates :name,
          presence: true,
          length: { maximum: 20 ,
          too_long: "must have at most %{count} characters" }
```

is is exactly the specified number of characters long. Here's an example:

```
validates :name,
          presence: true,
          length: { is: 8 }
```

:in or :within defines a length interval. The first number specifies the minimum number of the range, and the second specifies the maximum. Here's an example:

```
validates :name,
          presence: true,
          length: { in: 2..20 }
```

You can use `tokenizer` to define how the attribute should be split for counting. The default is `lambda{ |value| value.split(//) }` (individual characters are counted). Here is an example (for counting words):

```
validates :content,
          presence: true,
          length: { in: 2..20 },
          tokenizer: lambda {|str| str.scan(/\w+/)}
```

numericality

With `numericality` you can check whether an attribute is a number. It's easier to explain if you see an example, as shown in Listing 3-32.

Listing 3-32. app/models/product.rb

```
class Product < ApplicationRecord
  validates :name,
            presence: true,
            length: { in: 2..20 }

  validates :price,
            presence: true

  validates :weight,
            numericality: true
end
```

If you now use a `weight` that consists of letters or contains letters instead of numbers, you will get an error message.

```
$ rails console
Running via Spring preloader in process 27927
Loading development environment (Rails 5.2.0)
>> product = Product.create(name: 'Milk (1 liter)',
   price: 0.45, weight: 'abc')
   (0.1ms)  begin transaction
   (0.1ms)  rollback transaction
=> #<Product id: nQil, name: "Milk (1 liter)",
price: #<BigDecimal:7fca1ec90ed8,'0.45E0',9(27)>, weight: 0,
in_stock: nil, expiration_date: nil, created_at: nil, updated_at: nil>
>> product.errors.messages
=> {:weight=>["is not a number"]}
>> exit
```

💡 You can use `numericality` to define the content as a number even if an attribute is saved as a string in the database.

Options

`numericality` can be called with the following options.

The `only_integer` attribute can contain only an integer. The default is `false`. Here's an example:

```
validates :weight,
          numericality: { only_integer: true }
```

For `greater_than`, the number saved in the attribute must be greater than the specified value. Here's an example:

```
validates :weight,
          numericality: { greater_than: 100 }
```

For `greater_than_or_equal_to`, the number saved in the attribute must be greater than or equal to the specified value. Here's an example:

```
validates :weight,
          numericality: { greater_than_or_equal_to: 100 }
```

`equal_to` defines a specific value that the attribute must have. Here's an example:

```
validates :weight,
          numericality: { equal_to: 100 }
```

For `less_than`, the number saved in the attribute must be less than the specified value. Here's an example:

```
validates :weight,
          numericality: { less_than: 100 }
```

For `less_than_or_equal_to`, the number saved in the attribute must be less than or equal to the specified value. Here's an example:

```
validates :weight,
          numericality: { less_than_or_equal_to: 100 }
```

`odd` is the number saved in the attribute and must be an odd number. Here's an example:

```
validates :weight,
          numericality: { odd: true }
```

`even` is the number saved in the attribute and must be an even number. Here's an example:

```
validates :weight,
          numericality: { even: true }
```

uniqueness

With `uniqueness` you can define that the value of this attribute must be unique in the database. If you want a product in the database to have a unique name that appears nowhere else, then you can use the validation shown in Listing 3-33.

Listing 3-33. app/models/product.rb

```
class Product < ApplicationRecord
  validates :name,
            presence: true,
            uniqueness: true
end
```

If you now try to create a new Product with a name that already exists, then you get an error message.

```
$ rails console
Running via Spring preloader in process 27927
Loading development environment (Rails 5.2.0)
>> Product.last
  Product Load (0.2ms)  SELECT  "products".* FROM "products"
  ORDER BY "products"."id" DESC LIMIT 1
=> #<Product id: 4, name: "Milk (1 liter)", price:
#<BigDecimal:7fdccb1960b8,'0.45E0',9(27)>, weight: nil,
in_stock: nil, expiration_date: nil,
created_at: "2015-12-17 18:04:26",
updated_at: "2015-12-17 18:04:26">
>> product = Product.create(name: 'Milk (1 liter)')
   (0.1ms)  begin transaction
  Product Exists (0.2ms)  SELECT  1 AS one FROM "products"
  WHERE "products"."name" = 'Milk (1 liter)' LIMIT 1
   (0.1ms)  rollback transaction
=> #<Product id: nil, name: "Milk (1 liter)", price: nil,
weight: nil, in_stock: nil, expiration_date: nil,
created_at: nil, updated_at: nil>
>> product.errors.messages
=> {:name=>["has already been taken"]}
>> exit
```

> ⚠ The validation via `uniqueness` is no absolute guarantee that the attribute is unique in the database. A race condition could occur (see `http://en.wikipedia.org/wiki/Race_condition`). A detailed discussion of this effect would go beyond the scope of this book aimed at beginners (this phenomenon is extremely rare).

Options

`uniqueness` can be called with the following options.

`scope` defines a scope for the uniqueness. If you had a differently structured phone number database (with just one field for the phone number), then you could use this option to specify that a phone number must be saved only once per user. Here is what it would look like:

```
validates :name,
          presence: true,
          uniqueness: { scope: :user_id }
```

`case_sensitive` checks for uniqueness of uppercase and lowercase as well. The default is `false`. Here's an example:

```
validates :name,
          presence: true,
          uniqueness: { case_sensitive: true }
```

inclusion

With `inclusion` you can define from which values the content of this attribute can be created. For this example, you can demonstrate it using the attribute `in_stock`, as shown in Listing 3-34.

Listing 3-34. app/models/product.rb

```ruby
class Product < ApplicationRecord
  validates :name,
            presence: true

  validates :in_stock,
            inclusion: { in: [true, false] }
end
```

In your data model, a `Product` must be either `true` or `false` for `in_stock` (there must not be a `nil`). If you enter a different value than `true` or `false`, a validation error is returned.

```
$ rails console
Running via Spring preloader in process 27927
Loading development environment (Rails 5.2.0)
>> product = Product.create(name: 'Milk low-fat (1 liter)')
   (0.1ms)  begin transaction
   (0.1ms)  rollback transaction
=> #<Product id: nil, name: "Milk low-fat (1 liter)", price: nil, weight: nil,
in_stock: nil, expiration_date: nil, created_at: nil, updated_at: nil>
>> product.errors.messages
=> {:in_stock=>["is not included in the list"]}
>> exit
```

Options

`inclusion` can be called with the `message` option.

`message` is for outputting custom error messages. The default is `"is not included in the list"`. Here's an example:

```ruby
validates :in_stock,
          inclusion: { in: [true, false],
                       message: 'this one is not allowed' }
```

exclusion

exclusion is the inversion of inclusion. You can define from which values the content of this attribute must *not* be created, as shown in Listing 3-35.

Listing 3-35. app/models/product.rb

```
class Product < ApplicationRecord
  validates :name,
            presence: true

  validates :in_stock,
            exclusion: { in: [nil] }
end
```

Options

exclusion can be called with the message option.

message is for outputting custom error messages. Here's an example:

```
validates :in_stock,
          inclusion: { in: [nil],
                       message: 'this one is not allowed' }
```

format

With format you can define via a regular expression (see http://en.wikipedia.org/wiki/Regular_expression) how the content of an attribute can be structured.

With format you can, for example, carry out a simple validation of the syntax of an e-mail address.

```
validates :email,
          format: { with: /\A([^@\s]+)@((?:[-a-z0-9]+\.)+[a-z]{2,})\Z/i }
```

> It should be obvious that the e-mail address validation shown here is not complete. It is just meant to be an example. You can only use it to check the syntactic correctness of an e-mail address.

Options

validates_format_of can be called with the following options:

:message is for outputting a custom error message. The default is "is invalid".

Here's an example:

```
validates :email,
          format: { with: /\A([^@\s]+)@((?:[-a-z0-9]+\.)+[a-z]{2,})\Z/i,
                    message: 'is not a valid email address' }
```

General Validation Options

There are some options that can be used for all validations.

allow_nil

This allows the value nil. Here's an example:

```
validates :email,
          format: { with: /\A([^@\s]+)@((?:[-a-z0-9]+\.)+[a-z]{2,})\Z/i },
          allow_nil: true
```

allow_blank

This is the same as allow_nil, but additionally with an empty string. Here's an example:

```
validates :email,
          format: { with: /\A([^@\s]+)@((?:[-a-z0-9]+\.)+[a-z]{2,})\Z/i },
          allow_blank: true
```

on

With on, a validation can be limited to the events create, update, and safe. In the following example, the validation takes effect only when the record is initially created (during the create).

```
validates :email,
          format: { with: /\A([^@\s]+)@((?:[-a-z0-9]+\.)+[a-z]{2,})\Z/i },
          on: :create
```

if and unless

if and unless call the specified method and execute the validation only if the result of the method is true.

```
validates :name,
          presence: true,
          if: :today_is_monday?

def today_is_monday?
  Date.today.monday?
end
```

:proc calls a Proc object. The functionality of a Proc object is beyond the scope of this book. Here is an example of how to use it without describing the magic behind it:

```
validates :name,
          presence: true,
          if: Proc.new { |a| a.email == 'test@test.com' }
```

> ℹ️ If you want to dive more into Proc, you'll find documentation about it at
> https://ruby-doc.org/core-2.5.0/Proc.html.

Writing Custom Validations

Now and then, you will want to do a validation where you need some custom program logic. For such cases, you can define custom validations.

Defining Validations with Your Own Methods

Let's assume you are a big-shot hotel mogul and need a reservation system.

```
$ rails new my_hotel
  [...]
$ cd my_hotel
$ rails generate model reservation \
start_date:date end_date:date room_type
  [...]
$ rails db:migrate
  [...]
$
```

Then you specify in app/models/reservation.rb that the attributes start_date and end_date must be present every time, plus you use the method reservation_dates_must_make_sense to make sure that start_date is before end_date, as shown in Listing 3-36.

Listing 3-36. app/models/reservation.rb

```ruby
class Reservation < ApplicationRecord
  validates :start_date,
            presence: true

  validates :end_date,
            presence: true

  validate :reservation_dates_must_make_sense

  private
  def reservation_dates_must_make_sense
    if end_date <= start_date
      errors.add(:start_date, 'has to be before the end date')
    end
  end
end
```

With errors.add, you can add error messages for individual attributes. With errors. add_to_base, you can add error messages for the whole object.

Let's test the validation in the console by introducing Date.today + 1.day. It does exactly what you'd expect it to do.

```
$ rails console
Running via Spring preloader in process 27927
Loading development environment (Rails 5.2.0)
>> reservation = Reservation.new(start_date: Date.today, end_date:
Date.today)
=> #<Reservation id: nil, start_date: "2015-12-17", end_date: "2015-12-17",
room_type: nil, created_at: nil, updated_at: nil>
>> reservation.valid?
=> false
>> reservation.errors.messages
=> {:start_date=>["has to be before the end date"]}
>> reservation.end_date = Date.today + 1.day
=> Sat, 18 Apr 2015
>> reservation.valid?
=> true
>> reservation.save
[...]
=> true
>> exit
```

Further Documentation

The topic of validations is described well in the official Rails documentation at http://guides.rubyonrails.org/active_record_validations.html.

Migrations

SQL database tables are generated in Rails with *migrations*, and they can also be changed with migrations. If you create a model with rails generate model, a corresponding migration file is automatically created in the directory db/migrate/. I will explain this principle by using the example of a shop application. Let's create one first.

```
$ rails new shop
  [...]
$ cd shop
```

Then generate a Product model.

```
$ rails generate model product name 'price:decimal{7,2}' \
weight:integer in_stock:boolean expiration_date:date
      invoke   active_record
      create     db/migrate/20151217184823_create_products.rb
      create     app/models/product.rb
      invoke   test_unit
      create       test/models/product_test.rb
      create       test/fixtures/products.yml
$
```

The migrations file db/migrate/20151217184823_create_products.rb was created. Let's take a closer look at it; see Listing 3-37.

Listing 3-37. db/migrate/20151217184823_create_products.rb

```ruby
class CreateProducts < ActiveRecord::Migration[5.1]
  def change
    create_table :products do |t|
      t.string :name
      t.decimal :price, precision: 7, scale: 2
      t.integer :weight
      t.boolean :in_stock
      t.date :expiration_date

      t.timestamps null: false
    end
  end
end
```

The method change creates and deletes the database table in the case of a rollback. The migration files have embedded the current time in the file name and are processed in chronological order during a migration (in other words, when you call rails db:migrate).

```
$ rails db:migrate
== 20151217184823 CreateProducts: migrating =============================
-- create_table(:products)
   -> 0.0015s
== 20151217184823 CreateProducts: migrated (0.0016s) ====================
$
```

Only those migrations that have not been executed yet are processed. If you call
rails db:migrate again, nothing happens because the corresponding migration has
already been executed.

```
$ rails db:migrate
$
```

But if you manually delete the database with rm and then call rails db:migrate
again, the migration is repeated.

```
$ rm db/development.sqlite3
$ rails db:migrate
== 20151217184823 CreateProducts: migrating =============================
-- create_table(:products)
   -> 0.0017s
== 20151217184823 CreateProducts: migrated (0.0018s) ====================
$
```

After a while you will realize that you want to save not just the weight for some
products but also the height. So, you need another database field. There is an easy-to-
remember syntax for this: rails generate migration add*.

```
$ rails generate migration addHeightToProduct height:integer
     invoke  active_record
     create    db/migrate/20151217185307_add_height_to_product.rb
$
```

In the migration file called db/migrate/20151217185307_add_height_to_product.rb,
you once again find a change method, as shown in Listing 3-38.

Listing 3-38. db/migrate/20151217185307_add_height_to_product.rb

```
class AddHeightToProduct < ActiveRecord::Migration
  def change
    add_column :products, :height, :integer
  end
end
```

With `rails db:migrate`, you can start in the new migration.

```
$ rails db:migrate
== 20151217185307 AddHeightToProduct: migrating ============================
-- add_column(:products, :height, :integer)
   -> 0.0086s
== 20151217185307 AddHeightToProduct: migrated (0.0089s) ==================
$
```

In the *console* you can look at the new field. It was added after the field updated_at.

```
$ rails console
Running via Spring preloader in process 27927
Loading development environment (Rails 5.2.0)
>> Product.column_names
=> ["id", "name", "price", "weight", "in_stock", "expiration_date",
"created_at", "updated_at", "height"]
>> exit
```

What if you want to look at the previous state of things? No problem. You can easily go back to the previous version with `rails db:rollback`.

```
$ rails db:rollback
== 20151217185307 AddHeightToProduct: reverting ============================
-- remove_column(:products, :height, :integer)
   -> 0.0076s
== 20151217185307 AddHeightToProduct: reverted (0.0192s) ==================
$
```

Each migration has its own version number. You can find out the version number of the current status via `rails db:version`.

```
$ rails db:version
Current version: 20151217184823
$
```

> **!** Please note that all version numbers and timestamps apply only to the example printed here. If you re-create the example, you will of course get a different timestamp for your own example.

You will find the corresponding version in the directory db/migrate.

```
$ ls db/migrate/
20151217184823_create_products.rb
20151217185307_add_height_to_product.rb
$
```

You can go to a specific migration via `rails db:migrate VERSION=` and add the appropriate version number after the equal sign. The number zero represents the version zero, in other words, the start.

Let's try it.

```
$ rails db:migrate VERSION=0
== 20151217184823 CreateProducts: reverting ===============================
-- drop_table(:products)
   -> 0.0007s
== 20151217184823 CreateProducts: reverted (0.0032s) ======================
$
```

The table was deleted with all the data. You are back to square one.

Which Database Is Used?

The database table is created through the migration. As you can see, the table names automatically get the plural of the model's name (`Person` versus `people`). But in which database are the tables created? This is defined in the configuration file `config/database.yml`, as shown in Listing 3-39.

173

Listing 3-39. config/database.yml

```
# SQLite version 3.x
#    gem install sqlite3
#
#    Ensure the SQLite 3 gem is defined in your Gemfile
#    gem 'sqlite3'
#
default: &default
  adapter: sqlite3
  pool: 5
  timeout: 5000

development:
  <<: *default
  database: db/development.sqlite3

# Warning: The database defined as "test" will be erased and
# re-generated from your development database when you run "rake".
# Do not set this db to the same as development or production.
test:
  <<: *default
  database: db/test.sqlite3

production:
  <<: *default
  database: db/production.sqlite3
```

Three different databases are defined there in YAML format (see www.yaml.org/ or http://en.wikipedia.org/wiki/YAML). For us, only the development database is relevant for now (the first item). By default, Rails uses SQLite3 there. SQLite3 may not be the correct choice for the analysis of the weather data collected worldwide, but for a quick and straightforward development of Rails applications, you will quickly learn to appreciate it. In the Production environment, you can later still switch to "big" databases such as MySQL or PostgreSQL.

To satisfy your curiosity, let's take a quick look at the database with the command-line tool sqlite3:

```
$ sqlite3 db/development.sqlite3
SQLite version 3.8.5 2014-08-15 22:37:57
Enter ".help" for usage hints.
sqlite> .tables
schema_migrations
sqlite> .quit
$
```

There's nothing in it. Of course there's not; you have not yet run the migration.

```
$ rails db:migrate
== 20151217184823 CreateProducts: migrating ===============================
-- create_table(:products)
   -> 0.0019s
== 20151217184823 CreateProducts: migrated (0.0020s) ======================

== 20151217185307 AddHeightToProduct: migrating ===========================
-- add_column(:products, :height, :integer)
   -> 0.0007s
== 20151217185307 AddHeightToProduct: migrated (0.0008s) ==================

$ sqlite3 db/development.sqlite3
SQLite version 3.8.5 2014-08-15 22:37:57
Enter ".help" for usage hints.
sqlite> .tables
products           schema_migrations
sqlite> .schema products
CREATE TABLE "products" ("id" INTEGER PRIMARY KEY AUTOINCREMENT NOT NULL,
"name" varchar, "price" decimal(7,2), "weight" integer, "in_stock" boolean,
"expiration_date" date, "created_at" datetime NOT NULL, "updated_at" datetime
NOT NULL, "height" integer);
sqlite> .quit
```

The table schema_migrations is used for the versioning of the migrations. This table is created during the first migration carried out by Rails, if it does not yet exist.

Creating Index

I assume that you know what a database index is. If not, you will find a brief introduction at http://en.wikipedia.org/wiki/Database_index. In brief, you can use it to quickly search for a specific table column.

In your production database, you should index the field name in the products table. You create a new migration for that purpose.

```
$ rails generate migration create_index
      invoke  active_record
      create    db/migrate/20151217190442_create_index.rb
$
```

In the file db/migrate/20121120142002_create_index.rb, you create the index with add_index in the method self.up, and in the method self.down you delete it with remove_index, as shown in Listing 3-40.

Listing 3-40.   db/migrate/20121120142002_create_index.rb

```ruby
class CreateIndex < ActiveRecord::Migration
  def up
    add_index :products, :name
  end

  def down
    remove_index :products, :name
  end
end
```

With rails db:migrate, you create the index.

```
$ rails db:migrate
==  CreateIndex: migrating ==================================================
-- add_index(:products, :name)
   -> 0.0010s
==  CreateIndex: migrated (0.0011s) ========================================
$
```

Of course, you don't have to use the up and down methods. You can use change too. The migration for the new index would look like this:

```
class CreateIndex < ActiveRecord::Migration[5.1]
  def change
    add_index :products, :name
  end
end
```

> You can also create an index directly when you generate the model. In this case (an index for the attribute name), the command would look like this:

```
$ rails generate model product name:string:index
$ cat db/migrate/20151217191435_create_products.rb
class CreateProducts < ActiveRecord::Migration
  def change
    create_table :products do |t|
      t.string :name

      t.timestamps null: false
    end
    add_index :products, :name
  end
end
```

Automatically Added Fields (**id, created_at, and updated_at**)

Rails kindly adds the following fields automatically in the default migration:

- id:integer: This is the unique ID of the record. The field is automatically incremented by the database. For all SQL fans, this is equivalent to NOT NULL AUTO_INCREMENT.

177

- `created_at:datetime`: The field is filled automatically by ActiveRecord when a record is created.

- `updated_at:datetime`: The field is automatically updated to the current time whenever the record is edited.

So, you don't have to enter these fields yourself when generating the model.

At first you may ask yourself, "Is that really necessary? Does it make sense?" But after a while you will learn to appreciate these automatic fields. Omitting them would usually be false economy.

Further Documentation

The following web pages provide excellent further information on the topic of migration:

- `http://api.rubyonrails.org/classes/ActiveRecord/Migration.html`

- `http://api.rubyonrails.org/classes/ActiveRecord/ConnectionAdapters/TableDefinition.html`

  `http://railscasts.com/episodes/107-migrations-in-rails-2-1` (a bit dated but still good if you are trying to understand the basics)

- `www.dizzy.co.uk/ruby_on_rails/cheatsheets/rails-migrations`

Callbacks

Callbacks are defined programming hooks in the life of an `ActiveRecord` object. You can find a list of all callbacks at `http://api.rubyonrails.org/classes/ActiveRecord/Callbacks.html`. Here are the most frequently used callbacks:

- `before_validation`: Executed before the validation

- `after_validation`: Executed after the validation

- `before_save`: Executed before each save

- `before_create`: Executed before the first save

- `after_save`: Executed after every save

- `after_create`: Executed after the first save

A callback is always executed in the model. Let's assume you always want to save an e-mail address in a `User` model in lowercase but also give the user of the web interface the option to enter uppercase letters. You could use a `before_save` callback to convert the attribute `email` to lowercase via the method `downcase`.

Here's the Rails application:

```
$ rails new shop
  [...]
$ cd shop
$ rails generate model user email login
  [...]
$ rails db:migrate
  [...]
```

Listing 3-41 shows what the model `app/models/user.rb` would look like. The interesting stuff is the `before_save` part.

Listing 3-41. app/models/user.rb

```ruby
class User < ApplicationRecord
  validates :login,
            presence: true

  validates :email,
            presence: true,
            format: { :with => /\A([^@\s]+)@((?:[-a-z0-9]+\.)+[a-z]{2,})\Z/i }

  before_save :downcase_email

  private

  def downcase_email
    self.email = self.email.downcase
  end
end
```

179

Let's see in the console if it really works as you want it to work.

```
$ rails console
Running via Spring preloader in process 27927
Loading development environment (Rails 5.2.0)
>> User.create(login: 'smith', email: 'SMITH@example.com')
   (0.1ms)  begin transaction
  SQL (0.5ms)  INSERT INTO "users" ("login", "email", "created_at",
  "updated_at") VALUES (?, ?, ?, ?)  [["login", "smith"], ["email",
  "smith@example.com"], ["created_at", "2015-12-17 19:22:20.928994"],
  ["updated_at", "2015-12-17 19:22:20.928994"]]
   (9.0ms)  commit transaction
=> #<User id: 1, email: "smith@example.com", login: "smith", created_at:
"2015-12-17 19:22:20", updated_at: "2015-12-17 19:22:20">
>> exit
```

Even though the e-mail address was entered partly with capital letters, ActiveRecord has converted all letters automatically to lowercase via the before_save callback.

In the section "Default Values" you will find an example of defining a default value for a new object via an after_initialize callback.

Default Values

If you need specific default values for an ActiveRecord object, you can easily implement this with the after_initialize callback. This method is called by ActiveRecord when a new object is created. Let's assume you have a model Order and the minimum order quantity is always 1, so you can enter 1 directly as the default value when creating a new record.

Let's set up a quick example, shown here:

```
$ rails new shop
  [...]
$ cd shop
$ rails generate model order product_id:integer quantity:integer
  [...]
$ rails db:migrate
  [...]
```

You write an `after_initialize` callback into the file app/models/order.rb, as shown in Listing 3-42.

Listing 3-42. app/models/order.rb

```ruby
class Order < ApplicationRecord
  after_initialize :set_defaults

  private
  def set_defaults
    self.quantity ||= 1
  end
end
```

`||= 1` sets the value to 1 if it isn't set already.

Then now you check in the console whether a new order object automatically contains the quantity 1.

```
$ rails console
Running via Spring preloader in process 27927
Loading development environment (Rails 5.2.0)
>> order = Order.new
=> #<Order id: nil, product_id: nil, quantity: 1, created_at: nil,
updated_at: nil>
>> order.quantity
=> 1
>> exit
```

That's working fine!

CHAPTER 4

Scaffolding and REST

Scaffolding means simply that a basic *scaffold* for an application is created with a generator. This scaffold not only contains the *model* but also a simple web GUI (*views*) and of course a *controller*. The programming paradigm used for this is Representational State Transfer (REST).

You can find a definition of REST at `wikipedia.org/wiki/Representational_state_transfer`. My short and a bit oversimplified version is this: the inventor Roy Fielding described in 2000 how you can access data with a simple set of rules within the concept of CRUD and the specification of the Hypertext Transfer Protocol (HTTP). CRUD is the abbreviation for Create (SQL: `INSERT`), Read (SQL: `SELECT`), Update (SQL: `UPDATE`), and Delete (SQL: `DELETE`). This created URLs that are easy to read for humans and have a certain logic. In this chapter, you will see examples showing the individual paths for the different CRUD functions.

I think the greatest frustration with Rails arises regularly from the fact that many beginners use scaffolding to get quick results without having the proper basic knowledge of Ruby and without knowing what `ActiveRecord` is. They don't know what to do next. Fortunately, you have worked your way through Chapters 1–3, so you will be able to understand and use scaffolding straightaway.

Redirects and Flash Messages

Scaffolding uses redirects and flash messages. So, you have to make a little detour first to understand scaffolding.

Redirects

The name says it all, really. *Redirects* are commands that you can use within the controller to skip (i.e., redirect) to other web pages.

© Stefan Wintermeyer 2018
S. Wintermeyer, *Learn Rails 5.2*, https://doi.org/10.1007/978-1-4842-3489-1_4

> ℹ️   A redirect returns to the browser the response 302 Moved with the new target. So, each redirect does a round-trip to the browser and back.

Let's create a new Rails project for a suitable example.

```
$ rails new redirect_example
[...]
$ cd redirect_example
$ rails db:migrate
```

Before you can redirect, you need a controller with at least two different methods. Here is a ping-pong example:

```
$ rails generate controller Game ping pong
Running via Spring preloader in process 51759
      create  app/controllers/game_controller.rb
       route  get 'game/pong'
       route  get 'game/ping'
      invoke  erb
      create    app/views/game
      create    app/views/game/ping.html.erb
      create    app/views/game/pong.html.erb
      invoke  test_unit
      create    test/controllers/game_controller_test.rb
      invoke  helper
      create    app/helpers/game_helper.rb
      invoke    test_unit
      invoke  assets
      invoke    coffee
      create      app/assets/javascripts/game.coffee
      invoke    scss
      create      app/assets/stylesheets/game.scss
```

The controller app/controllers/game_controller.rb has the content shown in Listing 4-1.

Listing 4-1. app/controllers/game_controller.rb

```ruby
class GameController < ApplicationController
  def ping
  end

  def pong
  end
end
```

Now for the redirect: how can you set it up so you get immediately redirected to the method pong when you go to http://localhost:3000/game/ping? Easy, you say—you just change the route in config/routes.rb. And you are right. So, you don't necessarily need a redirect. But if you want to process something else in the method ping before redirecting, then this is only possible by using a redirect_to in the controller app/controllers/game_controller.rb, as shown in Listing 4-2.

Listing 4-2. app/controllers/game_controller.rb

```ruby
class GameController < ApplicationController
  def ping
    logger.info '+++  Example  +++'
    redirect_to game_pong_path
  end

  def pong
  end
end
```

But what is game_pong_path? Let's take a look at the routes generated for this Rails application:

```
$ rails routes
    Prefix Verb URI Pattern            Controller#Action
game_ping GET   /game/ping(.:format) game#ping
game_pong GET   /game/pong(.:format) game#pong
```

ⓘ   As you can see, the route to the action `ping` of the controller
`GameController` now gets the name game_ping (see the beginning of the line).
You could also write the redirect like this:

```
redirect_to :action => 'pong'
```

I will explain the details and the individual options of the redirect later in the context
of each specific case. For now, you just need to know that you can redirect not just to
another method but also to another controller or an entirely different web page.

When you try to go to `http://localhost:3000/game/ping`, you are automatically
redirected to `http://localhost:3000/game/pong`, and in the log output you see this:

```
Started GET "/game/ping" for 127.0.0.1 at 2015-04-15 17:50:04 +0200
Processing by GameController#ping as HTML
+++   Example   +++
Redirected to http://localhost:3000/game/pong
Completed 302 Found in 14ms (ActiveRecord: 0.0ms)

Started GET "/game/pong" for 127.0.0.1 at 2015-04-15 17:50:04 +0200
Processing by GameController#pong as HTML
  Rendered game/pong.html.erb within layouts/application (2.1ms)
Completed 200 OK in 2128ms (Views: 2127.4ms | ActiveRecord: 0.0ms)
```

redirect_to :back

If you want to redirect the user of your web application to the page the user was just on,
you can use `redirect_to :back`. This is useful in a scenario where your user first has to
log in to get access to a specific page.

Flash Messages

In my eyes, the term *flash messages* is somewhat misleading. Almost anyone would associate the term *flash* with more or less colorful web pages that were implemented with the Adobe Shockwave Flash plug-in. But in Ruby on Rails, flash messages are something completely different. They are messages that are displayed on the new page after a redirect, for example (see the section "Redirects").

Flash messages are good friends with redirects. The two often work together in a team to give the user feedback on an action just carried out. A typical example of a flash message is the system feedback when a user has logged in. Often the user is redirected back to the original page and gets the message "You are now logged in."

As an example, here again is the ping-pong scenario from the section "Redirects":

```
$ rails new pingpong
    [...]
$ cd pingpong
$ rails db:migrate
$ rails generate controller Game ping pong
    [...]
```

You fill app/controllers/game_controller.rb with the content shown in Listing 4-3.

Listing 4-3. app/controllers/game_controller.rb

```
class GameController < ApplicationController
  def ping
    redirect_to game_pong_path, notice: 'Ping-Pong!'
  end

  def pong
  end
end
```

Now you start the Rails web server with `rails server` and use the browser to go to `http://localhost:3000/game/ping`. You are redirected from `ping` to `pong`. But the flash message "Ping-Pong!" is nowhere to be seen. You first need to expand `app/views/layouts/application.html.erb`, as shown in Listing 4-4.

Listing 4-4. app/views/layouts/application.html.erb

```
<!DOCTYPE html>
<html>
  <head>
    <title>RedirectExample</title>
    <%= csrf_meta_tags %>

    <%= stylesheet_link_tag    'application', media: 'all', 'data-
    turbolinks-track': 'reload' %>
    <%= javascript_include_tag 'application', 'data-turbolinks-track':
    'reload' %>
  </head>

  <body>
    <% flash.each do |name, message| %>
      <p><i><%= "#{name}: #{message}" %></i></p>
    <% end %>
    <%= yield %>
  </body>
</html>
```

Now you see the flash message at the top of the page when you go to `http://localhost:3000/game/ping` in the browser, as shown in Figure 4-1.

Figure 4-1. *Flash message*

If you go to http://localhost:3000/game/pong, you still see the normal Pong page. But if you go to http://localhost:3000/game/ping, you are redirected to the Pong page, and then the flash message is displayed at the top.

> If you do not see a flash message that you were expecting, first check in the view to see whether the flash message is output there.

Different Types of Flash Messages

Flash messages are "automagically" passed to the view in a hash. By default, there are three different types: error, warning, and notice. You can also invent your own category and then get it in the view later.

You can set a flash message by writing the hash directly too, as shown here:

```
flash[:notice] = 'Ping-Pong!'
```

Please take a look at the official documentation at http://guides.rubyonrails. org/action_controller_overview.html#the-flash for more information.

Why Are There Flash Messages at All?

You may wonder why there are flash messages in the first place. Couldn't you just build them yourself if you need them? Yes, indeed. But flash messages have the advantage that they offer a defined approach that is the same for any programmer. So, you don't need to start from scratch every single time you need one.

Generating a Scaffold

Let's first use scaffolding to create a list of products for an online shop. First, you need to create a new Rails application.

```
$ rails new scaffold-shop
  [...]
$ cd scaffold-shop
$ rails db:migrate
```

Let's look at the scaffolding options.

```
$ rails generate scaffold
Usage:
  rails generate scaffold NAME [field[:type][:index] field[:type][:index]]
  [options]

[...]


Examples:
    `rails generate scaffold post`
    `rails generate scaffold post title body:text published:boolean`
    `rails generate scaffold purchase amount:decimal tracking_id:integer:uniq`
    `rails generate scaffold user email:uniq password:digest`
```

I'll keep it short: for the current state of knowledge, you can use rails generate scaffold just like rails generate model. Let's create the scaffold for the products.

```
$ rails generate scaffold product name 'price:decimal{7,2}'
Running via Spring preloader in process 38321
```

```
invoke   active_record
create     db/migrate/20180118065756_create_products.rb
create     app/models/product.rb
invoke     test_unit
create       test/models/product_test.rb
create       test/fixtures/products.yml
invoke   resource_route
 route      resources :products
invoke   scaffold_controller
create     app/controllers/products_controller.rb
invoke     erb
create       app/views/products
create       app/views/products/index.html.erb
create       app/views/products/edit.html.erb
create       app/views/products/show.html.erb
create       app/views/products/new.html.erb
create       app/views/products/_form.html.erb
invoke     test_unit
create       test/controllers/products_controller_test.rb
create       test/system/products_test.rb
invoke     helper
create       app/helpers/products_helper.rb
invoke       test_unit
invoke     jbuilder
create       app/views/products/index.json.jbuilder
create       app/views/products/show.json.jbuilder
create       app/views/products/_product.json.jbuilder
invoke   assets
invoke     coffee
create       app/assets/javascripts/products.coffee
invoke     scss
create       app/assets/stylesheets/products.scss
invoke   scss
create     app/assets/stylesheets/scaffolds.scss
```

As you can see, `rails generate scaffold` has already created the model. So, you can directly call `rails db:migrate`.

```
$ rails db:migrate
== 20180118065756 CreateProducts: migrating =================================
-- create_table(:products)
   -> 0.0014s
== 20180118065756 CreateProducts: migrated (0.0015s)
=========================
```

Let's create the first six products in `db/seeds.rb`.

```
Product.create(name: 'Apple', price: 1)
Product.create(name: 'Orange', price: 1)
Product.create(name: 'Pineapple', price: 2.4)
Product.create(name: 'Marble cake', price: 3)
```

Populate with the example data.

```
$ rails db:seed
```

The Routes

`rails generate scaffold` has created a route (more on this later in Chapter 5), a controller, and several views for you.

You could also have done all of this manually. Scaffolding is merely an automatism that does the work for you for some basic things. This is assuming that you always want to view, create, and delete records.

Without diving too deeply into the topic of routes, let's just take a quick look at the available routes for the example. You need to run `rails routes`.

```
$ rails routes
       Prefix Verb   URI Pattern                Controller#Action
     products GET    /products(.:format)        products#index
              POST   /products(.:format)        products#create
  new_product GET    /products/new(.:format)    products#new
 edit_product GET    /products/:id/edit(.:format) products#edit
      product GET    /products/:id(.:format)    products#show
```

```
PATCH   /products/:id(.:format)        products#update
PUT     /products/:id(.:format)        products#update
DELETE  /products/:id(.:format)        products#destroy
```

These are all the routes and consequently URLs available in this Rails application. All routes invoke actions (in other words, methods) in the ProductsController.

The Controller

Now it's about time you had a look at the file app/controllers/products_controller.rb. The scaffolding automatically creates the methods index, show, new, create, update, and destroy. These methods or actions are called by the routes.

Listing 4-5 shows the content of app/controllers/products_controller.rb.

Listing 4-5. app/controllers/products_controller.rb

```ruby
class ProductsController < ApplicationController
  before_action :set_product, only: [:show, :edit, :update, :destroy]

  # GET /products
  # GET /products.json
  def index
    @products = Product.all
  end

  # GET /products/1
  # GET /products/1.json
  def show
  end

  # GET /products/new
  def new
    @product = Product.new
  end

  # GET /products/1/edit
  def edit
  end
```

```ruby
  # POST /products
  # POST /products.json
  def create
    @product = Product.new(product_params)

    respond_to do |format|
      if @product.save
        format.html { redirect_to @product, notice: 'Product was
        successfully created.' }
        format.json { render :show, status: :created, location: @product }
      else
        format.html { render :new }
        format.json { render json: @product.errors, status: :unprocessable_
        entity }
      end
    end
  end

  # PATCH/PUT /products/1
  # PATCH/PUT /products/1.json
  def update
    respond_to do |format|
      if @product.update(product_params)
        format.html { redirect_to @product, notice: 'Product was
        successfully updated.' }
        format.json { render :show, status: :ok, location: @product }
      else
        format.html { render :edit }
        format.json { render json: @product.errors, status: :unprocessable_
        entity }
      end
    end
  end

  # DELETE /products/1
  # DELETE /products/1.json
  def destroy
```

```
    @product.destroy
    respond_to do |format|
      format.html { redirect_to products_url, notice: 'Product was
      successfully destroyed.' }
      format.json { head :no_content }
    end
  end

  private
    # Use callbacks to share common setup or constraints between actions.
    def set_product
      @product = Product.find(params[:id])
    end

    # Never trust parameters from the scary internet, only allow the white
    list through.
    def product_params
      params.require(:product).permit(:name, :price)
    end
end
```

Let's take a moment and go through this controller.

set_product

An action called before_action calls a private method to set an instance variable called @product for the actions :show, :edit, :update, and :destroy. That DRYs it up nicely.

```
before_action :set_product, only: [:show, :edit, :update, :destroy]

[...]

private
  # Use callbacks to share common setup or constraints between actions.
  def set_product
    @product = Product.find(params[:id])
  end
[...]
```

index

The index method sets the instance variable @products. It contains the result of Product.all.

```
# GET /products
# GET /products.json
def index
  @products = Product.all
end
```

show

The show method doesn't do anything. set_product before_action already set the instance variable @product. So, there is not more to do.

```
# GET /products/1
# GET /products/1.json
def show
end
```

new

The new method creates a new instance of Product and saves it in the instance variable @product.

```
# GET /products/new
def new
  @product = Product.new
end
```

edit

The edit method doesn't do anything. The action called set_product before_action already set the instance variable @product. So, there is nothing more to do.

```
# GET /products/1/edit
def edit
end
```

create

The create method uses Product.new to create a new instance of Product and store it in @product. The private method product_params is used to filter the trusted parameters with a white list. When @product is successfully saved, a redirect to the show action is initiated for HTML requests. If a validation error occurs, the new action will be rendered.

```ruby
# POST /products
# POST /products.json
def create
  @product = Product.new(product_params)

  respond_to do |format|
    if @product.save
      format.html { redirect_to @product, notice: 'Product was successfully
      created.' }
      format.json { render :show, status: :created, location: @product }
    else
      format.html { render :new }
      format.json { render json: @product.errors, status: :unprocessable_
      entity }
    end
  end
end

[...]

# Never trust parameters from the scary internet, only allow the white list
through.
def product_params
  params.require(:product).permit(:name, :price)
end
```

update

The update method tries to update @product with product_params. The private method product_params is used to filter the trusted parameters with a white list. When @product is successfully updated, a redirect to the show action is initiated for HTML requests. If a validation error occurs, the edit action will be rendered.

```ruby
# PATCH/PUT /products/1
# PATCH/PUT /products/1.json
def update
  respond_to do |format|
    if @product.update(product_params)
      format.html { redirect_to @product, notice: 'Product was successfully
      updated.' }
      format.json { render :show, status: :ok, location: @product }
    else
      format.html { render :edit }
      format.json { render json: @product.errors, status: :unprocessable_
      entity }
    end
  end
end

[...]

# Never trust parameters from the scary internet, only allow the white list
through.
def product_params
  params.require(:product).permit(:name, :price)
end
```

destroy

The destroy method destroys @product and redirects an HTML request to the index action.

```ruby
# DELETE /products/1
# DELETE /products/1.json
def destroy
  @product.destroy
  respond_to do |format|
    format.html { redirect_to products_url, notice: 'Product was
                  successfully destroyed.' }
    format.json { head :no_content }
  end
end
```

The Views

Now you start the Rails web server.

```
$ rails server
=> Booting Puma
=> Rails 5.2.0 application starting in development on http://localhost:3000
=> Run `rails server -h` for more startup options
Puma starting in single mode...
* Version 3.11.0 (ruby 2.5.0-p0), codename: Love Song
* Min threads: 5, max threads: 5
* Environment: development
* Listening on tcp://0.0.0.0:3000
Use Ctrl-C to stop
```

A little drum roll, please, for dramatic suspense...launch the web browser and go to the URL http://localhost:3000/products. You can see the list of products as a simple web page, as shown in Figure 4-2.

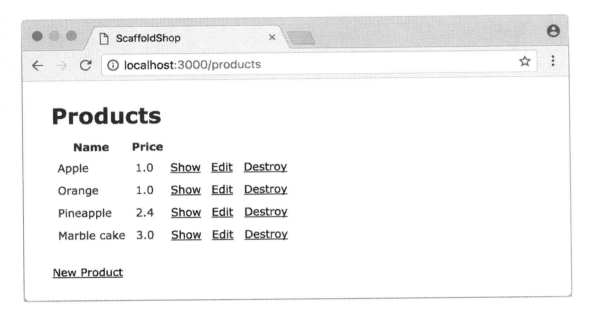

Figure 4-2. *Products index*

If you now click the link New Product, you will see an input form for a new record, as shown in Figure 4-3.

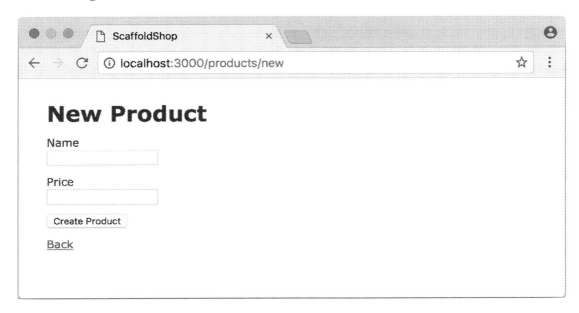

Figure 4-3. *New product form*

Use your browser's Back button to go back and click the Show link in the first line. You will then see the page shown in Figure 4-4.

Figure 4-4. *Showing a product*

If you now click Edit, you will see the editing view for this record, as shown in Figure 4-5.

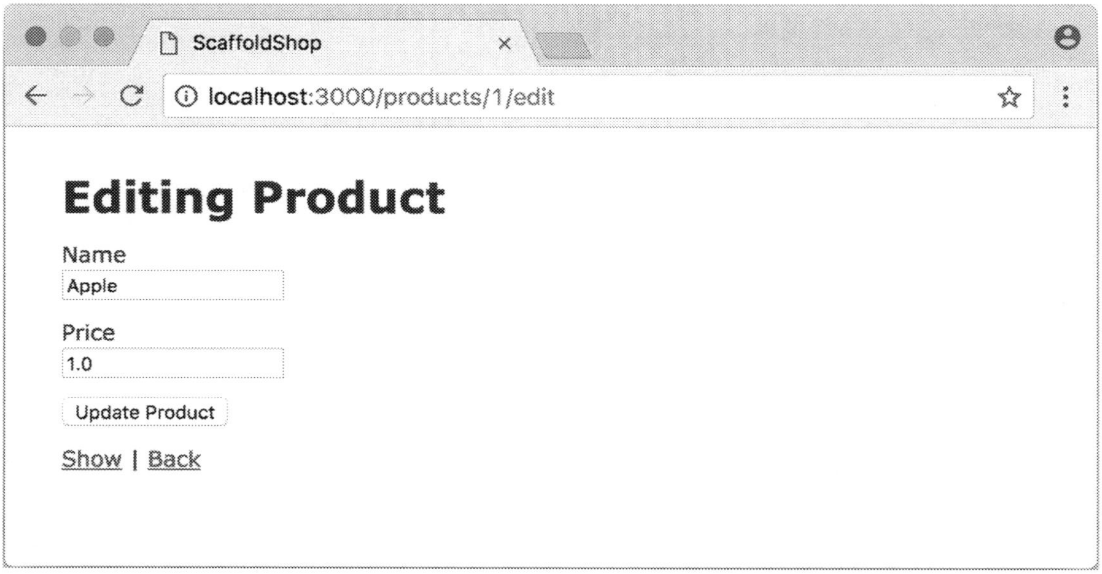

Figure 4-5. *Editing a product*

If you click Destroy on the index page, you can delete a record after confirming the message that pops up. Isn't that cool? Within less than ten minutes, you have written a web application that allows you to create, read/retrieve, update, and delete/destroy records. That is the scaffolding magic. You can save a lot of time.

Where Are the Views?

You can probably guess where the views are, but let's take a look at the directory app/views/products anyway.

```
$ tree app/views/products/
app/views/products/
├── _form.html.erb
├── _product.json.jbuilder
├── edit.html.erb
├── index.html.erb
├── index.json.jbuilder
```

```
├── new.html.erb
├── show.html.erb
└── show.json.jbuilder
```

There are two different file extensions. The html.erb file is for HTML requests, and the json.jbuilder file is for JSON requests.

For index, edit, new, and show, the corresponding views are located there. As new and edit both require a form for editing the data, this is stored in the partial _form. html.erb in accordance with the principle of DRY and is integrated into new.html.erb and edit.html.erb with a <%= render 'form' %>.

Let's open the file app/views/products/index.html.erb, as shown in Listing 4-6.

Listing 4-6. app/views/products/index.html.erb

```erb
<p id="notice"><%= notice %></p>

<h1>Products</h1>

<table>
  <thead>
    <tr>
      <th>Name</th>
      <th>Price</th>
      <th colspan="3"></th>
    </tr>
  </thead>

  <tbody>
    <% @products.each do |product| %>
      <tr>
        <td><%= product.name %></td>
        <td><%= product.price %></td>
        <td><%= link_to 'Show', product %></td>
        <td><%= link_to 'Edit', edit_product_path(product) %></td>
        <td><%= link_to 'Destroy', product, method: :delete, data: {
        confirm: 'Are you sure?' } %></td>
      </tr>
```

```
    <% end %>
  </tbody>
</table>

<br>

<%= link_to 'New Product', new_product_path %>
```

You are now an old hand when it comes to ERB, so you'll be able to read and understand the code without any problems.

link_to

In the views generated by the scaffold generator, you first came across the helper link_to. This creates <a hre ...> links. You can of course also enter a link manually via <a href="..."> in erb, but for links within a Rails project, link_to is more practical because you can use the names of the routes as a target. The code becomes much easier to read. In the previous example, there are the following routes:

```
$ rails routes
        Prefix Verb    URI Pattern                 Controller#Action
      products GET     /products(.:format)         products#index
               POST    /products(.:format)         products#create
   new_product GET     /products/new(.:format)     products#new
  edit_product GET     /products/:id/edit(.:format) products#edit
       product GET     /products/:id(.:format)     products#show
               PATCH   /products/:id(.:format)     products#update
               PUT     /products/:id(.:format)     products#update
               DELETE  /products/:id(.:format)     products#destroy
```

The first part of this route is the name of the route. With a new call, this is new_product. A link to new_product looks like the following in the erb code (you can see it at the end of the file app/views/products/index.html.erb):

```
<%= link_to 'New Product', new_product_path %>
```

In the HTML code of the generated page (http://localhost:3000/products), you can see the result.

```
<%= link_to 'New Product', new_product_path %>
```

With `link_to` you can also link to resources within a RESTful resource. Again, you can find examples for this in `app/views/products/index.html.erb`. In the table, a `show` link, an `edit` link, and a `destroy` link are rendered for each `product`.

```erb
<tbody>
  <% @products.each do |product| %>
    <tr>
      <td><%= product.name %></td>
      <td><%= product.price %></td>
      <td><%= link_to 'Show', product %></td>
      <td><%= link_to 'Edit', edit_product_path(product) %></td>
      <td><%= link_to 'Destroy', product, method: :delete, data: { confirm:
      'Are you sure?' } %></td>
    </tr>
  <% end %>
</tbody>
```

From the resource and the selected route, Rails automatically determines the required URL and the required HTTP verb (in other words, whether it is a POST, GET, PUT, or DELETE). For index and show calls, you need to observe the difference between singular and plural. `link_to 'Show', product` links to a single record, and `link_to 'Show', products_path` links to the index view.

Whether the name of the route is used with or without the suffix `_path` in `link_to` depends on whether Rails can "derive" the route from the other specified information. If only one object is specified (in this example, the variable `product`), then Rails automatically assumes that it is a show route.

Here are some examples:

ERD Code	Explanation
`link_to 'Show', Product.first`	Link to the first product
`link_to 'New Product', new_product_path`	Link to the web interface where a new product can be created
`link_to 'Edit', edit_product_path(Product.first)`	Link to the form where the first product can be edited
`link_to 'Destroy', Product.first, method: :delete`	Link to deleting the first product

form_for

In the partial used by new and edit, called app/views/products/_form.html.erb, you
will find the code shown in Listing 4-7 for the product form.

Listing 4-7. app/views/products/_form.html.erb

```erb
<%= form_with(model: product, local: true) do |f| %>
  <% if product.errors.any? %>
    <div id="error_explanation">
      <h2><%= pluralize(product.errors.count, "error") %> prohibited this
      product from being saved:</h2>

      <ul>
      <% product.errors.full_messages.each do |message| %>
        <li><%= message %></li>
      <% end %>
      </ul>
    </div>
  <% end %>

  <div class="field">
    <%= f.label :name %>
    <%= f.text_field :name %>
  </div>

  <div class="field">
    <%= f.label :price %>
    <%= f.text_field :price %>
  </div>

  <div class="actions">
    <%= f.submit %>
  </div>
<% end %>
```

In a block, the helper form_for takes care of creating the HTML form via which the user can enter the data for the record or edit it. If you delete a complete `<div class="field">` element here, this can no longer be used for input in the web interface. I am not going to comment on all possible form field variations at this point. The most frequently used ones will appear in examples later and be explained then (if they are not self-explanatory).

 You can find an overview of all form helpers at http://guides. rubyonrails.org/form_helpers.html.

When using validations in the model, any validation errors that occur are displayed in the following code at the head of the form:

```erb
<% if product.errors.any? %>
  <div id="error_explanation">
    <h2><%= pluralize(product.errors.count, "error") %> prohibited this
    product from being saved:</h2>

    <ul>
    <% product.errors.full_messages.each do |message| %>
      <li><%= message %></li>
    <% end %>
    </ul>
  </div>
<% end %>
```

Let's add a small validation to the app/models/product.rb model, as shown in Listing 4-8.

Listing 4-8. app/models/product.rb

```ruby
class Product < ApplicationRecord
  validates :name,
            presence: true
end
```

Whenever somebody wants to save a product that doesn't have a name, Rails will show the flash error in Figure 4-6.

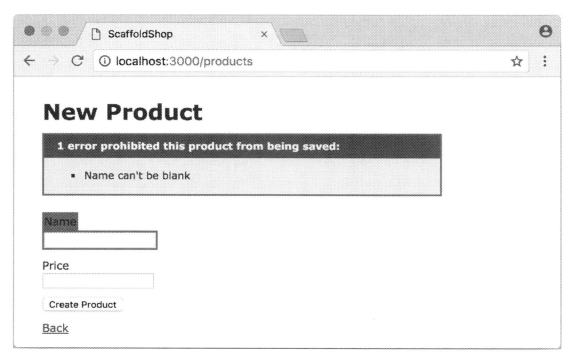

Figure 4-6. *Products error flash*

Access via JSON

By default, Rails' scaffolding generates not just access via HTML for human users but also a direct interface for machines. The same methods `index`, `show`, `new`, `create`, `update`, and `destroy` can be called via this interface, but in a format that is easier to read for machines. As an example, you will see the `index` action via which all data can be read in one go. With the same idea, data can be removed (`destroy`) or edited (`update`).

JSON (see `http://wikipedia.org/wiki/Json`) seems to be the new cool kid. So, let's use JSON.

If you do not require machine-readable access to data, you can remove the lines shown in Listing 4-9 from the file `Gemfile` (followed by the command `bundle`).

Listing 4-9. Gemfile

```
# Build JSON APIs with ease. Read more: https://github.com/rails/jbuilder
gem 'jbuilder', '~> 2.5'
```

Of course, you can delete the `format.json` lines manually too. But please don't forget to delete the JSON view files too.

JSON As Default

Right at the beginning of `app/controllers/products_controller.rb` you will find the entry for the `index` action, as shown in Listing 4-10.

Listing 4-10. app/controllers/products_controller.rb

```
# GET /products
# GET /products.json
def index
  @products = Product.all
end
```

The code is straightforward. In the instance variable `@products`, all the products are saved. The view `app/views/products/index.json.jbuilder` contains the code shown in Listing 4-11 to render the JSON.

Listing 4-11. app/views/products/index.json.jbuilder

```
json.array! @products, partial: 'products/product', as: :product
```

It renders the partial named `_product.json.jbuilder`, as shown in Listing 4-12.

Listing 4-12. app/views/products/_product.json.jbuilder

```
json.extract! product, :id, :name, :price, :created_at, :updated_at
json.url product_url(product, format: :json)
```

You can use your browser to fetch the JSON output. Just open
`http://localhost:3000/products.json` and view the result. I installed a JSON view
extension in my Chrome browser to get a nicer format, as shown in Figure 4-7.

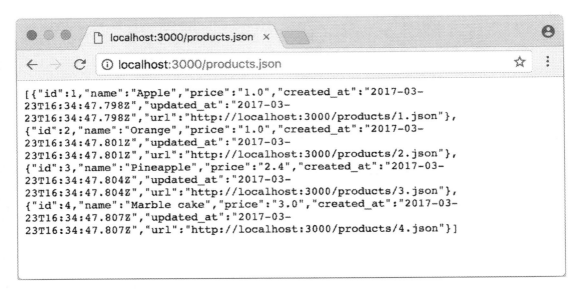

Figure 4-7. *Products index JSON*

If you do not want the JSON output, you need to delete the `json.jbuilder` files.

JSON and XML Together

If you ever need a JSON and XML interface in a Rails application, you just need to specify
both variants in the controller in the block `respond_to`. Listing 4-13 shows an example
with app/controllers/products_controller.rb in the `index` action.

Listing 4-13. app/controllers/products_controller.rb

```ruby
# GET /products
# GET /products.json
# GET /products.xml
def index
  @products = product.all

  respond_to do |format|
    format.html # index.html.erb
    format.json { render json: @products }
```

```
    format.xml { render xml: @products }
  end
end
```

When Should You Use Scaffolding?

You should never use scaffolding just for the sake of it. There are Rails developers who never use scaffolding and always build everything manually. I find scaffolding quite useful for quickly getting into a new project. But it is always just the beginning.

Example for a Minimal Project

Let's assume you need a web page quickly with which you can list products and represent them individually. But you do not require an editing or deleting function. In that case, a large part of the code created via scaffolding would be useless and have to be deleted. Let's try it as follows:

```
$ rails new read-only-shop
  [...]
$ cd read-only-shop
$ rails generate scaffold product name 'price:decimal{7,2}'
  [...]
$ rails db:migrate
  [...]
```

Now create db/seeds.rb with some demo products, as shown in Listing 4-14.

Listing 4-14. db/seeds.rb

```
Product.create(name: 'Apple', price: 1)
Product.create(name: 'Orange', price: 1)
Product.create(name: 'Pineapple', price: 2.4)
Product.create(name: 'Marble cake', price: 3)
```

Populate it with this data:

```
$ rails db:seed
```

Because you need only `index` and `show`, you should delete the views that not required.

```
$ rm app/views/products/_form.html.erb
$ rm app/views/products/new.html.erb
$ rm app/views/products/edit.html.erb
```

The `json.jbuilder` views are not needed either.

```
$ rm app/views/products/*.json.jbuilder
```

The file `app/controllers/products_controller.rb` can be simplified with an editor. It should look like Listing 4-15.

Listing 4-15. app/controllers/products_controller.rb

```ruby
class ProductsController < ApplicationController
  before_action :set_product, only: [:show]

  # GET /products
  # GET /products.json
  def index
    @products = Product.all
  end

  # GET /products/1
  # GET /products/1.json
  def show
  end

  private
    # Use callbacks to share common setup or constraints between actions.
    def set_product
      @product = Product.find(params[:id])
    end
end
```

You only need the routes for `index` and `show`. Please open the file `config/routes.rb` and edit it as shown in Listing 4-16.

Listing 4-16. config/routes.rb

```
Rails.application.routes.draw do
  resources :products, only: [:index, :show]
end
```

A rails routes command shows you that really only index and show are routed now.

```
$ rails routes
  Prefix Verb URI Pattern          Controller#Action
products GET   /products(.:format)       products#index
 product GET   /products/:id(.:format) products#show
```

If you now start the server with rails server and go to the URL
http://localhost:3000/products, you get an error message, as shown in Figure 4-8.

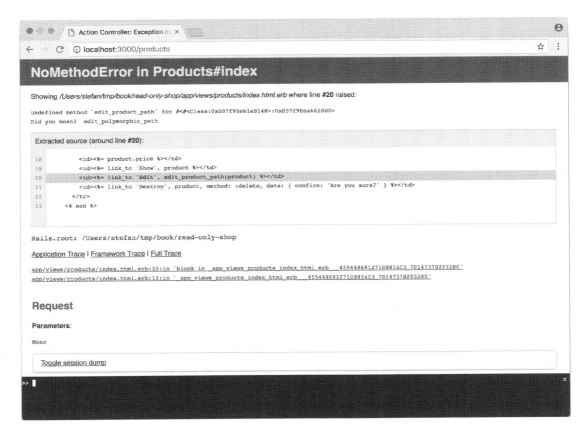

Figure 4-8. *Products error message*

The same message will be displayed in the log.

```
$ rails server
=> Booting Puma
=> Rails 5.2.0 application starting in development on http://localhost:3000
=> Run `rails server -h` for more startup options
Puma starting in single mode...
* Version 3.11.0 (ruby 2.5.0-p0), codename: Love Song
* Min threads: 5, max threads: 5
* Environment: development
* Listening on tcp://0.0.0.0:3000
Use Ctrl-C to stop
Started GET "/products" for 127.0.0.1 at 2017-03-23 17:47:43 +0100
   (0.2ms)  SELECT "schema_migrations"."version" FROM "schema_migrations"
   ORDER BY "schema_migrations"."version" ASC
Processing by ProductsController#index as HTML
  Rendering products/index.html.erb within layouts/application
  Product Load (0.2ms)  SELECT "products".* FROM "products"
  Rendered products/index.html.erb within layouts/application (126.3ms)
Completed 500 Internal Server Error in 149ms (ActiveRecord: 0.7ms)

ActionView::Template::Error (undefined method `edit_product_path' for
#<#<Class:0x007f98eb1e8148>:0x007f98ea6620d0>
Did you mean?  edit_polymorphic_path):
    17:            <td><%= product.name %></td>
    18:            <td><%= product.price %></td>
    19:            <td><%= link_to 'Show', product %></td>
    20:            <td><%= link_to 'Edit', edit_product_path(product) %></td>
    21:            <td><%= link_to 'Destroy', product, method: :delete, data:
                   { confirm: 'Are you sure?' } %></td>
    22:        </tr>
    23:      <% end %>

app/views/products/index.html.erb:20:in `block in _app_views_products_
index_html_erb___4554496912710881403_70147378203280'
app/views/products/index.html.erb:15:in `_app_views_products_index_html_erb
___4554496912710881403_70147378203280'
```

The error message states that you call the undefined method edit_product_path in the view app/views/products/index.html.erb. Because you route only index and show now, there are no more edit, destroy, or new methods anymore. So, you need to adapt the file app/views/products/index.html.erb in the editor as shown in Listing 4-17.

Listing 4-17. app/views/products/index.html.erb

```
<h1>Products</h1>

<table>
  <thead>
    <tr>
      <th>Name</th>
      <th>Price</th>
      <th></th>
    </tr>
  </thead>

  <tbody>
    <% @products.each do |product| %>
      <tr>
        <td><%= product.name %></td>
        <td><%= product.price %></td>
        <td><%= link_to 'Show', product %></td>
      </tr>
    <% end %>
  </tbody>
</table>
```

While you are at it, you can also edit app/views/products/show.html.erb accordingly; see Listing 4-18.

Listing 4-18. app/views/products/show.html.erb

```
<p>
  <strong>Name:</strong>
  <%= @product.name %>
</p>
```

```
<p>
  <strong>Price:</strong>
  <%= @product.price %>
</p>

<%= link_to 'Back', products_path %>
```

Now the application is finished. Start the Rails server with `rails server` and open the URL `http://localhost:3000/products` in the browser, as shown in Figure 4-9.

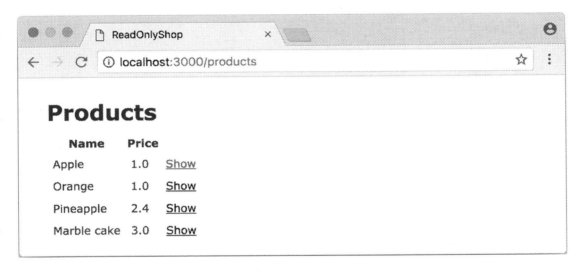

Figure 4-9. *Read-only products index*

ℹ️   In this example, I am not commenting on the required changes in the tests, as this is not an exercise for test-driven development (TDD) but is meant to demonstrate a way of working with scaffolding. TDD developers will quickly be able to adapt the tests.

Conclusion

Try working with scaffolds one time and without them the next. Then you will soon get a feel for whether they fit into your workflow. I find that scaffolding makes my work much easier for standard applications.

CHAPTER 5

Routes

In Chapters 2 and 4, you learned about *routes*. The configuration in `config/routes.rb` defines what happens in the Rails application when a user of a Rails application fetches a URL. A route can be static or dynamic and pass any dynamic values with variables to the controller. If several routes apply to the same URL, the one that is listed at the top of `config/routes.rb` wins.

💡 If you do not have much time, you can skip this chapter for now and come back to it later if you have any specific questions.

Let's first build a test Rails application so you can experiment.

```
$ rails new shop
  [...]
$ cd shop
$ rails db:migrate
```

With `rails routes`, you can display the routes of a project. Let's try it straightaway in the freshly created project.

```
$ rails routes
You don't have any routes defined!

Please add some routes in config/routes.rb.

For more information about routes, see the Rails guide:
http://guides.rubyonrails.org/routing.html.
```

© Stefan Wintermeyer 2018
S. Wintermeyer, *Learn Rails 5.2*, https://doi.org/10.1007/978-1-4842-3489-1_5

That's what I call a good error message. It's a new Rails project, so there are no routes yet.

HTTP GET Requests for Singular Resources

As you might know, the HTTP protocol uses different so-called verbs to access content on the web server (e.g., GET to request a page or POST to send a form to the server). First let's take a look at GET requests.

Create a controller with three pages.

```
$ rails generate controller Home index ping pong
      create  app/controllers/home_controller.rb
       route  get "home/pong"
       route  get "home/ping"
       route  get "home/index"
       [...]
```

Now `rails routes` lists a route for these three pages.

```
$ rails routes
    Prefix Verb URI Pattern            Controller#Action
home_index GET  /home/index(.:format)  home#index
 home_ping GET  /home/ping(.:format)   home#ping
 home_pong GET  /home/pong(.:format)   home#pong
```

The pages can be accessed at the following URLs after starting the Rails server with `rails server`:

- `http://localhost:3000/home/index` for `home_index GET /home/index(.:format)` `home#index`

- `http://localhost:3000/home/ping` for `home_ping GET /home/ping(.:format)` `home#ping` (see Figure 5-1)

- `http://localhost:3000/home/pong` for `home_pong GET /home/pong(.:format)` `home#pong`

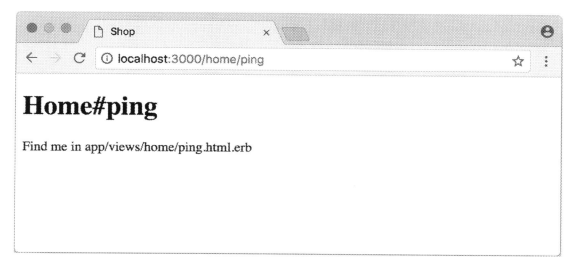

Figure 5-1. *Home ping*

With the output `home#index`, Rails tells you that the route `home/index` goes into the controller home and there to the action/method `index`. These routes are defined in the `config/routes.rb` file. `rails generate controller Home index ping pong` has automatically inserted the lines there shown in Listing 5-1.

Listing 5-1. config/routes.rb

```
get "home/index"
get "home/ping"
get "home/pong"
```

Naming a Route

A route should always have an internal name that doesn't change. In the section "HTTP Get Requests for Singular Resources," there is the following route:

```
home_pong GET /home/pong(.:format)   home#pong
```

This route has the automatically created name home_pong. Generally, you should always try to work with the name of the route within a Rails application. For example, you would point link_to to home_pong and not to /home/pong. This has the big advantage that you can later edit (in the best case, optimize) the routing for visitors externally and do not need to make any changes internally in the application. Of course, you need to enter the old names with :as in that case.

as

If you want to define the name of a route yourself, you can do so with as. For example, the following line:

```
get "home/pong", as: 'different_name'
```

results in the route shown here:

```
different_name GET   /home/pong(.:format)   home#pong
```

to

With to, you can define another destination for a route. For example, the following line:

```
get "home/applepie", to: "home#ping"
```

results in the route shown here:

```
home_applepie GET   /home/applepie(.:format) home#ping
```

Parameters

The routing engine does not just assign fixed routes; it also passes parameters that are part of the URL. A typical example would be date specifications (e.g., http://example. com/2010/12/ for all December postings).

To demonstrate this, let's create a mini blog application.

```
$ rails new blog
  [...]
$ cd blog
$ rails generate scaffold post subject content published_on:date
  [...]
$ rails db:migrate
  [...]
```

Put some example data in db/seeds.rb, as shown in Listing 5-2.

Listing 5-2. db/seeds.rb

```
Post.create(subject: 'A test', published_on: '01.10.2011')
Post.create(subject: 'Another test', published_on: '01.10.2011')
Post.create(subject: 'And yet one more test', published_on: '02.10.2011')
Post.create(subject: 'Last test', published_on: '01.11.2011')
Post.create(subject: 'Very final test', published_on: '01.11.2012')
```

With rails db:seed, you populate the database with this data:

```
$ rails db:seed
```

If you now start the Rails server with `rails server` and go to the page `http://localhost:3000/posts` in the browser, you will see the screen in Figure 5-2.

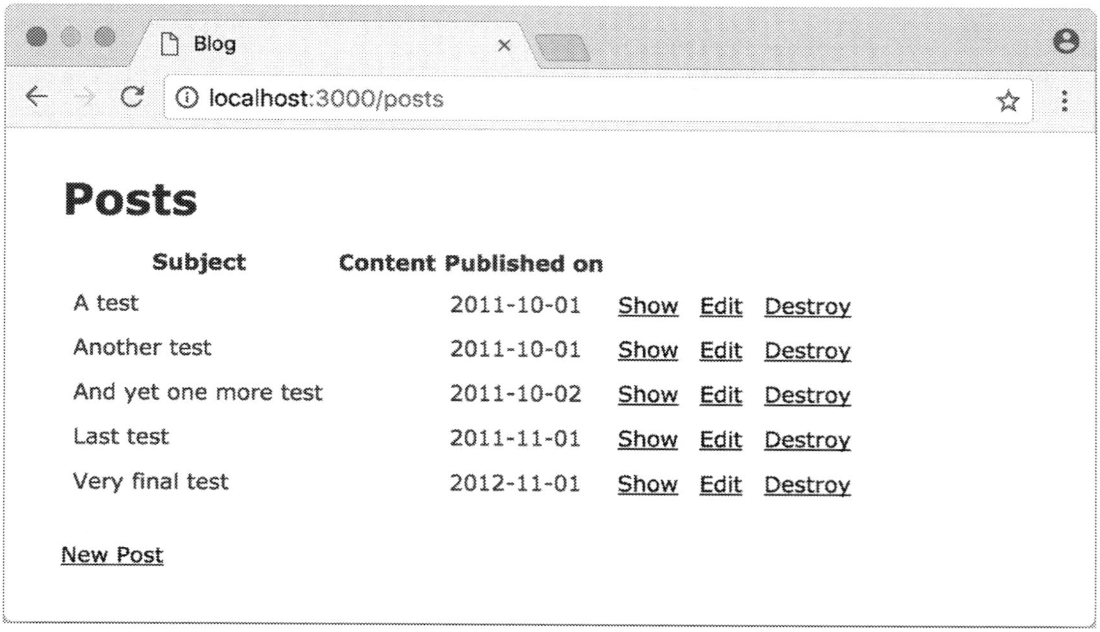

Figure 5-2. *Posts index*

For this kind of blog, it would of course be useful if you could render all entries for the year 2010 with the URL `http://localhost:3000/2010/` and all entries for October 1, 2010, with `http://localhost:3000/2010/10/01`. You can do this by using optional parameters. Enter the configuration shown in Listing 5-3 in `config/routes.rb`.

Listing 5-3. config/routes.rb

```
Blog::Application.routes.draw do
  resources :posts

  get ':year(/:month(/:day))', to: 'posts#index'
end
```

The round brackets represent optional parameters. In this case, you have to specify the year but not necessarily the month or day. `rails routes` shows the new route at the last line, as shown here:

```
$ rails routes
   Prefix Verb   URI Pattern                        Controller#Action
    posts GET    /posts(.:format)                   posts#index
          POST   /posts(.:format)                   posts#create
 new_post GET    /posts/new(.:format)               posts#new
edit_post GET    /posts/:id/edit(.:format)          posts#edit
     post GET    /posts/:id(.:format)               posts#show
          PATCH  /posts/:id(.:format)               posts#update
          PUT    /posts/:id(.:format)               posts#update
          DELETE /posts/:id(.:format)               posts#destroy
          GET    /:year(/:month(/:day))(.:format)   posts#index
```

If you do not change anything else, you still get the same result when calling http://localhost:3000/2011/ and http://localhost:3000/2011/10/01 as you did with http://localhost:3000/posts. But take a look at the output of `rails server` for the request http://localhost:3000/2011, as shown here:

```
Started GET "/2011/" for 127.0.0.1 at 2017-03-24 11:18:52 +0100
   (0.5ms)  SELECT "schema_migrations"."version" FROM "schema_migrations"
   ORDER BY "schema_migrations"."version" ASC
Processing by PostsController#index as HTML
  Parameters: {"year"=>"2011"}
  Rendering posts/index.html.erb within layouts/application
  Post Load (0.5ms)  SELECT "posts".* FROM "posts"
  Rendered posts/index.html.erb within layouts/application (14.7ms)
Completed 200 OK in 122ms (Views: 99.1ms | ActiveRecord: 1.0ms)
```

The route has been recognized, and "year" ⇒ "2011" has been assigned to the hash params (written misleadingly as Parameters in the output). Going to the URL http://localhost:3000/2010/12/24 results in the following output, as expected:

```
Started GET "/2010/12/24" for 127.0.0.1 at 2017-03-24 11:19:38 +0100
Processing by PostsController#index as HTML
  Parameters: {"year"=>"2010", "month"=>"12", "day"=>"24"}
```

```
  Rendering posts/index.html.erb within layouts/application
  Post Load (0.2ms)  SELECT "posts".* FROM "posts"
  Rendered posts/index.html.erb within layouts/application (2.9ms)
Completed 200 OK in 14ms (Views: 11.4ms | ActiveRecord: 0.2ms)
```

In the case of the URL http://localhost:3000/2010/12/24, the following values have been saved in the hash params: "year"⇒"2010", "month"⇒"12", and "day"⇒"24".

In the controller, you can access params[] to access the values defined in the URL. You simply need to adapt the index method in app/controllers/posts_controller.rb to output the posts entered for the corresponding date, month, or year, as shown in Listing 5-4.

Listing 5-4. app/controllers/posts_controller.rb

```ruby
# GET /posts
# GET /posts.json
def index
  # Check if the URL requests a date.
  if Date.valid_date? params[:year].to_i, params[:month].to_i,
    params[:day].to_i
    start_date = Date.parse("#{params[:day]}.#{params[:month]}.#{params
    [:year]}")
    end_date = start_date

  # Check if the URL requests a month
  elsif Date.valid_date? params[:year].to_i, params[:month].to_i, 1
    start_date = Date.parse("1.#{params[:month]}.#{params[:year]}")
    end_date = start_date.end_of_month

  # Check if the URL requests a year
  elsif params[:year] && Date.valid_date?(params[:year].to_i, 1, 1)
    start_date = Date.parse("1.1.#{params[:year]}")
    end_date = start_date.end_of_year
  end

  if start_date && end_date
    @posts = Post.where(published_on: start_date..end_date)
  else
```

```
    @posts = Post.all
  end
end
```

If you now go to `http://localhost:3000/2011/10/01`, you can see all `posts` for October 1, 2011, as shown in Figure 5-3.

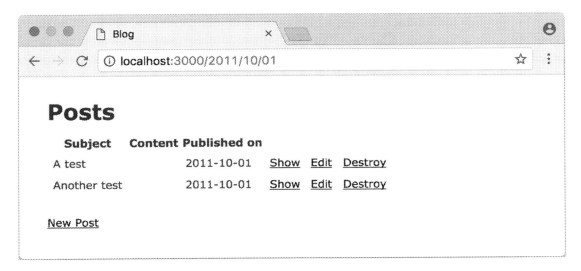

Figure 5-3. *Posts for October 1, 2011*

Constraints

In the section "Parameters," I showed you how you can read out parameters from the URL and pass them to the controller. The entry defined in `config/routes.rb` is shown here:

```
get ':year(/:month(/:day))', to: 'posts#index'
```

Unfortunately, this has one important disadvantage: it does not verify the individual elements. For example, the URL `http://localhost:3000/just/an/example` will be matched as usual and then of course results in an error, as shown in Figure 5-4.

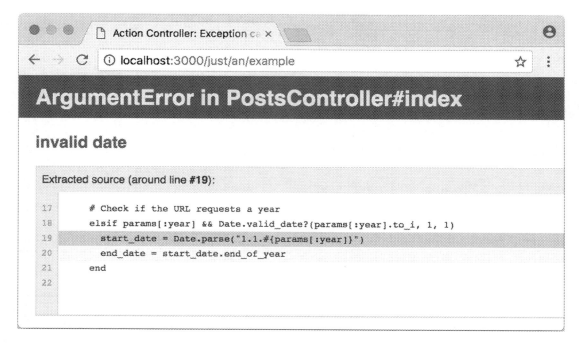

Figure 5-4. Invalid date

In the log output in log/development.log, you can see the following entry:

```
Started GET "/just/an/example" for 127.0.0.1 at 2017-03-24 13:18:21 +0100
Processing by PostsController#index as HTML
  Parameters: {"year"=>"just", "month"=>"an", "day"=>"example"}
Completed 500 Internal Server Error in 2ms (ActiveRecord: 0.0ms)

ArgumentError (invalid date):

app/controllers/posts_controller.rb:19:in `parse'
app/controllers/posts_controller.rb:19:in `index'
```

Obviously, Date.parse("example.an.just") does not work. A date is made up of numbers, not letters.

Constraints can define the content of the URL more precisely via regular expressions. In the case of the example blog, the config/routes.rb file with constraints would look like Listing 5-5.

Listing 5-5. config/routes.rb

```
Blog::Application.routes.draw do
  resources :posts

  get ':year(/:month(/:day))', to: 'posts#index',
  constraints: { year: /\d{4}/, month: /\d{2}/, day: /\d{2}/ }
end
```

> ⚠ Please note that you cannot use regex anchors such as ^ in regular expressions in a constraint.

If you go to the URL again with this configuration, Rails gives you an error message, "No route matches," as shown in Figure 5-5.

Figure 5-5. *No route error*

Redirects

The current application answers the request in the format YYYY/MM/DD (four digits for the year, two digits for the month, and two digits for the day). That is OK for machines, but maybe a human would request a single-digit month (like January) and a single-digit day without adding the extra 0 to make it two digits. You can fix that with a couple of redirect rules that catch these URLs and redirect them to the correct ones. See Listing 5-6.

Listing 5-6. config/routes.rb

```
Blog::Application.routes.draw do
  resources :posts

  get ':year/:month/:day', to: redirect("/%{year}/0%{month}/0%{day}"),
  constraints: { year: /\d{4}/, month: /\d{1}/, day: /\d{1}/ }
  get ':year/:month/:day', to: redirect("/%{year}/0%{month}/%{day}"),
  constraints: { year: /\d{4}/, month: /\d{1}/, day: /\d{2}/ }
  get ':year/:month/:day', to: redirect("/%{year}/%{month}/0%{day}"),
  constraints: { year: /\d{4}/, month: /\d{2}/, day: /\d{1}/ }
  get ':year/:month', to: redirect("/%{year}/0%{month}"),
  constraints: { year: /\d{4}/, month: /\d{1}/ }

  get ':year(/:month(/:day))', to: 'posts#index',
  constraints: { year: /\d{4}/, month: /\d{2}/, day: /\d{2}/ }
end
```

With this set of redirect rules, you can ensure that a user of the page can also enter single-digit days and months and still end up in the right place or be redirected to the correct format.

ⓘ   Redirects in `config/routes.rb` are by default HTTP redirects with the code 301 ("Moved Permanently"). So, even search engines will benefit from this.

---

root :to ⇒ welcome#index

Rails provides a shortcut for the / (root) route. Assuming you want to render the index view of the posts controller, you have to use the configuration shown in Listing 5-7.

Listing 5-7. config/routes.rb

```
Blog::Application.routes.draw do
  resources :posts

  root :to => posts#index
end
```

If you don't want to show any of the resource pages, you can create a new controller (e.g., Page) with an index view.

```
$ rails new controller Page index
```

Then you can use the following configuration to present it as your index (root) page.

```
Blog::Application.routes.draw do
  resources :posts

  get 'page/index'
  root :to => page#index
end
```

resources

resources provides routes for a RESTful resource. Let's try it with the mini blog application, shown here:

```
$ rails new blog
  [...]
$ cd blog
$ rails generate scaffold post subject content published_on:date
  [...]
$ rails db:migrate
  [...]
```

The scaffold generator automatically creates a `resources` route in `config/routes.rb`, as shown in Listing 5-8.

Listing 5-8. config/routes.rb

```
Blog::Application.routes.draw do
  resources :posts
end
```

ℹ️ New routes are always added at the beginning of `config/routes.rb` with `rails generate` scripts.

The resulting routes are shown here:

```
$ rails routes
    Prefix Verb   URI Pattern               Controller#Action
     posts GET    /posts(.:format)          posts#index
           POST   /posts(.:format)          posts#create
  new_post GET    /posts/new(.:format)      posts#new
 edit_post GET    /posts/:id/edit(.:format) posts#edit
      post GET    /posts/:id(.:format)      posts#show
           PATCH  /posts/:id(.:format)      posts#update
           PUT    /posts/:id(.:format)      posts#update
           DELETE /posts/:id(.:format)      posts#destroy
```

You have already encountered these RESTful routes in Chapter 4. They are required for displaying and editing records.

Selecting Specific Routes with only: or except:

If you want to use only specific routes from the finished set of RESTful routes, you can limit them with :only or :except.

config/routes.rb, as shown in Listing 5-9, defines only the routes for index and show.

Listing 5-9. config/routes.rb

```
Blog::Application.routes.draw do
  resources :posts, only: [:index, :show]
end
```

With rails routes you can check the result, as shown here:

```
$ rails routes
Prefix Verb URI Pattern          Controller#Action
 posts GET   /posts(.:format)      posts#index
  post GET   /posts/:id(.:format)  posts#show
```

except works exactly the other way around, as shown in Listing 5-10.

Listing 5-10. config/routes.rb

```
Blog::Application.routes.draw do
  resources :posts, except: [:index, :show]
end
```

Now all routes except for index and show are possible, as shown here:

```
$ rails routes
   Prefix Verb    URI Pattern                 Controller#Action
    posts POST    /posts(.:format)            posts#create
 new_post GET     /posts/new(.:format)        posts#new
edit_post GET     /posts/:id/edit(.:format)   posts#edit
     post PATCH   /posts/:id(.:format)        posts#update
          PUT     /posts/:id(.:format)        posts#update
          DELETE  /posts/:id(.:format)        posts#destroy
```

⚠️ When using only and except, please make sure you also adapt the views generated by the scaffold generator. For example, there is a link on the index page to the new view with <%= link_to 'New Post', new_post_path %>, but this view no longer exists in the previous example.

Nested Resources

Nested resources refer to routes of resources that work with an association. These can be addressed precisely via routes. Let's create a blog with Post and a second resource Comment.

```
$ rails new nested-blog
  [...]
$ cd nested-blog
  [...]
$ rails generate scaffold post subject body:text
  [...]
$ rails generate scaffold comment post:references content
  [...]
$ rails db:migrate
  [...]
```

Now you associate the two resources. In the file app/models/post.rb, you add a has_many, as shown in Listing 5-11.

Listing 5-11. app/models/post.rb

```
class Post < ApplicationRecord
  has_many :comments
end
```

The file app/models/comment.rb has its counterpart, belongs_to, as shown in Listing 5-12.

Listing 5-12. app/models/comment.rb

```
class Comment < ApplicationRecord
  belongs_to :post
end
```

The routes generated by the scaffold generator look like this:

```
$ rails routes
       Prefix Verb    URI Pattern                  Controller#Action
     comments GET     /comments(.:format)          comments#index
              POST    /comments(.:format)          comments#create
 new_comment GET     /comments/new(.:format)      comments#new
edit_comment GET     /comments/:id/edit(.:format) comments#edit
      comment GET     /comments/:id(.:format)      comments#show
              PATCH   /comments/:id(.:format)      comments#update
              PUT     /comments/:id(.:format)      comments#update
              DELETE  /comments/:id(.:format)      comments#destroy
        posts POST    /posts(.:format)             posts#create
    new_post GET     /posts/new(.:format)         posts#new
   edit_post GET     /posts/:id/edit(.:format)    posts#edit
         post PATCH   /posts/:id(.:format)         posts#update
              PUT     /posts/:id(.:format)         posts#update
              DELETE  /posts/:id(.:format)         posts#destroy
```

So, you can get the first post with /posts/1 and all the comments with /comments. By using nesting, you can get all the comments with a post_id of 1 via /posts/1/comments.

To achieve this, you need to change config/routes.rb, as shown in Listing 5-13.

Listing 5-13. config/routes.rb

```
Blog::Application.routes.draw do
  resources :posts do
    resources :comments
  end
end
```

This gives you the desired routes, as shown here:

```
$ rails routes
            Prefix Verb    URI Pattern                         Controller#Action
     post_comments GET     /posts/:post_id/                    comments#index
                           comments(.:format)
                   POST    /posts/:post_id/                    comments#create
                           comments(.:format)
  new_post_comment GET     /posts/:post_id/                    comments#new
                           comments/new(.:format)
 edit_post_comment GET     /posts/:post_id/comments/           comments#edit
                           :id/edit(.:format)
      post_comment GET     /posts/:post_id/                    comments#show
                           comments/:id(.:format)
                   PATCH   /posts/:post_id/                    comments#update
                           comments/:id(.:format)
                   PUT     /posts/:post_id/                    comments#update
                           comments/:id(.:format)
                   DELETE  /posts/:post_id/                    comments#destroy
                           comments/:id(.:format)
             posts GET     /posts(.:format)                    posts#index
                   POST    /posts(.:format)                    posts#create
          new_post GET     /posts/new(.:format)                posts#new
         edit_post GET     /posts/:id/edit(.:format)           posts#edit
              post GET     /posts/:id(.:format)                posts#show
                   PATCH   /posts/:id(.:format)                posts#update
                   PUT     /posts/:id(.:format)                posts#update
                   DELETE  /posts/:id(.:format)                posts#destroy
```

But you still need to make some changes in the file app/controllers/comments_
controller.rb. This ensures that only the Comments of the specified Post can be
displayed or changed, as shown in Listing 5-14.

Listing 5-14. app/controllers/comments_controller.rb

```ruby
class CommentsController < ApplicationController
  before_action :set_post
  before_action :set_comment, only: [:show, :edit, :update, :destroy]

  def index
    @comments = @post.comments
  end

  def show
  end

  def new
    @comment = @post.comments.build
  end

  def edit
  end

  def create
    @comment = @post.comments.build(comment_params)

    respond_to do |format|
      if @comment.save
        format.html { redirect_to post_comment_path(@post, @comment),
        notice: 'Comment was successfully created.' }
        format.json { render :show, status: :created, location: @comment }
      else
        format.html { render :new }
        format.json { render json: @comment.errors, status: :unprocessable_
        entity }
      end
    end
  end
```

```ruby
def update
  respond_to do |format|
    if @comment.update(comment_params)
      format.html { redirect_to post_comments_path(@post, @comment),
      notice: 'Comment was successfully updated.' }
      format.json { render :show, status: :ok, location: @comment }
    else
      format.html { render :edit }
      format.json { render json: @comment.errors, status: :unprocessable_
      entity }
    end
  end
end

def destroy
  @comment.destroy
  respond_to do |format|
    format.html { redirect_to post_comments_url(@post), notice: 'Comment
    was successfully destroyed.' }
    format.json { head :no_content }
  end
end

private
  def set_post
    @post = Post.find(params[:post_id])
  end

  def set_comment
    @comment = @post.comments.find(params[:id])
  end

  def comment_params
    params.require(:comment).permit(:content)
  end
end
```

Unfortunately, this is only half the story because the views still link to the old routes. So, you need to adapt each view in accordance with the nested route.

236

Please note that you need to change the form_with call to form_with(model: [post, comment], local: true). But you don't need the post_id field anymore because that information is already in the URL. See Listing 5-15, Listing 5-16, Listing 5-17, Listing 5-18, and Listing 5-19.

Listing 5-15. app/views/comments/_form.html.erb

```
<%= form_with(model: [post, comment], local: true) do |f| %>
  <% if comment.errors.any? %>
    <div id="error_explanation">
      <h2><%= pluralize(comment.errors.count, "error") %> prohibited this
      comment from being saved:</h2>

      <ul>
      <% comment.errors.full_messages.each do |message| %>
        <li><%= message %></li>
      <% end %>
      </ul>
    </div>
  <% end %>

  <div class="field">
    <%= f.label :content %>
    <%= f.text_field :content %>
  </div>

  <div class="actions">
    <%= f.submit %>
  </div>
<% end %>
```

Listing 5-16. app/views/comments/edit.html.erb

```
<h1>Editing Comment</h1>

<%= render 'form', comment: @comment, post: @post %>

<%= link_to 'Show', post_comment_path(@post, @comment) %> |
<%= link_to 'Back', post_comments_path(@post) %>
```

Listing 5-17. app/views/comments/index.html.erb

```erb
<p id="notice"><%= notice %></p>

<h1>Comments</h1>

<table>
  <thead>
    <tr>
      <th>Post</th>
      <th>Content</th>
      <th colspan="3"></th>
    </tr>
  </thead>

  <tbody>
    <% @comments.each do |comment| %>
      <tr>
        <td><%= comment.post %></td>
        <td><%= comment.content %></td>
        <td><%= link_to 'Show', post_comment_path(@post, comment) %></td>
        <td><%= link_to 'Edit', edit_post_comment_path(@post, comment) %></td>
        <td><%= link_to 'Destroy', post_comment_url(@post, comment),
        method: :delete, data: { confirm: 'Are you sure?' } %></td>
      </tr>
    <% end %>
  </tbody>
</table>

<br>

<%= link_to 'New Comment', new_post_comment_path(@post) %>
```

Listing 5-18. app/views/comments/new.html.erb

```
<h1>New Comment</h1>

<%= render 'form', comment: @comment, post: @post %>

<%= link_to 'Back', post_comments_path(@post) %>
```

Listing 5-19. app/views/comments/show.html.erb

```
<p id="notice"><%= notice %></p>

<p>
  <strong>Post:</strong>
  <%= @comment.post %>
</p>

<p>
  <strong>Content:</strong>
  <%= @comment.content %>
</p>

<%= link_to 'Edit', edit_post_comment_path(@post,@comment) %> |
<%= link_to 'Back', post_comments_path(@post) %>
```

Please go ahead and experiment with the URLs listed under `rails routes`.
You can now generate a new post with `/posts/new` and a new comment for this post with
`/posts/:post_id/comments/new`.

If you want to see all comments of the first post, you can access that with the URL
`http://localhost:3000/posts/1/comments`. It would look like Figure 5-6.

Figure 5-6. *Listing comments*

Shallow Nesting

Sometimes it is a better option to use shallow nesting. For this example, the
config/routes.rb file would contain the routes shown in Listing 5-20.

Listing 5-20. config/routes.rb

```
Blog::Application.routes.draw do
  resources :posts do
    resources :comments, only: [:index, :new, :create]
  end

  resources :comments, except: [:index, :new, :create]
end
```

That would lead to the less messy `rails routes` output, as shown here:

```
$ rails routes
           Prefix  Verb   URI Pattern                            Controller#Action
    post_comments  GET    /posts/:post_id/comments(.:format)     comments#index
                   POST   /posts/:post_id/comments(.:format)     comments#create
new_post_comment   GET    /posts/:post_id/comments/new(.:format) comments#new
            posts  GET    /posts(.:format)                       posts#index
                   POST   /posts(.:format)                       posts#create
         new_post  GET    /posts/new(.:format)                   posts#new
        edit_post  GET    /posts/:id/edit(.:format)              posts#edit
             post  GET    /posts/:id(.:format)                   posts#show
                   PATCH  /posts/:id(.:format)                   posts#update
                   PUT    /posts/:id(.:format)                   posts#update
                   DELETE /posts/:id(.:format)                   posts#destroy
     edit_comment  GET    /comments/:id/edit(.:format)           comments#edit
          comment  GET    /comments/:id(.:format)                comments#show
                   PATCH  /comments/:id(.:format)                comments#update
                   PUT    /comments/:id(.:format)                comments#update
                   DELETE /comments/:id(.:format)                comments#destroy
```

Shallow nesting tries to combine the best of two worlds, and because it is often used, there is a shortcut. You can use the `config/routes.rb` shown in Listing 5-21 to achieve it.

Listing 5-21. config/routes.rb

```ruby
Blog::Application.routes.draw do
  resources :posts do
    resources :comments, shallow: true
  end
end
```

> ℹ️   Generally, you should never nest more deeply than one level, and nested resources should feel natural. After a while, you will get a feel for this. In my opinion, the most important point about RESTful routes is that they should feel logical. If you phone a fellow Rails programmer and say, "I've got a resource post and a resource comment here," then both parties should immediately be clear on how you address these resources via REST and how you can nest them.

Further Information on Routes

The topic of routes is far more complex than I can address here. For example, you can also involve other HTTP methods/verbs. The official routing documentation at `http://guides.rubyonrails.org/routing.html` will give you a lot of information and examples for these features and edge cases.

CHAPTER 6

Bundler and Gems

Gems are how you do package management in the world of Ruby.

> 💡 If you do not have much time, you can skip this chapter for now and come back to it later if you have any specific questions.

If a Ruby developer wants to offer a specific feature or a certain program or collection of programs to other Ruby developers, the developer can create a package. Those packages are called *gems*. They can then be installed with the command gem install.

> 💡 Take a look at `https://www.ruby-toolbox.com` to get an overview of the existing gems.

Rails itself is a gem, and every Rails project uses a lot of different gems. You as a developer can even add other gems. The program bundle helps the developer to install all these gems in the right version and to take the dependencies into account.

The file Gemfile generated by rails new indicates which gems are to be installed by Bundler, as shown in Listing 6-1.

Listing 6-1. Gemfile

```
source 'https://rubygems.org'
git_source(:github) { |repo| "https://github.com/#{repo}.git" }

ruby '2.5.0'

# Bundle edge Rails instead: gem 'rails', github: 'rails/rails'
```

© Stefan Wintermeyer 2018
S. Wintermeyer, *Learn Rails 5.2*, https://doi.org/10.1007/978-1-4842-3489-1_6

```ruby
gem 'rails', '~> 5.2.0'
# Use sqlite3 as the database for Active Record
gem 'sqlite3'
# Use Puma as the app server
gem 'puma', '~> 3.11'
# Use SCSS for stylesheets
gem 'sass-rails', '~> 5.0'
# Use Uglifier as compressor for JavaScript assets
gem 'uglifier', '>= 1.3.0'
# See https://github.com/rails/execjs#readme for more supported runtimes
# gem 'mini_racer', platforms: :ruby

# Use CoffeeScript for .coffee assets and views
gem 'coffee-rails', '~> 4.2'
# Turbolinks makes navigating your web application faster. Read more:
https://github.com/turbolinks/turbolinks
gem 'turbolinks', '~> 5'
# Build JSON APIs with ease. Read more: https://github.com/rails/jbuilder
gem 'jbuilder', '~> 2.5'
# Use Redis adapter to run Action Cable in production
# gem 'redis', '~> 4.0'
# Use ActiveModel has_secure_password
# gem 'bcrypt', '~> 3.1.7'

# Use ActiveStorage variant
# gem 'mini_magick', '~> 4.8'

# Use Capistrano for deployment
# gem 'capistrano-rails', group: :development

# Reduces boot times through caching; required in config/boot.rb
gem 'bootsnap', '>= 1.1.0', require: false

group :development, :test do
  # Call 'byebug' anywhere in the code to stop execution and get a debugger
  console
  gem 'byebug', platforms: [:mri, :mingw, :x64_mingw]
  # Adds support for Capybara system testing and selenium driver
```

```
  gem 'capybara', '~> 2.15'
  gem 'selenium-webdriver'
  # Easy installation and use of chromedriver to run system tests with Chrome
  gem 'chromedriver-helper'
end

group :development do
  # Access an interactive console on exception pages or by calling
  'console' anywhere in the code.
  gem 'web-console', '>= 3.3.0'
  gem 'listen', '>= 3.0.5', '< 3.2'
  # Spring speeds up development by keeping your application running in the
  background. Read more: https://github.com/rails/spring
  gem 'spring'
  gem 'spring-watcher-listen', '~> 2.0.0'
end

# Windows does not include zoneinfo files, so bundle the tzinfo-data gem
gem 'tzinfo-data', platforms: [:mingw, :mswin, :x64_mingw, :jruby]
```

The format used is easy to explain: the word gem is followed by the name of the gem and then, if required, a specification of the version of the gem.

For example, the line gem 'rails', '5.2.0' means "install the gem with the name rails in the version 5.2.0."

With ~> before the version number, you can determine that the newest version after this version number should be installed. As a result, the last digit is incremented, so for example gem 'rails', '~> 4.0.0' would correspondingly install Rails 4.0.1 but not 4.1 (for the latter, you would need to specify gem 'rails', '~> 4.1').

---

i   You have the option of installing certain gems only in certain environments. To do so, you need to enclose the corresponding lines in a group :name do loop.

Besides the file `Gemfile`, there is also the file `Gemfile.lock`, and the exact versions of the installed gems are listed there. For the previous example, it looks like Listing 6-2.

Listing 6-2. Gemfile.lock

```
GEM
  remote: https://rubygems.org/
  specs:
    actioncable (5.2.0)
      actionpack (= 5.2.0)
      nio4r (~> 2.0)
      websocket-driver (~> 0.6.1)
    actionmailer (5.2.0)
      actionpack (= 5.2.0)
      actionview (= 5.2.0)
      activejob (= 5.2.0)
      mail (~> 2.5, >= 2.5.4)
      rails-dom-testing (~> 2.0)
    actionpack (5.2.0)
      actionview (= 5.2.0)
      activesupport (= 5.2.0)
      rack (~> 2.0)
      rack-test (>= 0.6.3)
      rails-dom-testing (~> 2.0)
      rails-html-sanitizer (~> 1.0, >= 1.0.2)
      [...]
```

The advantage of `Gemfile.lock` is that it makes it possible for several developers to work on the same Rails project independently from one another and to still be sure that they are all working with the same gem versions. If a file version is locked in `Gemfile.lock`, this version is used by Bundler. This is also useful for deploying the Rails project later on a web server.

 Edit only `Gemfile` and never `Gemfile.lock`.

Thanks to this mechanism, you can use and develop several Rails projects with different gem version numbers in parallel.

bundle update

With bundle update, you can update gems to new versions. For example, here is a Rails project with the Rails version 4.2.1:

```
$ rails -v
Rails 4.2.1
$
```

In the file Gemfile, this version is listed, as shown in Listing 6-3.

Listing 6-3. Gemfile

```
source 'https://rubygems.org'

# Bundle edge Rails instead: gem 'rails', github: 'rails/rails'
gem 'rails', '4.2.1'
[...]
```

It's also listed in Gemfile.lock.

```
$ grep 'rails' Gemfile.lock
  [...]
  rails (= 4.2.1)
  [...]
$
```

Assume you are working with Rails 4.2.0 and you want to update it to Rails 4.2.4. You have to change the Gemfile from what's shown in Listing 6-4 to what's shown in Listing 6-5.

Listing 6-4. Gemfile

```
[...]
gem 'rails', '4.2.0'
[...]
```

Listing 6-5. Gemfile

```
[...]
gem 'rails', '4.2.4'
[...]
```

After this change, you can use `bundle update rails` to install the new Rails version (Bundler automatically takes the required dependencies into account).

```
$ bundle update rails
  [...]
$ rails -v
Rails 4.2.4
$
```

❗ After every gem update, you should first run `rake test` to make sure that a new gem version does not add any unwanted side effects.

---

bundle outdated

If you want to know which of the gems used by your Rails project are now available in a new version, you can do this via the command `bundle outdated`. Here's an example:

```
$ bundle outdated
The dependency tzinfo-data (>= 0) will be unused by any of the platforms
Bundler is installing for. Bundler is installing for ruby but the
dependency is only for x86-mingw32, x86-mswin32, x64-mingw32, java. To add
those platforms to the bundle, run `bundle lock --add-platform x86-mingw32
x86-mswin32 x64-mingw32 java`.
Fetching gem metadata from https://rubygems.org/.........
Fetching gem metadata from https://rubygems.org/.
Resolving dependencies....

Outdated gems included in the bundle:
  * archive-zip (newest 0.10.0, installed 0.7.0)
  * websocket-driver (newest 0.7.0, installed 0.6.5)
```

To update them, you'll have to change the version numbers in Gemfile and run a bundle update command.

bundle exec

bundle exec is required whenever a program such as rake is used in a Rails project and is present in a different version than the rest of the system. The resulting error message is always easy to implement.

You have already activated rake 0.10, but your Gemfile requires rake 0.9.2.2. Using bundle exec may solve this.

In this case, it helps to invoke the command with a preceding bundle exec command, as shown here:

```
$ bundle exec rake db:migrate
```

binstubs

In some environments, using bundle exec is too complicated. In that case, you can install programs with the correct version via bundle install --binstubs in the directory bin.

```
$ bundle install --binstubs
Using rake 12.3.0
Using concurrent-ruby 1.0.5
Using i18n 0.9.1
[...]
Using turbolinks 5.1.0
Using uglifier 4.1.3
Using web-console 3.5.1
Bundle complete! 18 Gemfile dependencies, 76 gems now installed.
Use `bundle info [gemname]` to see where a bundled gem is installed.
```

Afterward, you can always use these programs. Here's an example:

```
$ bin/rake db:migrate
==  CreateUsers: migrating ================================================
-- create_table(:users)
   -> 0.0018s
==  CreateUsers: migrated (0.0019s) =======================================
```

Popular Gems

At https://www.ruby-toolbox.com you'll find most of the available gems. The main problem with gems is that many times you have no idea how active the community is that developed a gem. It's a major headache to upgrade a Rails application that uses neglected gems. So, you can check out the gem's home page and GitHub repository before installing a gem.

I'll show you a couple of gems that are essential for many developers. But please do your due diligence first before you include a gem!

acts_as_list

Let's create a to-do list application that displays a couple of to-dos that can be edited by the user. You just need one scaffold for this. Let's call the model task. Here is the basic setup:

```
$ rails new to-do-list
  [...]
$ cd to-do-list
$ rails generate scaffold task name completed:boolean
  [...]
$ rails db:migrate
  [...]
$ rails server
```

ℹ️   Naming is always important within a Rails project. I've seen many examples of a to-do list application where the `Task` model has a field called `task`. Don't do that. If you have an instance variable called `@task`, it is cleaner to have a `@task.name` than a `@task.task`, which is just confusing.

Order Your Tasks

A common idea for any to-do list is the feature to order the tasks. For that you'll need to have some sort of `position` field in your model. Because this is such a common problem, there is a nice gem ready to go for this. It's called `acts_as_list`. To use it, you have to add the line shown in Listing 6-6 to the `Gemfile` and run the bundler.

Listing 6-6. Gemfile

```
[...]
gem 'acts_as_list'
[...]

$ bundle
```

To use it, you have to add a `position` field to the `task` model.

```
$ rails generate migration AddPositionToTask position:integer
  [...]
$ rails db:migrate
```

If you already have a full database table of tasks, you will want to change the migration to something like this, which sets the `position` field:

```
class AddPositionToTask < ActiveRecord::Migration[5.2]
  def change
    add_column :tasks, :position, :integer
    Task.order(:updated_at).each.with_index(1) do |task, index|
      task.update_column :position, index
    end
  end
end
```

The last change is a change to the task model to make it use `acts_as_list`, as shown in Listing 6-7.

Listing 6-7. app/models/task.rb

```
class Task < ApplicationRecord
  acts_as_list
end
```

For any new entry of the tasks table, `acts_as_list` will set the `position` field automatically. But that is not all. You can use these methods to move the position of a task and reorder the list:

- `task.move_lower`
- `task.move_higher`
- `task.move_to_bottom`
- `task.move_to_top`

You also have access to these useful methods:

- `task.first?`
- `task.last?`
- `task.in_list?`
- `task.not_in_list?`
- `task.higher_item`
- `task.higher_items`
- `task.lower_item`
- `task.lower_items`

It's not rocket science, but it's so much easier to use an existing gem than to reinvent the wheel.

Don't forget to change the `index` action in your `tasks_controller.rb` file to display the tasks in the right order, as shown in Listing 6-8.

Listing 6-8. app/controllers/tasks_controller.rb

```ruby
[...]
def index
  @tasks = Task.order(:position)
end
[...]
```

Check Done Tasks in Your Index View

Wouldn't it be nice to have a way of checking done tasks in the /tasks index view instead of having to use the edit view every time? This could be done with a link to a yet to be created check action in app/controllers/tasks_controller.rb. But there is a cleaner, more RESTful way: you can use the update action from a little form in each table row.

Listing 6-9 shows the example code snippet for app/views/tasks/index.html.erb.

Listing 6-9. app/views/tasks/index.html.erb

```erb
[...]
<% @tasks.each do |task| %>
  <tr>
    <td><%= task.description %></td>
    <td><%= task.completed %></td>
    <td>
      <% unless task.completed %>
        <%= form_with(model: task, local: true) do |form| %>
          <%= form.hidden_field :completed, value: true %>
          <div class="actions">
            <%= form.submit 'Check!', :name => 'check' %>
          </div>
        <% end %>
      <% end %>
    </td>
```

```
    <td><%= link_to 'Show', task %></td>
    <td><%= link_to 'Edit', edit_task_path(task) %></td>
    <td><%= link_to 'Destroy', task, method: :delete, data: { confirm: 'Are
    you sure?' } %></td>
  </tr>
<% end %>
[...]
```

Find more information and the complete documentation about `acts_as_list` at `https://github.com/swanandp/acts_as_list`.

Authentication

Most Rails applications need some kind of authentication system. The old RailsCast episode at `http://railscasts.com/episodes/250-authentication-from-scratch-revised` shows how to do that by yourself. It is not that complicated, but it is also nice to do authentication with a ready-to-go gem that not only handles passwords but also sends one-time password e-mails and does the Facebook and Twitter magic. This saves you a lot of time that you can instead invest in your application.

Take a look at `https://www.ruby-toolbox.com/categories/rails_authentication`, which sorts the most popular authentication gems. I've used a couple of them, but I don't have a clear favorite.

If you have the time, try two to three for yourself. If you don't have the time, go with devise by Plataformatec (`https://github.com/plataformatec/devise`).

Authorization

Authentication is only half the battle. You need to have a system to limit access to special parts of your Rails application to specific users or user groups. In other words, you need an authorization system. Again, you can create such a system by yourself; it is not rocket science. But if you are in a hurry, go to `https://www.ruby-toolbox.com/categories/rails_authorization` to find a list of available gems for this.

However, do not use the outdated `cancan` by the Rails legend Ryan Bates (the inventor of `http://railscasts.com`). It is an orphan. Use `cancancan`, which is an up-to-date fork. You'll find it at `https://github.com/cancancommunity/cancancan`.

Simple Form

Many Rails developers use the `simple_form` gem (`https://github.com/plataformatec/simple_form`) to make their lives easier. It helps you create forms in an easier way than the default scaffolds. Please see for yourself. I found this topic a double-edged sword. I try to stay as vanilla as possible, but I see the attractiveness of `simple_form`.

Further Information on Bundler

The topic of Bundler is far more complex than can be described here. If you want to find out more about Bundler, please visit the following web sites:

- `http://gembundler.com/`
- `http://railscasts.com/episodes/201-bundler-revised`

CHAPTER 7

Forms

In this chapter, I'll talk about forms.

The Data-Input Workflow

To understand forms, you need take a look at the data workflow. Understanding it better will help you to understand how forms work.

Here is an example application:

```
$ rails new testapp
[...]
$ cd testapp
$ rails generate scaffold Person first_name last_name
[...]
$ rails db:migrate
[...]
$ rails server
[...]
```

Usually you will create forms by using the scaffold. Let's go through the flow the data.

Request the people#new Form

When you request the http://localhost:3000/people/new URL, the router answers with the following route:

```
new_person GET    /people/new(.:format)        people#new
```

The controller app/controllers/people_controller.rb runs the code shown in Listing 7-1.

257

© Stefan Wintermeyer 2018
S. Wintermeyer, *Learn Rails 5.2*, https://doi.org/10.1007/978-1-4842-3489-1_7

Listing 7-1. app/controllers/people_controller.rb

```ruby
# GET /people/new
def new
  @person = Person.new
end
```

So, a new instance of Person is created and stored in the instance variable @person.

Rails takes @person and starts processing the view file app/views/people/new.html.erb, as shown in Listing 7-2.

Listing 7-2. app/views/people/new.html.erb

```erb
<h1>New Person</h1>

<%= render 'form', person: @person %>


<%= link_to 'Back', people_path %>
```

render 'form' renders the file app/views/people/_form.html.erb and sets the local variable person to the content of @person, as shown in Listing 7-3.

Listing 7-3. app/views/people/_form.html.erb

```erb
<%= form_with(model: person, local: true) do |form| %>
  <% if person.errors.any? %>
    <div id="error_explanation">
      <h2><%= pluralize(person.errors.count, "error") %> prohibited this
      person from being saved:</h2>

      <ul>
      <% person.errors.full_messages.each do |message| %>
        <li><%= message %></li>
      <% end %>
      </ul>
    </div>
  <% end %>

  <div class="field">
    <%= form.label :first_name %>
```

```
      <%= form.text_field :first_name %>
    </div>

    <div class="field">
      <%= form.label :last_name %>
      <%= form.text_field :last_name %>
    </div>

    <div class="actions">
      <%= form.submit %>
    </div>
<% end %>
```

Next, form_with(model: person, local: true) embeds the two text_fields :first_name and :last_name instances plus a submit button.

Here is the resulting HTML:

```
[...]
<form action="/people" accept-charset="UTF-8" method="post">
<input name="utf8" type="hidden" value="&#x2713;" />
<input type="hidden" name="authenticity_token" value="lSt...hbIg==" />

  <div class="field">
    <label for="person_first_name">First name</label>
    <input type="text" name="person[first_name]" />
  </div>

  <div class="field">
    <label for="person_last_name">Last name</label>
    <input type="text" name="person[last_name]" />
  </div>

  <div class="actions">
    <input type="submit" name="commit" value="Create Person"
    data-disable-with="Create Person" />
  </div>
</form>
[...]
```

This form uses the post method to upload the data to the server.

Push the Data to the Server

Go ahead and enter **Stefan** in the first_name field and **Wintermeyer** in the last_name field and click the Submit button. The browser uses the post method to upload the data to the URL /people. The log shows the following:

```
Started POST "/people" for 127.0.0.1 at 2018-01-18 12:56:46 +0100
Processing by PeopleController#create as HTML
  Parameters: {"utf8"=>"✓", "authenticity_token"=>"OwS2r9...",
"person"=>{"first_name"=>"Stefan", "last_name"=>"Wintermeyer"},
"commit"=>"Create Person"}
   (0.1ms)  begin transaction
  Person Create (0.6ms)  INSERT INTO "people" ("first_name", "last_name",
"created_at", "updated_at") VALUES (?, ?, ?, ?)  [["first_name", "Stefan"],
["last_name", "Wintermeyer"], ["created_at", "2018-01-18 11:56:46.889256"],
["updated_at", "2018-01-18 11:56:46.889256"]]
   (0.9ms)  commit transaction
Redirected to http://localhost:3000/people/1
Completed 302 Found in 9ms (ActiveRecord: 1.6ms)
```

What happened in Rails? The router answers the request with this route:

```
POST    /people(.:format)            people#create
```

The controller app/controllers/people_controller.rb runs the code shown in Listing 7-4.

Listing 7-4. app/controllers/people_controller.rb

```ruby
def create
  @person = Person.new(person_params)

  respond_to do |format|
    if @person.save
      format.html { redirect_to @person, notice: 'Person was successfully
      created.' }
      format.json { render :show, status: :created, location: @person }
```

```
    else
      format.html { render :new }
      format.json { render json: @person.errors, status: :unprocessable_
      entity }
    end
  end
end
[...]

# Never trust parameters from the scary internet, only allow the white list
through.
def person_params
  params.require(:person).permit(:first_name, :last_name)
end
```

A new instance variable called @person is created. It represents a new Person
instance that was created with the parameters that were sent from the browser to the
Rails application. The parameters are checked in the person_params method, which is
a whitelist. That is done so the user does not inject parameters that you don't want to be
injected.

Once @person is saved, a redirect_to @person is triggered, which is
http://localhost:3000/people/1 in this example.

Present the New Data

The redirect to http://localhost:3000/people/1 is traceable in the log file, as shown here:

```
Started GET "/people/1" for 127.0.0.1 at 2018-01-18 12:56:46 +0100
Processing by PeopleController#show as HTML
  Parameters: {"id"=>"1"}
  Person Load (0.2ms)  SELECT  "people".* FROM "people"
  WHERE "people"."id" = ? LIMIT ?  [["id", 1], ["LIMIT", 1]]
  Rendering people/show.html.erb within layouts/application
  Rendered people/show.html.erb within layouts/application (0.9ms)
Completed 200 OK in 27ms (Views: 20.8ms | ActiveRecord: 0.2ms)
```

The router answers this request with the following:

```
person GET     /people/:id(.:format)        people#show
```

This gets handled by the show method in app/controllers/people_controller.rb.

Generic Forms

A form doesn't have to be hardwired to an ActiveRecord object. You can use the form_tag helper to create a form by yourself. Here is an example of http://guides. rubyonrails.org/form_helpers.html (which is the official Rails guide about forms) to show how to create a search form that is not connected to a model:

```
<%= form_with(url: '/search') do |f| %>
  <%= f.label(:q, "Search for:") %>
  <%= f.text_field(:q, id: :q) %>
  <%= f.submit("Search") %>
<% end %>
```

It results in this HTML code:

```
<form accept-charset="UTF-8" action="/search" method="get">
  <label for="q">Search for:</label>
  <input id="q" name="q" type="text" />
  <input name="commit" type="submit" value="Search" />
</form>
```

To handle this, you'd have to create a new route in config/routes.rb and write a method in a controller to handle it.

FormTagHelper

There is not just a helper for text fields. Take a look at the official API documentation for all FormTagHelpers at http://api.rubyonrails.org/classes/ActionView/Helpers/ FormTagHelper.html to get an overview. Because you use scaffold to create a form, there is no need to memorize them. It is just important to know where to look in case you need something else.

Alternatives

Many Rails developers use the Simple Form gem as an alternative to the standard way of defining forms. It is worth a try because you can really save time and some trouble. Simple Form is available as a gem at `https://github.com/plataformatec/simple_form`.

## CHAPTER 8

Cookies and Sessions

In this chapter, I'll talk about cookies and sessions.

Cookies

With a cookie, you can store information on the web browser's system in the form of strings as key-value pairs that the web server has previously sent to this browser. The information is later sent from the browser to the server in the HTTP header. A cookie (if configured accordingly) is not deleted from the browser system by restarting the browser or by restarting the system. Of course, the browser's human user can manually delete the cookie.

ℹ A browser does not have to accept cookies, and it does not have to save them either. But we live in a world where almost every page uses cookies. So, most users will have the cookie functionality enabled. For more information on cookies, please visit Wikipedia at `http://en.wikipedia.org/wiki/Http_cookie`.

A cookie has a limited size (the maximum is 4KB). You should remember that the information in the saved cookies is sent from the browser to the server. So, you should use cookies to store only small amounts of data (for example, a customer ID) to avoid the protocol overhead from becoming too big.

Rails provides a hash with the name `cookies[]` that you can use transparently. Rails automatically takes care of the technological details in the background.

© Stefan Wintermeyer 2018
S. Wintermeyer, *Learn Rails 5.2*, https://doi.org/10.1007/978-1-4842-3489-1_8

To demonstrate how cookies work, I will show how to build a Rails application that places a cookie on a page, reads it out on another page, and displays the content. The cookie is deleted on a third page.

```
$ rails new cookie_jar
  [...]
$ cd cookie_jar
$ rails db:migrate
$ rails generate controller home set_cookies show_cookies delete_cookies
  [...]
```

Populate the controller file app/controllers/home_controller.rb, as shown in Listing 8-1.

Listing 8-1. app/controllers/home_controller.rb

```ruby
class HomeController < ApplicationController
  def set_cookies
    cookies[:user_name]      = "Smith"
    cookies[:customer_number] = "1234567890"
  end

  def show_cookies
    @user_name       = cookies[:user_name]
    @customer_number = cookies[:customer_number]
  end

  def delete_cookies
    cookies.delete :user_name
    cookies.delete :customer_number
  end
end
```

Listing 8-2 shows the view file app/views/home/show_cookies.html.erb.

Listing 8-2. app/views/home/show_cookies.html.erb

```
<table>
  <tr>
    <td>User Name:</td>
    <td><%= @user_name %></td>
  </tr>
  <tr>
    <td>Customer Number:</td>
    <td><%= @customer_number %></td>
  </tr>
</table>
```

Start the Rails server with `rails server` and go to the URL `http://localhost:3000/home/show_cookies` in your browser. You will not see any values, as shown in Figure 8-1.

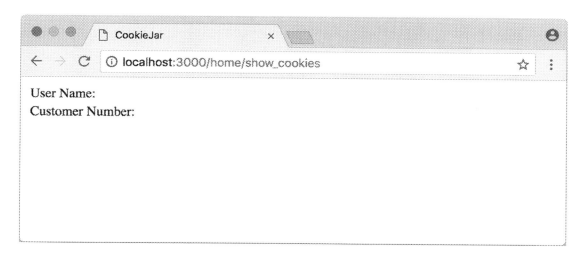

Figure 8-1. *Cookies empty*

Now go to the URL `http://localhost:3000/home/set_cookies` and then back to `http://localhost:3000/home/show_cookies`. Now you will see the values that you have set in the method `set_cookies`, as shown in Figure 8-2.

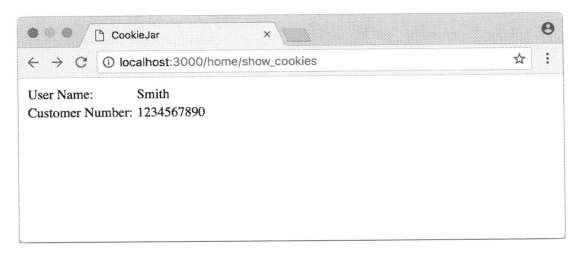

Figure 8-2. *Cookies set*

By requesting the page `http://localhost:3000/home/delete_cookies`, you can delete the cookies.

The cookies you have placed in this way stay alive in the browser until you close the browser completely.

Permanent Cookies

Cookies are usually set to give the application a way of recognizing users when they visit again later. Between these visits to the web site, much time can go by, and the user may well close the browser in the meantime. To store cookies for longer than the current browser session, you can use the method `permanent`. You can expand the previous example by adding the method shown in Listing 8-3 in `app/controllers/home_controller.rb`.

Listing 8-3. app/controllers/home_controller.rb

```ruby
class HomeController < ApplicationController
  def set_cookies
    cookies.permanent[:user_name]       = "Smith"
    cookies.permanent[:customer_number] = "1234567890"
  end

  def show_cookies
    @user_name       = cookies[:user_name]
    @customer_number = cookies[:customer_number]
  end

  def delete_cookies
    cookies.delete :user_name
    cookies.delete :customer_number
  end
end
```

> ❗ `permanent` here does not really mean permanent. You cannot set a cookie permanently. When you set a cookie, it always needs a `valid until` stamp that the browser can use to automatically delete old cookies. With the method `permanent`, this value is set to today's date in 20 years.

Signed Cookies

With normally placed cookies, you have no option on the application side to find out whether the user of the application has changed the cookie. This can quickly lead to security problems because changing the content of a cookie in the browser is no great mystery. The solution is to sign the cookies with a key that is known only to you. This key is automatically created via a random generator with each `rails new` command and is located in the file `config/secrets.yml`, as shown in Listing 8-4.

Listing 8-4. config/secrets.yml

```
development:
  secret_key_base: f4c3[...]095b
```

```
test:
  secret_key_base: d6ef[...]052a
```

```
# Do not keep production secrets in the repository,
# instead read values from the environment.
production:
  secret_key_base: <%= ENV["SECRET_KEY_BASE"] %>
```

As mentioned in the comment before the production key, it is not a good idea to store the production key in the source code of your project. It's better to store it as an environment variable and let the Rails project read it from there.

To sign cookies, you can use the method signed, which you use for writing and reading the cookie. You can expand the previous example by adding the method shown in Listing 8-5 in app/controllers/home_controller.rb.

Listing 8-5. app/controllers/home_controller.rb

```ruby
class HomeController < ApplicationController
  def set_cookies
    cookies.permanent.signed[:user_name]       = "Smith"
    cookies.permanent.signed[:customer_number] = "1234567890"
  end

  def show_cookies
    @user_name       = cookies.signed[:user_name]
    @customer_number = cookies.signed[:customer_number]
  end

  def delete_cookies
    cookies.delete :user_name
    cookies.delete :customer_number
  end
end
```

The content of the cookie is now encrypted every time you set the cookie. The user can read the name of the cookie, but not the value.

Sessions

As HTTP is a stateless protocol, you will encounter special problems when developing applications. An individual web page has no connection to the next web page, and they do not even know about one another. But since a user wants to register only once on a web site, not over and over again on each individual page, this can pose a problem. The solution is called a *session*, and Rails offers sessions to the programmer transparently as with the session[] hash. Rails automatically creates a new session for each new visitor of the web page. This session is saved by default as a cookie, so it is subject to the 4KB limit. You can also store the sessions in the database (see the section "Saving Sessions in the Database"). An independent and unique session ID is created automatically, and the cookie is deleted by default when the web browser is closed.

The beauty of a Rails session is that you can save not only strings there as with cookies, but any object, hashes, and arrays as well. So, you can, for example, use it to conveniently implement a shopping cart in an online shop.

Breadcrumbs via Sessions

As an example, let's create an application with a controller and three views. When a view is visited, the previously visited views are displayed in a little list.

Here is the basic application:

```
$ rails new breadcrumbs
  [...]
$ cd breadcrumbs
$ rails db:migrate
$ rails generate controller Home ping pong index
  [...]
```

First you create a method with which you can save the last three URLs in the session and set an instance variable called @breadcrumbs to be able to neatly retrieve the values in the view. To that end, you set up a before_action in app/controllers/home_controller.rb, as shown in Listing 8-6.

Listing 8-6. app/controllers/home_controller.rb

```ruby
class HomeController < ApplicationController
  before_action :set_breadcrumbs

  def ping
  end

  def pong
  end

  def index
  end

  private
  def set_breadcrumbs
    if session[:breadcrumbs]
      @breadcrumbs = session[:breadcrumbs]
    else
      @breadcrumbs = Array.new
    end

    @breadcrumbs.push(request.url)

    if @breadcrumbs.count > 4
      # shift removes the first element
      @breadcrumbs.shift
    end

    session[:breadcrumbs] = @breadcrumbs
  end
end
```

Now you use app/views/layouts/application.html.erb to display the last entries at the top of each page, as shown in Listing 8-7.

Listing 8-7. app/views/layouts/application.html.erb

```erb
<!DOCTYPE html>
<html>
  <head>
    <title>Breadcrumbs</title>
    <%= csrf_meta_tags %>

    <%= stylesheet_link_tag    'application', media: 'all', 'data-
    turbolinks-track': 'reload' %>
    <%= javascript_include_tag 'application', 'data-turbolinks-track':
    'reload' %>
  </head>

  <body>
    <% if @breadcrumbs && @breadcrumbs.any? %>
      <h3>Surf History</h3>
      <ul>
        <% @breadcrumbs[0..2].each do |breadcrumb| %>
          <li><%= link_to breadcrumb, breadcrumb %></li>
        <% end %>
      </ul>
    <% end %>

    <%= yield %>
  </body>
</html>
```

Start the Rails server with `rails server` and go to `http://localhost:3000/home/ping`, `http://localhost:3000/home/pong`, or `http://localhost:3000/home/index`; at the top you will always see the last three pages that you have visited. Of course, this works only on the second page because you do not yet have a history on the first page you visit.

reset_session

Occasionally, there are situations where you want to reset a session (in other words, delete the current session and start a new, fresh session). For example, if you log out of a web application, the session will be reset. This is easily done, and you can quickly integrate it into your breadcrumb application.

> **i**   With the switch -s, the generator doesn't overwrite existing files. In this example, that would be the home_controller.rb file.

```
$ rails generate controller Home reset -s
Running via Spring preloader in process 49668
      skip   app/controllers/home_controller.rb
     route   get 'home/reset'
    invoke   erb
     exist     app/views/home
    create     app/views/home/reset.html.erb
    invoke   test_unit
      skip     test/controllers/home_controller_test.rb
    invoke   helper
 identical     app/helpers/home_helper.rb
    invoke     test_unit
    invoke   assets
    invoke     coffee
 identical       app/assets/javascripts/home.coffee
    invoke     css
 identical       app/assets/stylesheets/home.css
```

The correspondingly expanded controller, named app/controllers/home_controller.rb, looks like Listing 8-8.

Listing 8-8. app/controllers/home_controller.rb

```ruby
class HomeController < ApplicationController
  before_action :set_breadcrumbs

  def ping
  end

  def pong
  end

  def index
  end

  def reset
    reset_session
    @breadcrumbs = nil
  end

  private
  def set_breadcrumbs
    if session[:breadcrumbs]
      @breadcrumbs = session[:breadcrumbs]
    else
      @breadcrumbs = Array.new
    end

    @breadcrumbs.push(request.url)

    if @breadcrumbs.count > 4
      # shift removes the first element
      @breadcrumbs.shift
    end

    session[:breadcrumbs] = @breadcrumbs
  end
end
```

So, you can delete the current session by going to the URL http://localhost:3000/home/reset.

> ❗ It's important not just to invoke `reset_session`, but you need to also set the instance variable `@breadcrumbs` to `nil`. Otherwise, the old breadcrumbs would still appear in the view.

Saving Sessions in the Database

Saving the entire session data in a cookie on the user's browser is not always the best solution. Among other reasons, the limit of 4KB can pose a problem. But it's no big obstacle; you can relocate the storing of the session from the cookie to the database with the gem at `https://github.com/rails/activerecord-session_store`. The session ID is of course still saved in a cookie, but the other session data is stored in the database on the server.

To install the gem, you have to add the line shown in Listing 8-9 at the end of the file `Gemfile`.

Listing 8-9. Gemfile

```
gem 'activerecord-session_store'
```

After that, run the `bundle install` command.

```
$ bundle install
[...]
```

Next, you have to run `rails generate active_record:session_migration` and `rails db:migrate` to create the needed table in the database.

```
$ rails generate active_record:session_migration
      create  db/migrate/20150428183919_add_sessions_table.rb
$ rails db:migrate
== 20150428183919 AddSessionsTable: migrating ===============================
-- create_table(:sessions)
   -> 0.0019s
-- add_index(:sessions, :session_id, {:unique=>true})
   -> 0.0008s
-- add_index(:sessions, :updated_at)
   -> 0.0008s
== 20150428183919 AddSessionsTable: migrated (0.0037s) ====================
```

Finally, change the `session_store` value in the file `config/initializers/session_store.rb` to `:active_record_store`, as shown in Listing 8-10.

Listing 8-10. config/initializers/session_store.rb

```
Rails.application.config.session_store :active_record_store, :key =>
'_my_app_session'
```

You're finished. Start the server again with `rails server` and Rails will save all sessions in the database.

CHAPTER 9

Tests

I have been programming for more than 30 years, and most of the time I have managed quite well without test-driven development (TDD). I am not going to be mad at you if you decide to just skip this chapter. You can create Rails applications without tests, and you are not likely to garner any bad karma as a result (at least, I hope not, but you can never be entirely sure with the whole karma thing).

If you should decide to go for TDD, then I can promise you that it is enlightening. The basic idea of TDD is that you write a test for each programming function to check that function. In the pure TDD teaching, this test is written before the actual programming. Yes, you will have a lot more to do initially. But later, you can run all the tests and see that the application works exactly as you wanted it to work. The real advantage becomes apparent only after a few weeks or months when you look at the project again and write an extension or new variation. Then you can safely change the code and check that it still works properly by running the tests. This avoids a situation where you find yourself saying "Oops, that went a bit wrong; I just didn't think of that particular problem."

Often, the advantage of TDD is evident when writing a program. Tests can reveal many careless mistakes that you would otherwise have stumbled across only much later.

This chapter is a brief overview of the topic of test-driven development with Rails. If you want to find out more, you can dive into the official Rails documentation at `http://guides.rubyonrails.org/testing.html`.

 TDD is just like driving a car. The only way to learn it is by doing it.

© Stefan Wintermeyer 2018
S. Wintermeyer, *Learn Rails 5.2*, https://doi.org/10.1007/978-1-4842-3489-1_9

Example for a User in a Web Shop

Let's start with a user scaffold in an imaginary web shop, as shown here:

```
$ rails new webshop
  [...]
$ cd webshop
$ rails generate scaffold user login_name first_name last_name
birthday:date
    [...]
    invoke    test_unit
    create      test/models/user_test.rb
    create      test/fixtures/users.yml
    [...]
    invoke    test_unit
    create      test/controllers/users_controller_test.rb
    create      test/system/users_test.rb
    invoke    helper
    create      app/helpers/users_helper.rb
    invoke      test_unit
    [...]
$ rails db:migrate
    [...]
```

You already know all about scaffolds (if not, please read Chapter 4), so you know
what the application you have just created does. The scaffold created a few tests (they are
easy to recognize because the word test is in the file names).

The complete test suite of a Rails project is processed with the command rails test.
Let's see what a test produces at this stage of development:

```
$ rails test
Running via Spring preloader in process 2440
Run options: --seed 62885
```

 # Running:

. . . .

```
Finished in 1.361143s, 5.1427 runs/s, 6.6121 assertions/s.
7 runs, 9 assertions, 0 failures, 0 errors, 0 skips
```

The output 7 runs, 9 assertions, 0 failures, 0 errors, 0 skips looks good. By default, a test will run through in a standard scaffold.

Let's edit app/models/user.rb and insert a few validations (if these are not entirely clear to you, please read the section "Validation" in Chapter X), as shown in Listing 9-1.

Listing 9-1. app/models/user.rb

```
class User < ApplicationRecord
  validates :login_name,
            presence: true,
            length: { minimum: 10 }

  validates :last_name,
            presence: true
end
```

Then execute rails test again, as shown here:

```
$ rails test
Running via Spring preloader in process 89164
Run options: --seed 40163
```

 # Running:

....F

```
Failure:
UsersControllerTest#test_should_update_user [/.../webshop/test/controllers/
users_controller_test.rb:38]:
Expected response to be a <3XX: redirect>, but was a <200: OK>

bin/rails test test/controllers/users_controller_test.rb:36
```

F

```
Failure:
UsersControllerTest#test_should_create_user [/.../webshop/test/controllers/
users_controller_test.rb:19]:
"User.count" didn't change by 1.
Expected: 3
  Actual: 2

bin/rails test test/controllers/users_controller_test.rb:18


.

Finished in 0.262099s, 26.7075 runs/s, 30.5228 assertions/s.

7 runs, 8 assertions, 2 failures, 0 errors, 0 skips
```

Boom! This time you have the output 2 `failures`. The error happens in
`UsersControllerTest#test_should_update_user` and `UsersControllerTest#test_`
`should_create_user`. The explanation for this is in the validation. The example data
created by the scaffold generator went through in the first `rails test` test (without
validation). The errors occurred only the second time (with validation).

This example data is created as `fixtures_tests` tests in YAML format in the
directory `test/fixtures/`. Let's take a look at the example data for `User` in the file
`test/fixtures/users.yml`; see Listing 9-2.

Listing 9-2. test/fixtures/users.yml

```
one:
  login_name: MyString
  first_name: MyString
  last_name: MyString
  birthday: 2018-01-25

two:
  login_name: MyString
  first_name: MyString
  last_name: MyString
  birthday: 2018-01-25
```

There are two example records in Listing 9-2 that do not fulfill the requirements of the validation. The login_name record should have a length of at least ten. Let's change the login_name record in test/fixtures/users.yml accordingly; see Listing 9-3.

Listing 9-3. test/fixtures/users.yml

```
one:
  login_name: MyString12
  first_name: MyString
  last_name: MyString
  birthday: 2018-01-25

two:
  login_name: MyString12
  first_name: MyString
  last_name: MyString
  birthday: 2018-01-25
```

Now, the rails test command completes without any errors again.

```
$ rails test
Running via Spring preloader in process 89807
Run options: --seed 50152

# Running:

.......

Finished in 0.271182s, 25.8129 runs/s, 33.1880 assertions/s.

7 runs, 9 assertions, 0 failures, 0 errors, 0 skips
```

Now you know that valid data has to be contained in test/fixtures/users.yml so that the standard test created via the scaffolding will succeed. But you need nothing more. The next step is to change test/fixtures/users.yml to the minimum needed (for example, you do not need a first_name field), as shown in Listing 9-4.

Listing 9-4. test/fixtures/users.yml

```
one:
  login_name: MyString12
  last_name: Mulder

two:
  login_name: MyString12
  last_name: Scully
```

To be on the safe side, let's run another `rails test` command after making the changes (you really can't do that often enough).

```
$ rails test
Running via Spring preloader in process 89972
Run options: --seed 40198

# Running:

.......

Finished in 0.255256s, 27.4234 runs/s, 35.2587 assertions/s.

7 runs, 9 assertions, 0 failures, 0 errors, 0 skips
```

❗ All fixtures are loaded into the database when a test is started. You need to keep this in mind for your test, especially if you use `uniqueness` in your validation.

Functional Tests

Let's take a closer look at the point where the original errors occurred, as shown here:

```
Failure:
UsersControllerTest#test_should_create_user
[/.../webshop/test/controllers/users_controller_test.rb:19]:
"User.count" didn't change by 1.
Expected: 3
  Actual: 2
```

In UsersControllerTest, the user could not be created. The controller tests are located in the directory test/functional/. Let's now take a good look at the file test/controllers/users_controller_test.rb, as shown in Listing 9-5.

Listing 9-5. test/controllers/users_controller_test.rb

```ruby
require 'test_helper'

class UsersControllerTest < ActionDispatch::IntegrationTest
  setup do
    @user = users(:one)
  end

  test "should get index" do
    get users_url
    assert_response :success
  end

  test "should get new" do
    get new_user_url
    assert_response :success
  end

  test "should create user" do
    assert_difference('User.count') do
      post users_url, params: { user: { birthday: @user.birthday,
      first_name: @user.first_name, last_name: @user.last_name,
      login_name: @user.login_name } }
    end

    assert_redirected_to user_url(User.last)
  end

  test "should show user" do
    get user_url(@user)
    assert_response :success
  end
```

```
test "should get edit" do
  get edit_user_url(@user)
  assert_response :success
end

test "should update user" do
  patch user_url(@user), params: { user: { birthday: @user.birthday,
  first_name: @user.first_name, last_name: @user.last_name,
  login_name: @user.login_name } }
  assert_redirected_to user_url(@user)
end

test "should destroy user" do
  assert_difference('User.count', -1) do
    delete user_url(@user)
  end

  assert_redirected_to users_url
end
end
```

At the beginning, you will find a setup instruction.

```
setup do
  @user = users(:one)
end
```

These three lines of code mean that for the start of each individual test, an instance called @user with the data of the item one from the file test/fixtures/users.yml is created. setup is a predefined callback that—if present—is started by Rails before each test. The opposite of setup is teardown. A teardown—if present—is called automatically after each test.

> ℹ️   For every test (in other words, at each run of `rails test`), a fresh and therefore empty test database is created automatically. This is a different database than the one you access by default via `rails console` (that is, the development database). The databases are defined in the configuration file `config/database.yml`. If you want to do debugging, you can access the test database with `rails console test`.

This functional test then tests various web page functions. First, you access the index page.

```
test "should get index" do
  get users_url
  assert_response :success
end
```

The command `get users_url` accesses the page /users. A response of `assert_response :success` means that the page was delivered.

Let's look more closely at the `should create user` problem from earlier.

```
test "should create user" do
  assert_difference('User.count') do
    post users_url, params: { user: { birthday: @user.birthday,
    first_name: @user.first_name, last_name: @user.last_name,
    login_name: @user.login_name } }
  end

  assert_redirected_to user_url(User.last)
end
```

The block `assert_difference('User.count') do ... end` expects a change by the code contained within it. `User.count` should result in +1.

The last line, `assert_redirected_to user_path(User.last)`, checks whether after the newly created record the redirection to the corresponding view show occurs.

Without describing each individual functional test line by line, it's becoming clear what these tests do: they execute real queries to the web interface (or actually to the controllers), and so they can be used for testing the controllers.

Unit Tests

For testing the validations that you have entered in `app/models/user.rb`, unit tests are more suitable. Unlike the functional tests, these test only the model, not the controller's work.

The unit tests are located in the directory `test/models/`. But a look into the file `test/models/user_test.rb` is rather sobering, as shown in Listing 9-6.

Listing 9-6. test/models/user_test.rb

```ruby
require 'test_helper'

class UserTest < ActiveSupport::TestCase
  # test "the truth" do
  #   assert true
  # end
end
```

By default, the scaffold only writes a commented-out dummy test.

A unit test always consists of the following structure:

```ruby
test "an assertion" do
  assert something_is_true
end
```

The word `assert` already indicates that you are dealing with an assertion in this context. If this assertion is `true`, the test will complete, and all is well. If this assertion is `false`, the test fails, and you have an error in the program (you can specify the output of the error as a string at the end of the assert line).

If you take a look at `http://guides.rubyonrails.org/testing.html`, you'll see that there are some other `assert` variations. Here are a few examples:

- `assert( boolean, [msg] )`

- `assert_equal( obj1, obj2, [msg] )`

- `assert_not_equal( obj1, obj2, [msg] )`

- `assert_same( obj1, obj2, [msg] )`

- `assert_not_same( obj1, obj2, [msg] )`

- assert_nil(obj, [msg])

- assert_not_nil(obj, [msg])

- assert_match(regexp, string , [msg])

- assert_no_match(regexp, string , [msg])

Let's breathe some life into the first test in test/unit/user_test.rb, as shown in Listing 9-7.

Listing 9-7. test/unit/user_test.rb

```ruby
require 'test_helper'

class UserTest < ActiveSupport::TestCase
  test 'a user with no attributes is not valid' do
    user = User.new
    assert_not user.save, 'Saved a user with no attributes.'
  end
end
```

This test checks whether a newly created User that does not contain any data is valid (it shouldn't be).

You can run a rails test command for the complete test suite.

```
$ rails test
Running via Spring preloader in process 91049
Run options: --seed 8014

# Running:

........

Finished in 0.248883s, 32.1436 runs/s, 40.1795 assertions/s.

8 runs, 10 assertions, 0 failures, 0 errors, 0 skips
```

Now you integrate two asserts in a test to check whether the two fixture entries in test/fixtures/users.yml are really valid. The first one is just a shorter version of the empty user test.

```ruby
require 'test_helper'

class UserTest < ActiveSupport::TestCase
  test 'an empty user is not valid' do
    assert !User.new.valid?, 'Saved an empty user.'
  end

  test "the two fixture users are valid" do
    assert User.new(last_name: users(:one).last_name, login_name:
    users(:one).login_name ).valid?, 'First fixture is not valid.'
    assert User.new(last_name: users(:two).last_name, login_name:
    users(:two).login_name ).valid?, 'Second fixture is not valid.'
  end
end
```

Then once more there's a rails test command.

```
$ rails test
Running via Spring preloader in process 91434
Run options: --seed 57493

# Running:

.........

Finished in 0.256179s, 35.1317 runs/s, 46.8422 assertions/s.

9 runs, 12 assertions, 0 failures, 0 errors, 0 skips
```

Fixtures

With *fixtures* you can generate example data for tests. The default format for this is YAML. You can find the files for this in the directory test/fixtures/; they are automatically created with rails generate scaffold. But of course you can also define your own files. All fixtures are loaded into the test database by default with every test.

You can find examples for alternative formats (e.g., CSV) at `http://api.`
`rubyonrails.org/classes/ActiveRecord/Fixtures.html`.

Static Fixtures

The simplest variant for fixtures is static data. The fixture for User used in the section
"Example for a User in a Web Shop" statically should look like Listing 9-8 (please change
the content of the file accordingly).

Listing 9-8. test/fixtures/users.yml

```
one:
  login_name: fox.mulder
  last_name: Mulder

two:
  login_name: dana.scully
  last_name: Scully
```

You simply write the data in YAML format into the corresponding file.

Fixtures with erb

Static YAML fixtures are sometimes not smart enough to do the job. In these cases, you
can work with erb.

If you want to dynamically enter today's date 20 years ago for a birthday, then you
can simply do it with erb in `test/fixtures/users.yml`, as shown in Listing 9-9.

Listing 9-9. test/fixtures/users.yml

```
one:
  login_name: fox.mulder
  last_name: Mulder
  birthday: <%= 20.years.ago.to_s(:db) %>

two:
  login_name: dana.scully
  last_name: Scully
  birthday: <%= 20.years.ago.to_s(:db) %>
```

Integration Tests

Integration tests are tests that work like functional tests, but they can span several controllers and additionally analyze the content of a generated view. So, you can use them to re-create complex workflows within a Rails application. As an example, I will show how to write an integration test that tries to create a new user via the web GUI but omits the login_name value and consequently gets corresponding flash error messages.

A rails generate scaffold command generates unit and functional tests but not integration tests. You can do this either manually in the directory test/integration/ or more comfortably with rails generate integration_test. So, let's create an integration test.

```
$ rails generate integration_test invalid_new_user_workflow
Running via Spring preloader in process 91538
      invoke  test_unit
      create    test/integration/invalid_new_user_workflow_test.rb
```

You can now populate the file test/integration/invalid_new_user_workflow_test.rb with the test shown in Listing 9-10.

Listing 9-10. test/integration/invalid_new_user_workflow_test.rb

```ruby
require 'test_helper'

class InvalidNewUserWorkflowTest < ActionDispatch::IntegrationTest
  fixtures :all

  test 'try to create a new user without a login' do
    @user = users(:one)

    get '/users/new'
    assert_response :success

    post users_url, params: { user: { last_name: @user.last_name } }
    assert_equal '/users', path
    assert_select 'li', "Login name can't be blank"
    assert_select 'li', "Login name is too short (minimum is 10 characters)"
  end
end
```

Let's run all the tests.

```
$ rails test
Running via Spring preloader in process 91837
Run options: --seed 4153

# Running:

..........

Finished in 0.277714s, 36.0083 runs/s, 57.6132 assertions/s.

10 runs, 16 assertions, 0 failures, 0 errors, 0 skips
```

The example clearly shows that you can program without manually using a web browser to try it. Once you have written a test for the corresponding workflow, you can rely in the future on the fact that it will run through; in other words, you don't have to try it manually in the browser as well.

rails stats

With rails stats, you can get an overview of your Rails project. Here's an example:

```
$ rails stats
```

Name	Lines	LOC	Classes	Methods	M/C	LOC/M
Controllers	77	53	2	9	4	3
Helpers	4	4	0	0	0	0
Jobs	2	2	1	0	0	0
Models	11	10	2	0	0	0
Mailers	4	4	1	0	0	0
Channels	8	8	2	0	0	0
JavaScripts	31	4	0	1	0	2
Libraries	0	0	0	0	0	0
Controller tests	48	38	1	7	7	3
Helper tests	0	0	0	0	0	0
Model tests	14	12	1	2	2	4
Mailer tests	0	0	0	0	0	0

```
| Integration tests   |      17 |     13 |       1 |       1 |   1 |     11 |
| System tests        |       9 |      3 |       1 |       0 |   0 |      0 |
+---------------------+--------+--------+---------+---------+-----+-------+
| Total               |     225 |    151 |      12 |      20 |   1 |      5 |
+---------------------+--------+--------+---------+---------+-----+-------+
   Code LOC: 88      Test LOC: 63      Code to Test Ratio: 1:0.7
```

In this project, there are a total of 88 lines of code (LOCs) in the controllers, helpers, and models. There are a total of 63 LOCs for tests. This gives you a test relation of 1:1.0.7. Logically, this does not say anything about the quality of tests.

More on Testing

This chapter just scratched the surface of the topic of TDD in Rails. Take a look at `http://guides.rubyonrails.org/testing.html` for more information. There you will also find several good examples on this topic.

One cool feature of Ruby on Rails testing is the ability to run the tests in real browsers (e.g., Chrome) and to take screenshots while doing so.

CHAPTER 10

Active Job

Sometimes a specific piece of code takes a long time to run but doesn't need to run right away. An example is sending an e-mail after creating an order at the end of an online shopping workflow. It can take a long time to send an e-mail, but you don't want your user to wait for that to happen within the controller. It makes more sense to use a queueing mechanism for these tasks.

Active Job provides such a queueing system. You can create jobs that are processed asynchronously by the active job.

Create a New Job

The quickest way to create a new job is to use the job generator. Let's create an example job that waits for ten seconds and then logs an info message, as shown here:

```
$ rails new shop
  [...]
$ cd shop
$ rails db:migrate
$ rails generate job example
Running via Spring preloader in process 5301
      invoke  test_unit
      create    test/jobs/example_job_test.rb
      create  app/jobs/example_job.rb
$
```

All jobs are created in the app/jobs directory. Please change the app/jobs/example_job.rb file accordingly, as shown in Listing 10-1.

© Stefan Wintermeyer 2018
S. Wintermeyer, *Learn Rails 5.2*, https://doi.org/10.1007/978-1-4842-3489-1_10

Listing 10-1. app/jobs/example_job.rb

```ruby
class ExampleJob < ApplicationJob
  queue_as :default

  def perform(*args)
    sleep 10
    logger.info "Just waited 10 seconds."
  end
end
```

You can test the job in your console with ExampleJob.perform_later, which creates it.

```
$ rails console
Running via Spring preloader in process 98485
Loading development environment (Rails 5.2.0)
>> ExampleJob.perform_later
Enqueued ExampleJob (Job ID: 21526c3c-7839-49e7-975e-2a176a07dbc4) to
Async(default)
Performing ExampleJob (Job ID: 21526c3c-7839-49e7-975e-2a176a07dbc4) from
Async(default)
=> #<ExampleJob:0x007fceee71f498 @arguments=[], @job_id="21526c3c-7839-49e7-
975e-2a176a07dbc4", @queue_name="default", @priority=nil, @executions=0,
@provider_job_id="4c814d91-45d1-4c3e-a57a-3bfd08c1c56f">
```

Now you have to wait ten seconds to see the following output in the console:

```
Just waited 10 seconds.
Performed ExampleJob (Job ID: bb6e9781-8ffb-4bf2-8dfc-8ac983ed8bf6)
from Async(default) in 10012.97ms

?> exit
```

   The file log/development.log contains the logging output.

You'll find a more concrete example of using jobs in Chapter 11 where an e-mail gets sent.

Set the Time for Future Execution

The set method provides two arguments that can be used to set the execution of a job in the future.

- wait

  ExampleJob.set(wait: 1.hour).perform_later

- wait_until

  ExampleJob.set(wait_until: Date.tomorrow.noon).perform_later

Configure the Job Server Back End

The page http://api.rubyonrails.org/classes/ActiveJob/QueueAdapters.html lists all the available back ends. To use one of them, you have to install the needed gem. Listing 10-2 shows an example of using the popular Sidekiq. To use the gem, you have to add it to the Gemfile and run a bundle install command afterward.

Listing 10-2. Gemfile

```
[...]
gem 'sidekiq'
```

```
$ bundle install
```

In config/application.rb, you can configure the use of it, as shown in Listing 10-3.

Listing 10-3. config/application.rb

```
require_relative 'boot'

require 'rails/all'

# Require the gems listed in Gemfile, including any gems
# you've limited to :test, :development, or :production.
Bundler.require(*Rails.groups)
```

```ruby
module Shop
  class Application < Rails::Application
    # Initialize configuration defaults for originally generated Rails version.
    config.load_defaults 5.2

    # Settings in config/environments/* take precedence over those
    # specified here.
    # Application configuration should go into files in config/initializers
    # -- all .rb files in that directory are automatically loaded.

    # Sidekiq Configuration
    config.active_job.queue_adapter = :sidekiq
  end
end
```

CHAPTER 11

Action Mailer

Even if you mainly use Ruby on Rails to generate web pages, it sometimes is useful to be able to send an e-mail.

So, let's build an example with minimal user management for a web shop that automatically sends an e-mail to the user when a new user is created, as shown here:

```
$ rails new webshop
  [...]
$ cd webshop
$ rails generate scaffold User name email
  [...]
$ rails db:migrate
  [...]
```

For the user model, create a minimal validation in app/models/user.rb so that you can be sure that each user has a name and a syntactically correct e-mail address (see Listing 11-1).

Listing 11-1. app/models/user.rb

```ruby
class User < ApplicationRecord
  validates :name,
            presence: true

  validates :email,
            presence: true,
            format: { with: /\A([^@\s]+)@((?:[-a-z0-9]+\.)+[a-z]{2,})\Z/i }
end
```

© Stefan Wintermeyer 2018
S. Wintermeyer, *Learn Rails 5.2*, https://doi.org/10.1007/978-1-4842-3489-1_11

There is a generator with the name mailer that creates the files required for mailing. First, take a look at the output of rails generate mailer, without passing any further arguments, as shown here:

```
$ rails generate mailer
Running via Spring preloader in process 99958
Usage:
  rails generate mailer NAME [method method] [options]

[...]

Example:
========

    rails generate mailer Notifications signup forgot_password invoice

    creates a Notifications mailer class, views, and test:
        Mailer:     app/mailers/notifications_mailer.rb
        Views:      app/views/notifications_mailer/signup.text.erb [...]
        Test:       test/mailers/notifications_mailer_test.rb
```

That is just as expected. Let's now create the mailer notification, as shown here:

```
$ rails generate mailer Notification new_account
Running via Spring preloader in process 201
      create  app/mailers/notification_mailer.rb
      invoke  erb
      create    app/views/notification_mailer
      create    app/views/notification_mailer/new_account.text.erb
      create    app/views/notification_mailer/new_account.html.erb
      invoke  test_unit
      create    test/mailers/notification_mailer_test.rb
      create    test/mailers/previews/notification_mailer_preview.rb
```

In the file app/mailers/notification_mailer.rb you will find the controller for it, as shown in Listing 11-2.

Listing 11-2. app/mailers/notification_mailer.rb

```ruby
class NotificationMailer < ApplicationMailer

  # Subject can be set in your I18n file at config/locales/en.yml
  # with the following lookup:
  #
  #   en.notification_mailer.new_account.subject
  #
  def new_account
    @greeting = "Hi"

    mail to: "to@example.org"
  end
end
```

In it, you change the new_account method to accept a parameter with
new_account(user) and some code to use to send the confirmation e-mail; see Listing 11-3.

Listing 11-3. app/mailers/notification_mailer.rb

```ruby
class NotificationMailer < ApplicationMailer
  def new_account(user)
    @user = user
    mail(to: user.email, subject: "Account #{user.name} is active")
  end
end
```

Now you can create the view for this method. Actually, you have to breathe life into two files.

- app/views/notification_mailer/new_account.text.erb
- app/views/notification_mailer/new_account.html.erb

If you want to send a non-HTML e-mail, you can delete the file app/views/
notification_mailer/new_account.html.erb. Otherwise, Action Mailer will generate
an e-mail that can be read as a traditional text e-mail (see Listing 11-4) or as a modern
HTML e-mail (see Listing 11-5).

Listing 11-4. app/views/notification_mailer/new_account.text.erb

```
Hello <%= @user.name %>,

your new account is active.

Have a great day!
  A Robot
```

Listing 11-5. app/views/notification_mailer/new_account.html.erb

```
<p>Hello <%= @user.name %>,</p>
<p>your new account is active.</p>
<p>Have a great day!</br>
  A Robot</p>
```

As you want to send this e-mail after the creation of a User, you still need to add an after_create callback that triggers the delivery, as shown in Listing 11-6.

Listing 11-6. app/models/user.rb

```ruby
class User < ApplicationRecord
  validates :name,
            presence: true

  validates :email,
            presence: true,
            format: { with: /\A([^@\s]+)@((?:[-a-z0-9]+\.)+[a-z]{2,})\Z/i }

  after_create :send_welcome_email

  private
  def send_welcome_email
    NotificationMailer.new_account(self).deliver_later
  end
end
```

Let's create a new User in the console.

ℹ️   It'll take a moment for Action Mailer to send the e-mail. It's using Active Job to queue it. Be patient.

```
$ rails console
Running via Spring preloader in process 1795
Loading development environment (Rails 5.2.0)
>> User.create(name: "Wintermeyer", email: "sw@wintermeyer-consulting.de")
   (0.1ms)  begin transaction
  User Create (0.4ms)  INSERT INTO "users" ("name", "email", "created_at",
"updated_at") VALUES (?, ?, ?, ?)  [["name", "Wintermeyer"], ["email",
"sw@wintermeyer-consulting.de"], ["created_at", "2018-01-27 16:21:32.093810"],
["updated_at", "2018-01-27 16:21:32.093810"]]
Enqueued ActionMailer::DeliveryJob (Job ID: de33ce3d-9671-4957-8b89-
65b8d3000820) to Async(mailers) with arguments: "NotificationMailer",
"new_account", "deliver_now", #<GlobalID:0x007ffe488addf8 @uri=#<URI::GID
gid://shop4/User/1>>
   (3.2ms)  commit transaction
=> #<User id: 1, name: "Wintermeyer", email: "sw@wintermeyer-consulting.
de", created_at: "2018-01-27 16:21:32", updated_at: "2018-01-27 16:21:32">
>>   User Load (0.3ms)  SELECT  "users".* FROM "users" WHERE "users"."id" =
? LIMIT ?  [["id", 1], ["LIMIT", 1]]
Performing ActionMailer::DeliveryJob (Job ID: de33ce3d-9671-4957-8b89-
65b8d3000820) from Async(mailers) with arguments: "NotificationMailer",
"new_account", "deliver_now", #<GlobalID:0x007ffe45f84120 @uri=#<URI::GID
gid://shop4/User/1>>
  Rendering notification_mailer/new_account.html.erb within layouts/mailer
  Rendered notification_mailer/new_account.html.erb within layouts/mailer (6.7ms)
  Rendering notification_mailer/new_account.text.erb within layouts/mailer
  Rendered notification_mailer/new_account.text.erb within layouts/mailer (0.4ms)
NotificationMailer#new_account: processed outbound mail in 792.9ms
Sent mail to sw@wintermeyer-consulting.de (31.8ms)
```

```
Date: Sat, 27 Jan 2018 17:21:43 +0100
From: from@example.com
To: sw@wintermeyer-consulting.de
Message-ID: <5a6ca717456a9_183a3fff24456d442550@sw.mail>
Subject: Account Wintermeyer is active
Mime-Version: 1.0
Content-Type: multipart/alternative;
 boundary="--==_mimepart_5a6ca7174371d_183a3fff24456d44254be";
 charset=UTF-8
Content-Transfer-Encoding: 7bit

----==_mimepart_5a6ca7174371d_183a3fff24456d44254be
Content-Type: text/plain;
 charset=UTF-8
Content-Transfer-Encoding: 7bit

Hello Wintermeyer,

your new account is active.

Have a great day!
  A Robot

----==_mimepart_5a6ca7174371d_183a3fff24456d44254be
Content-Type: text/html;
 charset=UTF-8
Content-Transfer-Encoding: 7bit

<!DOCTYPE html>
<html>
  <head>
    <meta http-equiv="Content-Type" content="text/html; charset=utf-8" />
    <style>
      /* Email styles need to be inline */
    </style>
  </head>

  <body>
    <p>Hello Wintermeyer,</p>
```

```
<p>your new account is active.</p>
<p>Have a great day!</br>
  A Robot</p>

  </body>
</html>

----==_mimepart_5a6ca7174371d_183a3fff24456d44254be--

Performed ActionMailer::DeliveryJob (Job ID: de33ce3d-9671-4957-8b89-
65b8d3000820) from Async(mailers) in 842.52ms
>> exit
```

That was straightforward. In development mode, you can see the e-mail in the log. In production mode, it is sent to the configured SMTP gateway.

ℹ   Take a look at the files `app/views/layouts/mailer.html.erb` and `app/views/layouts/mailer.text.erb` to set a generic envelope (e.g., add CSS) for your e-mail content. It works like `app/views/layouts/application.html.erb` for HTML views.

Configuring the E-mail Server

Rails can use a local `sendmail` or an external SMTP server to deliver the e-mails.

Sending via Local Sendmail

If you want to send the e-mail in the traditional way via local `sendmail`, then you need to insert the lines shown in Listing 11-7 into your configuration file, which is `config/environments/development.rb` for your Development environment or `config/environments/production.rb` for your Production environment.

Listing 11-7.   config/environments/development.rb

```
config.action_mailer.delivery_method = :sendmail
config.action_mailer.perform_deliveries = true
config.action_mailer.raise_delivery_errors = true
```

Sending via Direct SMTP

If you want to send the e-mail directly via an SMTP server (for example, Google Mail), then you need to insert the lines shown in Listing 11-8 into your configuration file, which is config/environments/development.rb for your Development environment or config/environments/production.rb for your Production environment.

Listing 11-8. config/environments/development.rb

```
config.action_mailer.delivery_method = :smtp
config.action_mailer.smtp_settings = {
  address:              "smtp.gmail.com",
  port:                 587,
  domain:               'example.com',
  user_name:            '<username>',
  password:             '<password>',
  authentication:       'plain',
  enable_starttls_auto: true   }
```

Of course, you need to adapt the values for :domain, :user_name, and :password in accordance with your configuration.

Custom X-Header

If you feel the urge to integrate an additional X-header, then this is no problem. Listing 11-9 shows an example for expanding the file app/mailers/notification_mailer.rb.

Listing 11-9. app/mailers/notification_mailer.rb

```
class NotificationMailer < ApplicationMailer
  def new_account(user)
    @user = user
    headers["X-Priority"] = '3'
    mail(to: user.email, subject: "The account #{user.name} is active.")
  end
end
```

This means the sent e-mail looks like this:

```
Sent mail to sw@wintermeyer-consulting.de (50ms)
Date: Sat, 27 Jan 2018 17:35:21 +0200
From: from@example.com
To: sw@wintermeyer-consulting.de
Message-ID: <4fc63e39e356a_aa083fe366028cd8803c7@MacBook.local.mail>
Subject: The new account Wintermeyer is active.
Mime-Version: 1.0
Content-Type: text/plain;
 charset=UTF-8
Content-Transfer-Encoding: 7bit
X-Priority: 3

Hello Wintermeyer,

your new account is active.

Have a great day!
  A Robot
```

Attachments

E-mail attachments can be defined too.

As an example, in app/mailers/notification_mailer.rb you add the Rails image app/assets/images/rails.png to an e-mail as an attachment, as shown in Listing 11-10.

Listing 11-10. app/mailers/notification_mailer.rb

```ruby
class NotificationMailer < ApplicationMailer
  def new_account(user)
    @user = user
    attachments['rails.png'] =
      File.read("#{Rails.root}/app/assets/images/rails.png")
    mail(to: user.email, subject: "The account #{user.name} is active.")
  end
end
```

Inline Attachments

For *inline attachments* in HTML e-mails, you need to use the method inline when calling attachments. In the example, the controller app/mailers/notification_mailer.rb looks like Listing 11-11.

Listing 11-11. app/mailers/notification_mailer.rb

```
class NotificationMailer < ApplicationMailer
  def new_account(user)
    @user = user
    attachments.inline['rails.png'] =
      File.read("#{Rails.root}/app/assets/images/rails.png")
    mail(to: user.email, subject: "The account #{user.name} is active.")
  end
end
```

In the HTML e-mail, you can access the hash attachments[] via image_tag. In the example, the app/views/notification_mailer/new_account.html.erb file will look like Listing 11-12.

Listing 11-12. app/views/notification_mailer/new_account.html.erb

```
<!DOCTYPE html>
<html>
  <head>
    <meta content="text/html; charset=UTF-8" http-equiv="Content-Type" />
  </head>
  <body>
    <%= image_tag attachments['rails.png'].url, :alt => 'Rails Logo' %>
    <p>Hello <%= @user.name %>,</p>

    <p>your new account is active.</p>

    <p><i>Have a great day!</i></p>
    <p>A Robot</p>
  </body>
</html>
```

Further Information

The Rails online documentation has an extensive entry on Action Mailer at `http://guides.rubyonrails.org/action_mailer_basics.html`.

CHAPTER 12

Internationalization

If you are in the lucky situation of creating web pages in English only, then you can skip this chapter completely.

But even if you want to create a web page that uses only one language (other than English), you will need to dive into this chapter. It is not enough to just translate the views. If you use scaffolding, you will still need to take care of the not yet translated validation errors.

The class I18n is responsible for everything having to do with translation in the Rails application. It offers two important methods for this purpose.

- `I18n.translate` or `I18n.t`: Takes care of inserting previously defined text blocks. These can contain variables.

- `I18n.localize` or `I18n.l`: Takes care of adapting time and date specifications to the local format.

With `I18n.locale`, you define the language you want to use in the current call. In the configuration file `config/application.rb`, the entry `config.i18n.default_locale` sets the default value for `I18n.locale`. If you do not make any changes there, this value is set by default to `:en` for English.

For special cases such as displaying numbers, currencies, and times, special helpers are available. For example, if you want to create a German web page, you can ensure that the number 1000.23 can be correctly displayed with a decimal comma as 1.000,23 on the German page and with a decimal point on an English web page as 1,000.23.

Let's create an example application that includes the rails-i18n gem by Sven Fuchs (`https://github.com/svenfuchs/i18n`). It provides a couple of language files with translations and format information.

```
$ rails new shop-i18n
  [...]
$ cd shop-i18n
```

© Stefan Wintermeyer 2018
S. Wintermeyer, *Learn Rails 5.2*, https://doi.org/10.1007/978-1-4842-3489-1_12

```
$ rails db:migrate
$ echo "gem 'rails-i18n'" >> Gemfile
$ bundle
  [...]
$
```

In the console, you can see the different output of a number depending on the language setting, as shown here:

```
$ rails console
Running via Spring preloader in process 3337
Loading development environment (Rails 5.2.0)
>> price = 1000.23
=> 1000.23
>> helper.number_to_currency(price, locale: :de)
=> "1.000,23 €"
>> helper.number_to_currency(price, locale: :en)
=> "$1,000.23"
>> helper.number_to_currency(price, locale: :fr)
=> "1 000,23 €"
>> exit
```

I18n.t

With I18n.t, you can retrieve previously defined translations. The translations are saved by default in YAML format in the directory config/locales/.

In config/locales/, you can find an example file called config/locales/en.yml with the content in Listing 12-1.

Listing 12-1. config/locales/en.yml

```
en:
  hello: "Hello world"
```

In the Rails console, you can see how I18n.t works, as shown here:

```
$ rails console
Running via Spring preloader in process 3487
```

```
Loading development environment (Rails 5.2.0)
>> I18n.t :hello
=> "Hello world"
>> I18n.locale
=> :en
>> exit
```

Let's first create a config/locales/de.yml file with the content shown in Listing 12-2.

Listing 12-2. config/locales/de.yml

```
de:
  hello: "Hallo Welt"
```

Now you have to tell Rails to load this file by adding those files to config.i18n.load_path in config/application.rb, as shown in Listing 12-3.

Listing 12-3. config/application.rb

```
require_relative 'boot'

require 'rails/all'

# Require the gems listed in Gemfile, including any gems
# you've limited to :test, :development, or :production.
Bundler.require(*Rails.groups)

module ShopI18n
  class Application < Rails::Application
    # Initialize configuration defaults for originally generated Rails version.
    config.load_defaults 5.2

    # Settings in config/environments/* take precedence over those specified here.
    # Application configuration should go into files in config/initializers
    # -- all .rb files in that directory are automatically loaded.

    # Load i18n translation files
    config.i18n.load_path +=
      Dir[Rails.root.join('my', 'locales', '*.{rb,yml}').to_s]
  end
end
```

In the console, you can set the system language using I18n.locale = :de to German.

```
$ rails console
Running via Spring preloader in process 4009
Loading development environment (Rails 5.2.0)
>> I18n.locale = :de
=> :de
>> I18n.t :hello
=> "Hallo Welt"
```

I18n.t looks by default for the entry in the language defined in I18n.locale. It does not matter if you are working with I18n.t or I18n.translate. Nor does it matter if you are searching for a symbol or a string.

```
>> I18n.locale = :en
=> :en
>> I18n.t :hello
=> "Hello world"
>> I18n.t 'hello'
=> "Hello world"
>> I18n.translate 'hello'
=> "Hello world"
```

If a translation does not exist, you get an error message that says translation missing:. This also applies if a translation is missing in only one language (then all other languages will work, but for the missing translation you will get the error message). In that case, you can define a default with default: 'any default value', as shown here:

```
>> I18n.t 'asdfasdfasdf'
=> "translation missing: en.asdfasdfasdf"
>> I18n.t 'asdfasdfasdf', default: 'asdfasdfasdf'
=> "asdfasdfasdf"
>> exit
```

In the YAML structure, you can also specify several levels. Please amend the `config/ locale/en.yml` file as shown in Listing 12-4.

Listing 12-4. config/locale/en.yml

```
en:
  hello: "Hello world"
  example:
    test: "A test"
  aaa:
    bbb:
      test: "Another test"
```

You can display the different levels within the string with dots or with a `:scope` for the symbols. You can also mix both options.

```
$ rails console
Running via Spring preloader in process 4243
Loading development environment (Rails 5.2.0)
>> I18n.t 'example.test'
=> "A test"
>> I18n.t 'aaa.bbb.test'
=> "Another test"
>> I18n.t :test, scope: [:aaa, :bbb]
=> "Another test"
>> I18n.t :test, scope: 'aaa.bbb'
=> "Another test"
>> exit
```

It's up to you which structure you choose to save your translations in the YAML files. But the structure described in the section "A Rails Application in Only One Language: German" does make some things easier, and that's why you are going to use it for this application as well.

315

Using I18n.t in the View

In the view, you can use I18n.t as follows:

```
<%= t :hello-world %>
```

```
<%= I18n.t :hello-world %>
```

```
<%= I18n.translate :hello-world %>
```

```
<%= I18n.t 'hello-world' %>
```

```
<%= I18n.t 'aaa.bbb.test' %>
```

```
<%= link_to I18n.t('views.destroy'), book, confirm:
I18n.t('views.are_you_sure'), method: :delete %>
```

Localized Views

In Rails, there is a useful option of saving several variations of a view as *localized views*, each of which represents a different language. This technique is independent of the potential use of I18n.t in these views. The file name results from the view name, the language code (for example, de for German), and html.erb for erb pages. Each of these is separated by a dot. So, the German variation of the index.html.erb page would get the file name index.de.html.erb.

Your views directory could then look like this:

```
|-app
|---views
|-----products
|-------_form.html.erb
|-------_form.de.html.erb
|-------edit.html.erb
|-------edit.de.html.erb
|-------index.html.erb
|-------index.de.html.erb
|-------new.html.erb
|-------new.de.html.erb
|-------show.html.erb
```

```
|-------show.de.html.erb
|-----page
|-------index.html.erb
|-------index.de.html.erb
```

The language set with `config.i18n.default_locale` is used automatically if no
language was encoded in the file name. In a new and not yet configured Rails project,
this will be English. You can configure it in the file `config/application.rb`.

A Rails Application in Only One Language: German

In a Rails application aimed only at German users, it is unfortunately not enough to
just translate all the views into German. The approach is in many respects similar to
a multilingual Rails application (see the section "Multilingual Rails Applications").
Correspondingly, there will be a certain amount of repetition. I am going to show you the
steps you need to watch out for by using a simple application as an example.

Let's go through all the changes using the example of a bibliography application, as
shown here:

```
$ rails new bibliography
  [...]
$ cd bibliography
$ rails generate scaffold book title number_of_pages:integer \
  'price:decimal{7,2}'
  [...]
$ rails db:migrate
  [...]
$ echo "gem 'rails-i18n'" >> Gemfile
$ bundle
$
```

To get examples of validation errors, please insert the validations shown in Listing 12-5
into app/models/book.rb.

317

Listing 12-5. app/models/book.rb

```ruby
class Book < ApplicationRecord
  validates :title,
            presence: true,
            uniqueness: true,
            length: { within: 2..255 }

  validates :price,
            presence: true,
            numericality: { greater_than: 0 }
end
```

Please search the configuration file `config/application.rb` for the value `config.i18n.default_locale` and set it to `:de` for German. In the same context, you then also insert two directories in the previous line for the translations of the models and the views. This directory structure is not a technical requirement but makes it easier to keep track of things if your application becomes big, as shown in Listing 12-6.

Listing 12-6. config/application.rb

```ruby
require_relative 'boot'

require 'rails/all'

# Require the gems listed in Gemfile, including any gems
# you've limited to :test, :development, or :production.
Bundler.require(*Rails.groups)

module ShopI18n
  class Application < Rails::Application
    # Initialize configuration defaults for originally generated Rails version.
    config.load_defaults 5.2

    # Settings in config/environments/* take precedence over those specified here.
    # Application configuration should go into files in config/initializers
    # -- all .rb files in that directory are automatically loaded.
```

```
# Load i18n translation files
config.i18n.load_path +=
  Dir[Rails.root.join('config', 'locales', 'models', '*', '*.yml').to_s]
config.i18n.load_path +=
  Dir[Rails.root.join('config', 'locales', 'views', '*', '*.yml').to_s]
# Set de as the default language
config.i18n.default_locale = :de
  end
end
```

You then still need to create the corresponding directories.

```
$ mkdir -p config/locales/models/book
$ mkdir -p config/locales/views/book
```

Now you need to generate a language configuration file for German or simply download a ready-made one by Sven Fuchs from his GitHub repository at https://github.com/svenfuchs/rails-i18n, as shown here:

```
$ cd config/locales
$ curl -O \
  https://raw.githubusercontent.com/svenfuchs/rails-i18n/master/rails/
locale/de.yml
  % Total  % Received % Xferd  Average Speed  Time    Time     Time   Current
                                Dload  Upload  Total   Spent    Left   Speed
100 5492 100 5492      0       0  20795       0  --:--:-- --:--:-- --:--:--   20803
$
```

If you know how Bundler works, you can also insert the line gem 'rails-i18n' into the file Gemfile and then execute bundle install. This gives you all the language files from the repository.

In the file config/locales/de.yml, you have all the required formats and generic wordings for German that you need for a normal Rails application (for example, days of the week, currency symbols, etc.). Take a look at it with your favorite editor to get a first impression.

Next, you need to tell Rails that a model book is not called book in German, but buch. The same applies to all attributes. So, you create the file `config/locales/models/book/de.yml` with the structure shown in Listing 12-7. As a side effect, you get the methods `Model.model_name.human` and `Model.human_attribute_name(attribute)`, with which you can insert the model and attribute names in the view.

Listing 12-7. config/locales/models/book/de.yml

```
de:
  activerecord:
    models:
      book: 'Buch'
    attributes:
      book:
        title: 'Titel'
        number_of_pages: 'Seitenanzahl'
        price: 'Preis'
```

In the file `config/locales/views/book/de.yml`, you insert a few values for the scaffold views, as shown in Listing 12-8.

Listing 12-8. config/locales/views/book/de.yml

```
de:
  views:
    show: Anzeigen
    edit: Editieren
    destroy: Löschen
    are_you_sure: Sind Sie sicher?
    back: Zurück
    edit: Editieren
    book:
      index:
        title: Bücherliste
        new: Neues Buch
      edit:
        title: Buch editieren
```

```
new:
  title: Neues Buch
flash_messages:
  book_was_successfully_created: 'Das Buch wurde angelegt.'
  book_was_successfully_updated: 'Das Buch wurde aktualisiert.'
```

Now, you still need to integrate a "few" changes into the views. You can use the
I18n.t helper, which can also be abbreviated as t in the view. I18n.t reads out the
corresponding item from the YAML file. In the case of a purely monolingual German
application, you could also write the German text directly into the view, but with this
method you can more easily switch to multilingual use if required. See Listing 12-9,
Listing 12-10, Listing 12-11, Listing 12-12, and Listing 12-13.

Listing 12-9. app/views/books/_form.html.erb

```erb
<%= form_with(model: book, local: true) do |form| %>
  <% if book.errors.any? %>
    <div id="error_explanation">
      <h2><%= t 'activerecord.errors.template.header', :model =>
      Book.model_name.human, :count => @book.errors.count %></h2>

      <ul>
      <% book.errors.full_messages.each do |message| %>
        <li><%= message %></li>
      <% end %>
      </ul>
    </div>
  <% end %>

  <div class="field">
    <%= form.label :title %>
    <%= form.text_field :title %>
  </div>

  <div class="field">
    <%= form.label :number_of_pages %>
    <%= form.number_field :number_of_pages %>
  </div>
```

```
  <div class="field">
    <%= form.label :price %>
    <%= form.text_field :price %>
  </div>

  <div class="actions">
    <%= form.submit %>
  </div>
<% end %>
```

Listing 12-10. app/views/books/edit.html.erb

```
<h1><%= t 'views.book.edit.title' %></h1>

<%= render 'form', book: @book %>

<%= link_to I18n.t('views.show'), @book %> |
<%= link_to I18n.t('views.back'), books_path %>
```

Listing 12-11. app/views/books/index.html.erb

```
<p id="notice"><%= notice %></p>

<h1><%= t 'views.book.index.title' %></h1>

<table>
  <thead>
    <tr>
      <th><%= Book.human_attribute_name(:title) %></th>
      <th><%= Book.human_attribute_name(:number_of_pages) %></th>
      <th><%= Book.human_attribute_name(:price) %></th>
      <th colspan="3"></th>
    </tr>
  </thead>

  <tbody>
    <% @books.each do |book| %>
      <tr>
        <td><%= book.title %></td>
        <td><%= number_with_delimiter(book.number_of_pages) %></td>
```

```
    <td><%= number_to_currency(book.price) %></td>
    <td><%= link_to I18n.t('views.show'), book %></td>
    <td><%= link_to I18n.t('views.edit'), edit_book_path(book) %></td>
    <td><%= link_to I18n.t('views.destroy'), book, method: :delete,
    data: { confirm: I18n.t('views.are_you_sure') } %></td>
  </tr>
<% end %>
  </tbody>
</table>

<br>

<%= link_to I18n.t('views.book.index.new'), new_book_path %>
```

Listing 12-12. app/views/books/new.html.erb

```
<h1><%= t 'views.book.new.title' %></h1>

<%= render 'form' %>

<%= link_to I18n.t('views.back'), books_path %>
```

Listing 12-13. app/views/books/show.html.erb

```
<p id="notice"><%= notice %></p>

<p>
  <strong><%= Book.human_attribute_name(:title) %>:</strong>
  <%= @book.title %>
</p>

<p>
  <strong><%= Book.human_attribute_name(:number_of_pages) %>:</strong>
  <%= number_with_delimiter(@book.number_of_pages) %>
</p>

<p>
  <strong><%= Book.human_attribute_name(:price) %>:</strong>
  <%= number_to_currency(@book.price) %>
</p>
```

```erb
<%= link_to I18n.t('views.edit'), edit_book_path(@book) %> |
<%= link_to I18n.t('views.back'), books_path %>
```

ℹ️   In the show and index views, I integrated the helpers number_with_delimiter and number_to_currency so the numbers are represented more attractively for the user.

Right at the end, you still need to adapt a few flash messages in the controller app/controllers/books_controller.rb, as shown in Listing 12-14.

Listing 12-14. app/controllers/books_controller.rb

```ruby
class BooksController < ApplicationController
  before_action :set_book, only: [:show, :edit, :update, :destroy]

  # GET /books
  # GET /books.json
  def index
    @books = Book.all
  end

  # GET /books/1
  # GET /books/1.json
  def show
  end

  # GET /books/new
  def new
    @book = Book.new
  end

  # GET /books/1/edit
  def edit
  end

  # POST /books
  # POST /books.json
```

```ruby
def create
  @book = Book.new(book_params)

  respond_to do |format|
    if @book.save
      format.html { redirect_to @book, notice: I18n.t('views.book.flash_
      messages.book_was_successfully_created') }
      format.json { render :show, status: :created, location: @book }
    else
      format.html { render :new }
      format.json { render json: @book.errors, status: :unprocessable_
      entity }
    end
  end
end

# PATCH/PUT /books/1
# PATCH/PUT /books/1.json
def update
  respond_to do |format|
    if @book.update(book_params)
      format.html { redirect_to @book, notice: I18n.t('views.book.flash_
      messages.book_was_successfully_updated') }
      format.json { render :show, status: :ok, location: @book }
    else
      format.html { render :edit }
      format.json { render json: @book.errors, status: :unprocessable_
      entity }
    end
  end
end

# DELETE /books/1
# DELETE /books/1.json
def destroy
  @book.destroy
  respond_to do |format|
```

```
        format.html { redirect_to books_url, notice: I18n.t('views.book.
        flash_messages.book_was_successfully_destroyed') }
        format.json { head :no_content }
      end
    end

    private
      # Use callbacks to share common setup or constraints between actions.
      def set_book
        @book = Book.find(params[:id])
      end

      # Never trust parameters from the scary internet, only allow the white
      list through.
      def book_params
        params.require(:book).permit(:title, :number_of_pages, :price)
      end
end
```

Now you can use the views generated by the scaffold generator entirely in German. The structure of the YAML files shown here can of course be adapted to your own preferences. The texts in the views and the controller are displayed with I18n.t. At this point, you could of course also integrate the German text directly if the application is purely in German.

Paths in German

The bibliography is completely in German, but the URLs are still in English. If you want to make all books available at the URL http://localhost:3000/buecher instead of the URL http://localhost:3000/books, then you need to add the entry shown in Listing 12-15 to config/routes.rb.

Listing 12-15. config/routes.rb

```
Bibliography::Application.routes.draw do
  resources :books, path: 'buecher', path_names:
    { new: 'neu', edit: 'editieren' }
end
```

As a result, you then have the following new paths:

```
$ rails routes
(in /Users/xyz/rails/project-42/bibliography)
     Prefix Verb   URI Pattern                    Controller#Action
      books GET    /buecher(.:format)             books#index
            POST   /buecher(.:format)             books#create
   new_book GET    /buecher/neu(.:format)         books#new
  edit_book GET    /buecher/:id/editieren(.:format) books#edit
       book GET    /buecher/:id(.:format)         books#show
            PATCH  /buecher/:id(.:format)         books#update
            PUT    /buecher/:id(.:format)         books#update
            DELETE /buecher/:id(.:format)         books#destroy
```

The brilliant thing with Rails routes is that you do not need to do anything else. The rest is managed transparently by the routing engine.

Multilingual Rails Applications

The approach for multilingual Rails applications is similar to the monolingual, all-German Rails application described in the section "A Rails Application in Only One Language: German." However, you need to define YAML language files for all the required languages and tell the Rails application which language it should currently use. You do this via I18n.locale.

Using I18n.locale for Defining the Default Language

Of course, a Rails application has to know in which language a web page should be represented. I18n.locale saves the current language and can be read by the application. I am going to show you this with a mini web shop example, as shown here:

```
$ rails new i18n-webshop
  [...]
$ cd i18n-webshop
$ echo "gem 'rails-i18n'" >> Gemfile
$ bundle
$
```

This web shop gets a home page, as shown here:

```
$ rails generate controller Page index
  [...]
$
```

You still need to enter it as a root page in `config/routes.rb`, as shown in Listing 12-16.

Listing 12-16. config/routes.rb

```
Rails.application.routes.draw do
  get 'page/index'
  root 'page#index'
end
```

Now populate the `app/views/page/index.html.erb` with the example shown in Listing 12-17.

Listing 12-17. app/views/page/index.html.erb

```
<h1>Example Webshop</h1>
<p>Welcome to this webshop.</p>

<p>
<strong>I18n.locale:</strong>
<%= I18n.locale %>
</p>
```

If you start the Rails server with `rails server` and go to `http://localhost:3000/` in the browser, then you see the web page shown in Figure 12-1.

Figure 12-1. *I18n index page*

As you can see, the default is set to en for English. Stop the Rails server with Ctrl+C and change the setting for the default language to German in the file config/application.rb, as shown in Listing 12-18.

Listing 12-18. config/application.rb

```
[...]
config.i18n.default_locale = :de
[...]
```

If you then start the Rails server and again go to http://localhost:3000/ in the web browser, you will see the web page shown in Figure 12-2.

Figure 12-2. *I18n index page default locale de*

The web page has not changed, but as output of `<%= I18n.locale %>` you now get de for German (Deutsch), not en for English as before.

Please stop the Rails server with Ctrl+C and change the setting for the default language to en for English in the file `config/application.rb`, as shown in Listing 12-19.

Listing 12-19. config/application.rb

```
[...]
config.i18n.default_locale = :en
[...]
```

You now know how to set the default for `I18n.locale` in the entire application, but that gets only half the job done. A user wants to be able to choose a language. There are various ways of achieving this. To make things clearer, you need a second page that displays German text.

Please create the file `app/views/page/index.de.html.erb` with the content shown in Listing 12-20.

Listing 12-20. app/views/page/index.de.html.erb

```
<h1>Beispiel Webshop</h1>
<p>Willkommen in diesem Webshop.</p>
```

```
<p>
<strong>I18n.locale:</strong>
<%= I18n.locale %>
</p>
```

Setting I18n.locale via the URL Path Prefix

The more stylish way of setting the language is to add it as a prefix to the URL. This enables search engines to manage different language versions better. You want `http://localhost:3000/de` to display the German version of your home page and `http://localhost:3000/en` to display the English version. The first step is to adapt `config/routes.rb`, as shown in Listing 12-21.

Listing 12-21. config/routes.rb

```
Rails.application.routes.draw do
  scope ':locale', locale: /en|de/ do
    get 'page/index'
    get '/', to: 'page#index'
  end

  root 'page#index'
end
```

Next, you need to set a `before_action` in app/controllers/application_controller.rb. This filter sets the parameter locale set by the route as `I18n.locale`, as shown in Listing 12-22.

Listing 12-22. app/controllers/application_controller.rb

```
class ApplicationController < ActionController::Base
  before_action :set_locale

  private
  def set_locale
    I18n.locale = params[:locale] || I18n.default_locale
  end
end
```

Now you have to allow the new locales to be loaded. Add the line in Listing 12-23 to your `config/application.rb` file.

Listing 12-23. config/application.rb

```
[...]
config.i18n.available_locales = [:en, :de]
[...]
```

To test it, start Rails with `rails server` and go to the URL `http://localhost:3000/de`, as shown in Figure 12-3.

Figure 12-3. *I18n root de*

Of course, you can also go to `http://localhost:3000/de/page/index`, as shown in Figure 12-4.

Figure 12-4. *I18n de page index*

If you go to http://localhost:3000/en and http://localhost:3000/en/page/index, you get the English version of each page.

But now you have a problem: by using the prefix, you initially get to a page with the correct language, but what if you want to link from that page to another page in your Rails project? Then you would need to manually insert the prefix into the link. Who wants that? Obviously, there is a clever solution for this problem. You can set global default parameters for URL generation by defining a method called default_url_options in the controller.

So, you just need to add this method in app/controllers/application_controller.rb, as shown in Listing 12-24.

Listing 12-24. app/controllers/application_controller.rb

```ruby
class ApplicationController < ActionController::Base
  before_action :set_locale

  def default_url_options
    { locale: I18n.locale }
  end

  private
  def set_locale
    I18n.locale = params[:locale] || I18n.default_locale
  end
end
```

As a result, all links created with link_to and url_for (on which link_to is based) are automatically expanded by the parameter locale. You do not need to do anything else. All links generated via the scaffold generator are automatically changed accordingly.

Navigation Example

To give the user the option of switching easily between the different language versions, it makes sense to offer two links at the top of the web page. You don't want the current language to be displayed as the active link. This can be achieved as shown in Listing 12-25 for all views in the file app/views/layouts/application.html.erb.

Listing 12-25. app/views/layouts/application.html.erb

```
<!DOCTYPE html>
<html>
  <head>
    <title>I18nWebshop</title>
    <%= csrf_meta_tags %>

    <%= stylesheet_link_tag    'application', media: 'all', 'data-
    turbolinks-track': 'reload' %>
    <%= javascript_include_tag 'application', 'data-turbolinks-track':
    'reload' %>
  </head>

  <body>
    <p>
      <%= link_to_unless I18n.locale == :en, "English", locale: :en %>
      |
      <%= link_to_unless I18n.locale == :de, "Deutsch", locale: :de %>
    </p>

    <%= yield %>
  </body>
</html>
```

The navigation is then displayed at the top of the page, as shown in Figure 12-5.

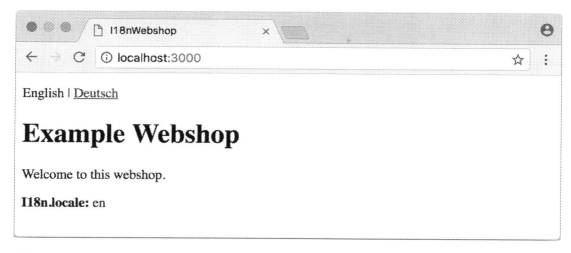

Figure 12-5. *I18n URL prefix*

Setting I18n.locale via the Accept Language HTTP Header of the Browser

When a user goes to your web page for the first time, you ideally want to immediately display the web page in the correct language for that user. To do this, you can read out the accept language field in the HTTP header. In every web browser, the user can set the preferred language (see `www.w3.org/International/questions/qa-lang-priorities`). The browser automatically informs the web server and consequently Ruby on Rails of this value.

Please edit `app/controllers/application_controller.rb` as shown in Listing 12-26.

Listing 12-26. app/controllers/application_controller.rb

```
class ApplicationController < ActionController::Base
  before_action :set_locale

  private
  def extract_locale_from_accept_language_header
    http_accept_language =
    request.env['HTTP_ACCEPT_LANGUAGE'].scan(/^[a-z]{2}/).first
    if ['de', 'en'].include? http_accept_language
      http_accept_language
    else
```

```
      'en'
    end
  end

  def set_locale
    I18n.locale = extract_locale_from_accept_language_header ||
    I18n.default_locale
  end
end
```

Do not forget to clean the settings from the section "Setting I18n.locale via the URL Path Prefix" out of config/routes.rb, as shown in Listing 12-27.

Listing 12-27. config/routes.rb

```
Rails.application.routes.draw do
  get "page/index"
  root 'page#index'
end
```

Now you always get the output in the language defined in the web browser. Please note that request.env['HTTP_ACCEPT_LANGUAGE'].scan(/^[a-z]{2}/).first does not catch all cases. For example, you should make sure that you support the specified language in your Rails application in the first place. There are some ready-made gems that can easily do this job for you. Take a look at https://www.ruby-toolbox.com/categories/i18n#http_accept_language to find them.

Saving I18n.locale in a Session

Often you want to save the value of I18n.locale in a session.

To set the value, let's create a controller in the web shop as an example, namely, the controller SetLanguage with the two actions english and german, as shown here:

```
$ rails generate controller SetLanguage english german
  [...]
$
```

In the file app/controllers/set_language_controller.rb, you populate the two actions as shown in Listing 12-28.

Listing 12-28. app/controllers/set_language_controller.rb

```ruby
class SetLanguageController < ApplicationController
  def english
    I18n.locale = :en
    set_session_and_redirect
  end

  def german
    I18n.locale = :de
    set_session_and_redirect
  end

  private
  def set_session_and_redirect
    session[:locale] = I18n.locale
  end
end
```

Finally, you also want to adapt the set_locale methods in the file app/controllers/application_controller.rb, as shown in Listing 12-29.

Listing 12-29. app/controllers/application_controller.rb

```ruby
class ApplicationController < ActionController::Base
  before_action :set_locale

  private
  def set_locale
    I18n.locale = session[:locale] || I18n.default_locale
    session[:locale] = I18n.locale
  end
end
```

After starting Rails with rails server, you can now set the language to German by going to the URL http://localhost:3000/set_language/german and to English by going to http://localhost:3000/set_language/english.

Navigation Example

To give the user the option of switching easily between the different language versions, it makes sense to offer two links at the top of the web page. You don't want the current language to be displayed as the active link. This can be achieved as shown in Listing 12-30 for all views in the file app/views/layouts/application.html.erb.

Listing 12-30. app/views/layouts/application.html.erb

```
<!DOCTYPE html>
<html>
  <head>
    <title>I18nWebshop</title>
    <%= csrf_meta_tags %>

    <%= stylesheet_link_tag    'application', media: 'all', 'data-
    turbolinks-track': 'reload' %>
    <%= javascript_include_tag 'application', 'data-turbolinks-track':
    'reload' %>
  </head>

  <body>
    <p>
      <%= link_to_unless I18n.locale == :en, "English", set_language_
      english_path %>
      |
      <%= link_to_unless I18n.locale == :de, "Deutsch", set_language_
      german_path %>
    </p>

    <%= yield %>
  </body>
</html>
```

The navigation is then displayed at the top of the page.

Setting I18n.locale via a Domain Extension

If you have several domains with the extensions typical for the corresponding languages, you can of course also use these extensions to set the language. For example, if a user visits the page www.example.com, the user would see the English version; if the user goes to http://www.example.de, then the German version would be displayed.

To achieve this, you would need to go into app/controllers/application_controller.rb and insert a before_action that analyzes the accessed domain and sets I18n.locale, as shown in Listing 12-31.

Listing 12-31. app/controllers/application_controller.rb

```ruby
class ApplicationController < ActionController::Base
  before_action :set_locale

  private
  def set_locale
    case request.host.split('.').last
    when 'de'
      I18n.locale = :de
    when 'com'
      I18n.locale = :en
    else
      I18n.locale = I18n.default_locale
    end
  end
end
```

To test this functionality, you can add the following items on your Linux or macOS development system in the file /etc/hosts:

```
localhost www.example.com
localhost www.example.de
```

Then you can go to the URLs www.example.com:3000 and www.example.de:3000 to see the corresponding language versions.

Which Approach Is the Best?

I believe that a combination of the approaches described earlier will lead to the best result. When I first visit a web page, I am happy if I find that the accept language HTTP header of my browser is read and implemented correctly. But it is also nice to be able to change the language later in the user configuration (in particular, for badly translated pages, English language is often better). Ultimately it has to be said that a page that is easy to represent is worth a lot for a search engine, and this also goes for the languages. Rails gives you the option of easily using all variations and even enables you to combine them.

Multilingual Scaffold Example

As an example, let's use a mini web shop in which you translate a product scaffold. The aim is to make the application available in German and English.

Here's the Rails application:

```
$ rails new i18n-webshop
  [...]
$ cd i18n-webshop
$ rails generate scaffold Product name description 'price:decimal{7,2}'
  [...]
$ rails db:migrate
  [...]
$ echo "gem 'rails-i18n'" >> Gemfile
$ bundle
$
```

You define the product model in app/models/product.rb, as shown in Listing 12-32.

Listing 12-32. app/models/product.rb

```
class Product < ApplicationRecord
  validates :name,
            presence: true,
            uniqueness: true,
            length: { within: 2..255 }
```

```ruby
validates :price,
          presence: true,
          numericality: { greater_than: 0 }
end
```

When selecting the language for the user, you use the URL prefix variation described in the section "Setting I18n.locale via the URL Path Prefix." You use the app/controllers/application_controller.rb file shown in Listing 12-33.

Listing 12-33. app/controllers/application_controller.rb

```ruby
class ApplicationController < ActionController::Base
  before_action :set_locale

  def default_url_options
    { locale: I18n.locale }
  end

  private
  def set_locale
    I18n.locale = params[:locale] || I18n.default_locale
  end
end
```

Listing 12-34 shows the config/routes.rb file.

Listing 12-34. config/routes.rb

```ruby
Rails.application.routes.draw do
  scope ':locale', locale: /en|de/ do
    resources :products
    get '/', to: 'products#index'
  end

  root 'products#index'
end
```

To allow the new locales to be loaded, add the line shown in Listing 12-35 to your config/application.rb file.

Listing 12-35. config/application.rb

```
[...]
config.i18n.available_locales = [:en, :de]
[...]
```

Then you insert the links for the navigation in the app/views/layouts/application.
html.erb file, as shown in Listing 12-36.

Listing 12-36. app/views/layouts/application.html.erb

```
<!DOCTYPE html>
<html>
  <head>
    <title>I18nWebshop</title>
    <%= csrf_meta_tags %>

    <%= stylesheet_link_tag    'application', media: 'all', 'data-
    turbolinks-track': 'reload' %>
    <%= javascript_include_tag 'application', 'data-turbolinks-track':
'reload' %>
  </head>

  <body>
    <p>
      <%= link_to_unless I18n.locale == :en, "English", locale: :en %>
      |
      <%= link_to_unless I18n.locale == :de, "Deutsch", locale: :de %>
    </p>

    <%= yield %>
  </body>
</html>
```

Start the Rails server with rails server.

```
$ rails server
[...]
```

If you go to http://localhost:3000, you see the normal English page, as shown in
Figure 12-6.

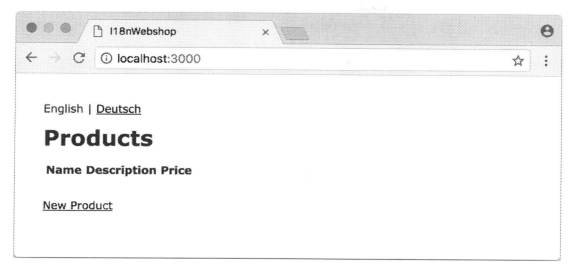

Figure 12-6. *I18n basic version*

If you click the option German, the URL and the language navigation links change, as shown in Figure 12-7.

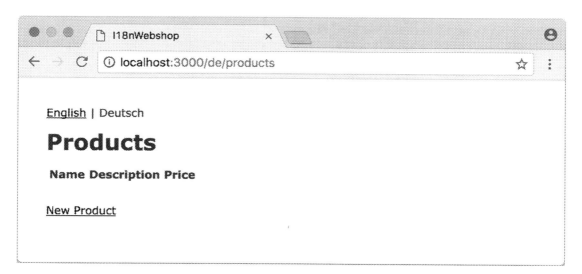

Figure 12-7. *I18n basic version de*

You still need to find a way to translate the individual elements of this page appropriately and as generically as possible.

Text Blocks in YAML Format

You need to define the individual text blocks for `I18n.t`. The corresponding directories still have to be created first.

```
$ mkdir -p config/locales/models/product
$ mkdir -p config/locales/views/product
$
```

To make sure that the YAML files created are indeed read in automatically, you need to insert the lines shown in Listing 12-37 in the file `config/application.rb`.

Listing 12-37. config/application.rb

```
[...]
# The default locale is :en and all translations from config/locales/*.rb,yml
# are auto loaded.
config.i18n.load_path += Dir[Rails.root.join('config', 'locales', 'models',
'*', '*.yml').to_s]
config.i18n.load_path += Dir[Rails.root.join('config', 'locales', 'views',
'*', '*.yml').to_s]
config.i18n.available_locales = [:en, :de]
[...]
```

German

Please create the file `config/locales/models/product/de.yml` with the content shown in Listing 12-38.

Listing 12-38. config/locales/models/product/de.yml

```
de:
  activerecord:
    models:
      product: 'Produkt'
    attributes:
      product:
        name: 'Name'
        description: 'Beschreibung'
        price: 'Preis'
```

In the file config/locales/views/product/de.yml, you insert a few values for the scaffold views, as shown in Listing 12-39.

Listing 12-39. config/locales/views/product/de.yml

```
de:
  views:
    show: Anzeigen
    edit: Editieren
    destroy: Löschen
    are_you_sure: Sind Sie sicher?
    back: Zurück
    edit: Editieren
    product:
      index:
        title: Liste aller Produkte
        new_product: Neues Produkt
      edit:
        title: Produkt editieren
      new:
        title: Neues Produkt
      flash_messages:
        product_was_successfully_created: 'Das Produkt wurde angelegt.'
        product_was_successfully_updated: 'Das Produkt wurde aktualisiert.'
        product_was_successfully_destroyed: 'Das Produkt wurde gelöscht.'
```

Finally, you can copy a ready-made default translation by Sven Fuchs from his GitHub repository at https://github.com/svenfuchs/rails-i18n.

```
$ cd config/locales/
$ curl -O https://raw.githubusercontent.com/svenfuchs/rails-i18n/master/
rails/locale/de.yml
  % Total    % Received % Xferd  Average Speed   Time    Time     Time  Current
                                 Dload  Upload   Total   Spent    Left  Speed
100  5027  100  5027    0     0  15756      0 --:--:-- --:--:-- --:--:-- 15758
$
```

> ℹ️   If you know how Bundler works, you can also insert the line gem `'rails-i18n'` into the file `Gemfile` and then execute `bundle install`. This gives you all language files from the repository.

The file `config/locales/de.yml` contains all the required formats and generic phrases for German that you need for a normal Rails application (for example, days of the week, currency symbols, etc.). Use your favorite editor to take a look at the file.

English

As most things are already present in the system for English, you just need to insert a few values for the scaffold views in the file `config/locales/views/product/en.yml`, as shown in Listing 12-40.

Listing 12-40. config/locales/views/product/en.yml

```
en:
  views:
    show: Show
    edit: Edit
    destroy: Delete
    are_you_sure: Are you sure?
    back: Back
    edit: Edit
    product:
      index:
        title: List of all products
        new_product: New product
      edit:
        title: Edit Product
      new:
        title: New product
      flash_messages:
        product_was_successfully_created: 'Product was created.'
        product_was_successfully_updated: 'Product was updated.'
```

Equipping Views with I18n.t

Please edit the listed view files as specified.

_form.html.erb

In the file app/views/products/_form.html.erb, you need to change the display of the
validation errors in the top section to I18n.t. The names of form errors are automatically
read in from activerecord.attributes.product, as shown in Listing 12-41.

Listing 12-41. app/views/products/_form.html.erb

```erb
<%= form_with(model: product, local: true) do |f| %>
  <% if product.errors.any? %>
    <div id="error_explanation">
      <h2><%= t 'activerecord.errors.template.header', model:
      Product.model_name.human, count: @product.errors.count %></h2>

      <ul>
      <% product.errors.full_messages.each do |message| %>
        <li><%= message %></li>
      <% end %>
      </ul>
    </div>
  <% end %>

  <div class="field">
    <%= f.label :name %>
    <%= f.text_field :name %>
  </div>

  <div class="field">
    <%= f.label :description %>
    <%= f.text_field :description %>
  </div>

  <div class="field">
    <%= f.label :price %>
    <%= f.text_field :price %>
  </div>
```

```
  <div class="actions">
    <%= f.submit %>
  </div>
<% end %>
```

edit.html.erb

In the file app/views/products/edit.html.erb, you need to integrate the heading and the links at the bottom of the page with I18n.t, as shown in Listing 12-42.

Listing 12-42. app/views/products/edit.html.erb

```
<h1><%= t 'views.product.edit.title' %></h1>

<%= render 'form', product: @product %>

<%= link_to I18n.t('views.show'), @product %> |
<%= link_to I18n.t('views.back'), products_path %>
```

index.html.erb

In the file app/views/products/index.html.erb, you need to change practically every line. In the table header I use human_attribute_name(), but you could also do it directly with I18n.t. The price of the product is specified with the helper number_to_currency. In a real application, you would have to specify a defined currency at this point as well, as shown in Listing 12-43.

Listing 12-43. app/views/products/index.html.erb

```
<p id="notice"><%= notice %></p>

<h1><%= t 'views.product.index.title' %></h1>

<table>
  <thead>
    <tr>
      <th><%= Product.human_attribute_name(:name) %></th>
      <th><%= Product.human_attribute_name(:description) %></th>
      <th><%= Product.human_attribute_name(:price) %></th>
```

```
      <th colspan="3"></th>
    </tr>
  </thead>

  <tbody>
    <% @products.each do |product| %>
      <tr>
        <td><%= product.name %></td>
        <td><%= product.description %></td>
        <td><%= product.price %></td>
        <td><%= link_to I18n.t('views.show'), product %></td>
        <td><%= link_to I18n.t('views.edit'), edit_product_path(product)
        %></td>
        <td><%= link_to I18n.t('views.destroy'), product,
        method: :delete, data: { confirm: I18n.t('views.are_you_sure') }
        %></td>
      </tr>
    <% end %>
  </tbody>
</table>

<br>

<%= link_to I18n.t('views.product.index.new_product'), new_product_path %>
```

new.html.erb

In the app/views/products/new.html.erb file, you need to adapt the heading and the
link, as shown in Listing 12-44.

Listing 12-44. app/views/products/new.html.erb

```
<h1><%= t 'views.product.new.title' %></h1>

<%= render 'form', product: @product %>

<%= link_to I18n.t('views.back'), products_path %>
```

show.html.erb

In the app/views/products/show.html.erb file, you again use human_attribute_
name() for the attributes. Plus, the links need to be translated with I18n.t. As with the
index view, you again use number_to_currency() to show the price in formatted form, as
shown in Listing 12-45.

Listing 12-45. app/views/products/show.html.erb

```
<p id="notice"><%= notice %></p>

<p>
  <strong><%= Product.human_attribute_name(:name) %>:</strong>
  <%= @product.name %>
</p>

<p>
  <strong><%= Product.human_attribute_name(:description) %>:</strong>
  <%= @product.description %>
</p>

<p>
  <strong><%= Product.human_attribute_name(:price) %>:</strong>
  <%= @product.price %>
</p>

<%= link_to I18n.t('views.edit'), edit_product_path(@product) %> |
<%= link_to I18n.t('views.back'), products_path %>
```

Translating Flash Messages in the Controller

Finally, you need to translate the two flash messages in app/controllers/products_
controller.rb for creating (create) and updating (update) records, again via I18n.t, as
shown in Listing 12-46.

Listing 12-46. app/controllers/products_controller.rb

```ruby
class ProductsController < ApplicationController
  before_action :set_product, only: [:show, :edit, :update, :destroy]
  # GET /products
  # GET /products.json
  def index
    @products = Product.all
  end

  # GET /products/1
  # GET /products/1.json
  def show
  end

  # GET /products/new
  def new
    @product = Product.new
  end

  # GET /products/1/edit
  def edit
  end

  # POST /products
  # POST /products.json
  def create
    @product = Product.new(product_params)

    respond_to do |format|
      if @product.save
        format.html { redirect_to @product, notice:
        I18n.t('views.product.flash_messages.product_was_successfully_
        created') }
        format.json { render :show, status: :created, location: @product }
      else
        format.html { render :new }
```

```ruby
        format.json { render json: @product.errors, status: :unprocessable_
        entity }
      end
    end
  end

  # PATCH/PUT /products/1
  # PATCH/PUT /products/1.json
  def update
    respond_to do |format|
      if @product.update(product_params)
        format.html { redirect_to @product, notice:
        I18n.t('views.product.flash_messages.product_was_successfully_
        updated') }
        format.json { render :show, status: :ok, location: @product }
      else
        format.html { render :edit }
        format.json { render json: @product.errors, status: :unprocessable_
        entity }
      end
    end
  end

  # DELETE /products/1
  # DELETE /products/1.json
  def destroy
    @product.destroy
    respond_to do |format|
      format.html { redirect_to products_url, notice:
      I18n.t('views.product.flash_messages.product_was_successfully_
      destroyed') }
      format.json { head :no_content }
    end
  end
```

```
private
  # Use callbacks to share common setup or constraints between actions.
  def set_product
    @product = Product.find(params[:id])
  end

  # Never trust parameters from the scary internet, only allow the white
  list through.
  def product_params
    params.require(:product).permit(:name, :description, :price)
  end
end
```

The Result

Now you can use the scaffold products both in German and in English. You can switch the language via the link at the top of the page.

Further Information

You can find the best source of information on this topic in the Rails documentation at `http://guides.rubyonrails.org/i18n.html`. This also shows how you can operate other back ends for defining the translations.

CHAPTER 13

Asset Pipeline

The asset pipeline offers Rails developers the opportunity to deliver CSS, JavaScript, and image files to the browser more optimally. Depending on the type of file, this can be through compression or a file name fingerprint. Different CSS files are combined into one big file. The fingerprinting enables the browser and any proxy in between to optimally cache the data so the browser can load these files more quickly on subsequent visits.

ℹ When running your web server on HTTP/2, it might be a good idea to break up this flow into smaller chunks to optimize HTTP caching. But that depends on the specifics of your web application.

Within the asset pipeline, you can program CSS, Sass, JavaScript, and CoffeeScript extensively and clearly to let them be delivered later as automatically compressed CSS and JavaScript files.

As an example, you will use once more a web shop with a product scaffold, as shown here:

```
$ rails new webshop
  [...]
$ cd webshop
$ rails generate scaffold product name 'price:decimal{7,2}'
  [...]
$ rails db:migrate
  [...]
```

© Stefan Wintermeyer 2018
S. Wintermeyer, *Learn Rails 5.2*, https://doi.org/10.1007/978-1-4842-3489-1_13

In the directory `app/assets`, you will then find the following files:

```
app/assets/
├── config
│   └── manifest.js
├── images
├── javascripts
│   ├── application.js
│   ├── cable.js
│   ├── channels
│   └── products.coffee
└── stylesheets
    ├── application.css
    ├── products.scss
    └── scaffolds.scss
```

The files `app/assets/javascripts/application.js` and `app/assets/stylesheets/application.css` are referred to as *manifest files*. They automatically include the other files in the relevant directory.

application.js

The file `app/assets/javascripts/application.js` has the content, as shown in Listing 13-1.

Listing 13-1. app/assets/javascripts/application.js

```
// [...]
//
//= require rails-ujs
//= require activestorage
//= require turbolinks
//= require_tree .
```

This file and all subfiles (which are integrated via `required_tree`) are merged into one file, and the asset pipeline optimizes it. The not yet optimized version can be downloaded in the Development environment with this URL: `http://localhost:3000/assets/application.js`.

application.css

The file app/assets/stylesheets/application.css has the content shown in Listing 13-2.

Listing 13-2. app/assets/stylesheets/application.css

```
/*
 * [...]
 *
 *= require_tree .
 *= require_self
 */
```

With the command `require_tree .`, all files in this directory are automatically integrated.

You can download the not yet optimized CSS at the URL `http://localhost:3000/assets/application.css`.

rails assets:precompile

When using the asset pipeline, you need to remember that you have to precompile the assets before starting the Rails server in the Production environment. This happens via the command `rails assets:precompile` with a prefixed RAILS_ENV=production value for the Production environment.

```
$ RAILS_ENV=production bin/rails assets:precompile
Yarn executable was not detected in the system.
Download Yarn at https://yarnpkg.com/en/docs/install
I, [2018-01-27T17:56:51.650389 #8573]  INFO -- : Writing /.../public/
assets/application-9eca361cfc054d474ebb4c8c6b16465dd4cd42664fe474b8d9a52573
c1e2d2e3.js
I, [2018-01-27T17:56:51.656011 #8573]  INFO -- : Writing /.../public/
assets/application-9eca361cfc054d474ebb4c8c6b16465dd4cd42664fe474b8d9a52573
c1e2d2e3.js.gz
I, [2018-01-27T17:56:51.700670 #8573]  INFO -- : Writing /.../public/
assets/application-35729bfbaf9967f119234595ed222f7ab14859f304ab0acc5451afb3
87f637fa.css
```

I, [2018-01-27T17:56:51.700920 #8573] INFO -- : Writing /.../public/
assets/application-35729bfbaf9967f119234595ed222f7ab14859f304ab0acc5451afb3
87f637fa.css.gz

If you forget to do this, you will find the following error message in the log:

ActionView::Template::Error (application.css isn't precompiled)

The files created by rails assets:precompile appear in the directory public/
assets.

```
public/assets/
├── application-35729bfbaf9967f119234595ed222f7ab14859f304ab0acc5451afb38
7f637fa.css
├── application-35729bfbaf9967f119234595ed222f7ab14859f304ab0acc5451afb387
f637fa.css.gz
├── application-443bf66d6410ac6de6fd02a73fd8279e83ae0baee64d3832cc67a0909
e8329d9.css
├── application-443bf66d6410ac6de6fd02a73fd8279e83ae0baee64d3832cc67a0909e
8329d9.css.gz
├── application-9eca361cfc054d474ebb4c8c6b16465dd4cd42664fe474b8d9a52573c
1e2d2e3.js
├── application-9eca361cfc054d474ebb4c8c6b16465dd4cd42664fe474b8d9a52573c1
e2d2e3.js.gz
├── application-b59f735b008e94c6f72a3b7c43cf31aea2ab324386b7a378482d17887
e683a61.js
└── application-b59f735b008e94c6f72a3b7c43cf31aea2ab324386b7a378482d17887e
683a61.js.gz
```

Go ahead and use your favorite editor to take a look at the created .css and .js files.
You will find minimized and optimized code. If the web server supports it, the zipped
.gz files are delivered directly, which speeds things up a bit more.

The difference in file size is enormous. The file application.js created in the
Development environment has a file size of 80 KB. The file js.gz created by rails
assets:precompile is only 20 KB. Users of cell phones in particular will be grateful for
the smaller file sizes.

The speed advantage incidentally lies not just in the file size but also in the fact that only one file is downloaded, not several. The HTTP/1.1 overhead for loading multiple files is time-consuming. Things are changing with HTTP/2, but that is beyond the scope of this book.

ℹ️   jQuery used to be an essential part of the JavaScript and Ruby on Rails world. Since Rails version 5.1, jQuery is no longer needed. Most people still use it, but you don't have to.

The Fingerprint

The fingerprint in the file name consists of a hash sum generated from the content of the relevant file. This fingerprint ensures optimal caching and prevents an old cache from being used if any changes are made to the content. It's a simple but effective method.

Coding Links to an Asset

All files under the directory app/assets are delivered in normal form by the Rails server. For example, you can go to the URL http://localhost:3000/assets/rails.png to view the Rails logo saved under app/assets/images/rails.png and can go to http://localhost:3000/assets/application.js to view the content of app/assets/javascripts/application.js. The Rails image rails.png is delivered 1:1, and the file application.js is first created by the asset pipeline.

But you should never enter these files as hardwired in a view. To make the most of the asset pipeline, you must use the helpers described here.

Coding a Link to an Image

You want to save all images in the directory app/assets/images/. The asset pipeline will search for them there. To actually use them in your erb code, you can use the image_tag helper. Assuming you have a file called app/assets/images/rails.png, you can re-create an <img> element with this code:

```
<%= image_tag "rails.png", alt: "Rails Logo" %>
```

In Development mode, the following HTML code results from this:

```
<img alt="Rails Logo" src="/assets/rails.png" />
```

In Production mode, you get an HTML code that points to a precompiled file with a fingerprint, as shown here:

```
<img alt="Rails Logo" src="/assets/rails-be...as0.png" />
```

Coding a Link to a JavaScript File

You can use the helper `javascript_include_tag` to retrieve a JavaScript file compiled by the asset pipeline. This is what it would look like in the view for the file app/assets/javascripts/application.js:

```
<%= javascript_include_tag "application" %>
```

Normally you don't have to care about this because the default app/views/layouts/application.html.erb takes care of it.

Coding a Link to a CSS File

A stylesheet compiled by the asset pipeline can be retrieved via the helper `stylesheet_link_tag`. In the view, it would look like this for the file app/assets/stylesheets/application.css:

```
<%= stylesheet_link_tag "application" %>
```

Normally you don't have to care about this because the default app/views/layouts/application.html.erb takes care of it.

Defaults in application.html.erb

Incidentally, the file app/views/layouts/application.html.erb that the scaffold generator creates by default already contains the coding links for these JavaScript and stylesheet files, as shown in Listing 13-3.

Listing 13-3. app/views/layouts/application.html.erb

```
<!DOCTYPE html>
<html>
  <head>
    <title>Webshop</title>
    <%= csrf_meta_tags %>

    <%= stylesheet_link_tag    'application', media: 'all', 'data-
    turbolinks-track': 'reload' %>
    <%= javascript_include_tag 'application', 'data-turbolinks-track':
    'reload' %>
  </head>

  <body>
    <%= yield %>
  </body>
</html>
```

CHAPTER 14

Caching

With the caching of web applications, most people tend to wait to implement it until they encounter performance problems. First the admin usually looks at the database and adds an index here and there. If that does not help, the admin then takes a look at the views and adds fragment caching. But this is not the best approach for working with caches. The aim of this chapter is to help you understand how key-based cache expiration works. You can then use this approach to plan new applications already on the database structure level in such a way that you can cache optimally during development.

There are two main arguments for using caching.

- The application becomes faster for the user. A faster web page results in happier users, which results in a better conversion rate.

- You need less hardware for the web server because you require less CPU and RAM resources for processing the queries.

If these two arguments are irrelevant for you, then there's no need to read this chapter. I will cover three caching methods.

- *HTTP caching*: This is the sledgehammer among the caching methods and the ultimate performance weapon. In particular, web pages that are intended for mobile devices should try to make the most of HTTP caching. If you use a combination of key-based cache expiration and HTTP caching, you save a huge amount of processing time on the server and also bandwidth.

- *Page caching*: This is the screwdriver among the caching methods. You can get a lot of performance out of the system, but it is not as good as HTTP caching.

- *Fragment caching*: This is the tweezers among the caching methods, so to speak. But do not underestimate it!

© Stefan Wintermeyer 2018
S. Wintermeyer, *Learn Rails 5.2*, https://doi.org/10.1007/978-1-4842-3489-1_14

The aim is to optimally combine all three methods.

The Example Application

You will use a simple phone book with a company model and an employees model.

Create the new Rails app, as shown here:

```
$ rails new phone_book
  [...]
$ cd phone_book
$ rails generate scaffold company name
  [...]
$ rails generate scaffold employee company:references \
  last_name first_name phone_number
  [...]
$ rails db:migrate
  [...]
```

Models

Listing 14-1 and Listing 14-2 show the setup for the two models.

Listing 14-1. app/models/company.rb

```ruby
class Company < ApplicationRecord
  validates :name,
            presence: true,
            uniqueness: true

  has_many :employees, dependent: :destroy

  def to_s
    name
  end
end
```

Listing 14-2. app/models/employee.rb

```ruby
class Employee < ApplicationRecord
  belongs_to :company, touch: true

  validates :first_name,
            presence: true

  validates :last_name,
            presence: true

  validates :company,
            presence: true

  def to_s
    "#{first_name} #{last_name}"
  end
end
```

Views

Go ahead and change the two company views, shown in Listing 14-3 and Listing 14-4, to list the number of employees in the index view and all the employees in the show view.

Listing 14-3. app/views/companies/index.html.erb

```erb
[...]
<table>
  <thead>
    <tr>
      <th>Name</th>
      <th>Number of employees</th>
      <th colspan="3"></th>
    </tr>
  </thead>

  <tbody>
    <% @companies.each do |company| %>
```

```
    <tr>
      <td><%= company.name %></td>
      <td><%= company.employees.count %></td>
      [...]
    </tr>
  <% end %>
  </tbody>
</table>
[...]
```

Listing 14-4. app/views/companies/show.html.erb

```
<p id="notice"><%= notice %></p>

<p>
  <strong>Name:</strong>
  <%= @company.name %>
</p>

<% if @company.employees.any? %>
<h1>Employees</h1>

<table>
  <thead>
    <tr>
      <th>Last name</th>
      <th>First name</th>
      <th>Phone number</th>
    </tr>
  </thead>

  <tbody>
    <% @company.employees.each do |employee| %>
      <tr>
        <td><%= employee.last_name %></td>
        <td><%= employee.first_name %></td>
        <td><%= employee.phone_number %></td>
      </tr>
    <% end %>
```

```
    </tbody>
</table>
<% end %>

<%= link_to 'Edit', edit_company_path(@company) %> |
<%= link_to 'Back', companies_path %>
```

Example Data

To easily populate the database, you can use the Faker gem (see `http://faker.`
`rubyforge.org/`). With Faker, you can generate random names and phone numbers.
Please add the line shown in Listing 14-5 in the `Gemfile`.

Listing 14-5. Gemfile

```
[...]
gem 'faker'
[...]
```

Then start `bundle`, as shown here:

```
$ bundle
```

With `db/seeds.rb`, you can create 30 companies with a random number of
employees in each case, as shown in Listing 14-6.

Listing 14-6. db/seeds.rb

```ruby
30.times do
  company = Company.new(:name => Faker::Company.name)
  if company.save
    SecureRandom.random_number(100).times do
      company.employees.create(
        first_name:   Faker::Name.first_name,
        last_name:    Faker::Name.last_name,
        phone_number: Faker::PhoneNumber.phone_number
      )
    end
  end
end
```

You can populate it via `rails db:seed`.

```
$ rails db:seed
```

You can start the application with `rails server` and retrieve the example data with a web browser by going to the URL `http://localhost:3000/companies` or `http://localhost:3000/companies/1`.

Normal Speed of the Pages to Optimize

In this chapter, you will optimize the example web pages. Start the Rails application in development mode with `rails server`. (The relevant time values, of course, depend on the hardware you are using.)

```
$ rails server
```

To access the web pages, use the command-line tool `curl` (`http://curl.haxx.se/`). Of course, you can also access the web pages with other web browsers. You can look at the time shown in the Rails log for creating the page. In reality, you need to add the time it takes for the page to be delivered to the web browser.

List of All Companies (Index View)

At the URL `http://localhost:3000/companies`, the user can see a list of all the saved companies with the relevant number of employees.

Generating the page takes 89ms on my machine.

```
Completed 200 OK in 89ms (Views: 79.0ms | ActiveRecord: 9.6ms)
```

Detailed View of a Single Company (Show View)

At the URL `http://localhost:3000/companies/1`, the user can see the details of the first company with all the employees.

Generating the page takes 51ms on my machine.

```
Completed 200 OK in 51ms (Views: 48.9ms | ActiveRecord: 0.9ms)
```

HTTP Caching

HTTP caching attempts to reuse already loaded web pages or files. For example, if you visit a web page such as `www.nytimes.com` or `www.wired.com` several times a day to read the latest news, then certain elements of that page (for example, the logo at the top of the page) will not be loaded again from the server on your second visit. Your browser already has these files in the local cache, which saves the loading time and bandwidth.

Within the Rails framework, your aim is to answer the question "Has a page changed?" in the controller. Normally, most of the time is spent on rendering the page in the view. I'd like to repeat that: most of the time is spent on rendering the page in the view!

Last-Modified

The web browser knows when it has downloaded a resource (e.g., a web page) and then placed it into its cache. On a second request, it can pass this information to the web server in an `If-Modified-Since:` header. The web server can then compare this information to the corresponding file and either deliver a newer version or return an `HTTP 304 Not Modified` code as response. In the case of a 304, the web browser delivers the locally cached version. Now you are going to say, "That's all very well for images, but it won't help me at all for dynamically generated web pages such as the `index` view of the companies." However, you are underestimating the power of Rails.

ℹ️   Please modify the times used in the examples in accordance with your own circumstances.

Go ahead and edit the `show` method in the controller file `app/controllers/companies_controller.rb`, as shown in Listing 14-7.

Listing 14-7. app/controllers/companies_controller.rb

```
# GET /companies/1
# GET /companies/1.json
def show
  fresh_when last_modified: @company.updated_at
end
```

After restarting the Rails application, take a look at the HTTP header of http://
localhost:3000/companies/1, as shown here:

```
$ curl -I http://localhost:3000/companies/1
HTTP/1.1 200 OK
X-Frame-Options: SAMEORIGIN
X-XSS-Protection: 1; mode=block
X-Content-Type-Options: nosniff
Last-Modified: Sat, 27 Jan 2018 18:38:05 GMT
[...]
```

The Last-Modified entry in the HTTP header was generated by fresh_when in the
controller. If you later go to the same web page and specify this time as well, then you do
not get the web page back; you get a 304 Not Modified message, as shown here:

```
$ curl -I http://localhost:3000/companies/1 --header 'If-Modified-Since:
Sat, 27 Jan 2018 18:38:05 GMT'
HTTP/1.1 304 Not Modified
 [...]
```

In the Rails log, you will find this:

```
Started HEAD "/companies/1" for 127.0.0.1 at 2018-01-27 18:24:21 +0100
Processing by CompaniesController#show as */*
  Parameters: {"id"=>"1"}
  Company Load (0.1ms)  SELECT  "companies".* FROM "companies" WHERE
  "companies"."id" = ? LIMIT ?  [["id", 1], ["LIMIT", 1]]
Completed 304 Not Modified in 2ms (ActiveRecord: 0.1ms)
```

It took Rails 2ms on my machine to answer this request, compared to the 51ms of the
standard variation. This is much faster! So, you have used fewer resources on the server
and saved a massive amount of bandwidth. The user will be able to see the page much
more quickly.

etag

Sometimes the update_at field of a particular object is not meaningful on its own. For
example, if you have a web page where users can log in and this page then generates web

page contents based on a role model, it can happen that user A as the admin is able to see an Edit link that is not displayed to user B as a normal user. In such a scenario, the Last-Modified header explained earlier does not help. Actually, it would do harm.

In these cases, you can use the etag header. The etag is generated by the web server and delivered when the web page is first visited. If the user visits the same URL again, the browser can then check whether the corresponding web page has changed by sending an If-None-Match: query to the web server.

Please edit the index and show methods in the controller file app/controllers/companies_controller.rb, as shown in Listing 14-8.

Listing 14-8. app/controllers/companies_controller.rb

```ruby
# GET /companies
# GET /companies.json
def index
  @companies = Company.all
  fresh_when etag: @companies
end

# GET /companies/1
# GET /companies/1.json
def show
  fresh_when etag: @company
end
```

A special Rails feature comes into play for the etag: Rails automatically sets a new CSRF token for each new visitor of the web site. This prevents cross-site request forgery attacks (see http://wikipedia.org/wiki/Cross_site_request_forgery). But it also means that each new user of a web page gets a new etag for the same page. To ensure that the same users also get identical CSRF tokens, these are stored in a cookie by the web browser and consequently sent back to the web server every time the web page is visited. You have to tell curl that you want to save all cookies in a file and transmit these cookies later if a request is received.

For saving, you use the -c cookies.txt parameter.

```
$ curl -I http://localhost:3000/companies -c cookies.txt
HTTP/1.1 200 OK
X-Frame-Options: SAMEORIGIN
```

```
X-XSS-Protection: 1; mode=block
X-Content-Type-Options: nosniff
ETag: W/"53830a75ef520df8ad8e1894cf1e5003"
  [...]
```

With the parameter `-b cookies.txt`, `curl` sends these cookies to the web server when a request arrives. Now you get the same etag for two subsequent requests.

```
$ curl -I http://localhost:3000/companies -b cookies.txt
HTTP/1.1 200 OK
X-Frame-Options: SAMEORIGIN
X-XSS-Protection: 1; mode=block
X-Content-Type-Options: nosniff
ETag: W/"53830a75ef520df8ad8e1894cf1e5003"
[...]

$ curl -I http://localhost:3000/companies -b cookies.txt
HTTP/1.1 200 OK
X-Frame-Options: SAMEORIGIN
X-Xss-Protection: 1; mode=block
X-Content-Type-Options: nosniff
ETag: W/"53830a75ef520df8ad8e1894cf1e5003"
[...]
```

You now use this etag to find out in the request with `If-None-Match` if the version you have cached is still up-to-date.

```
$ curl -I http://localhost:3000/companies -b cookies.txt --header 'If-None-
Match: W/"53830a75ef520df8ad8e1894cf1e5003"'
HTTP/1.1 304 Not Modified
X-Frame-Options: SAMEORIGIN
X-XSS-Protection: 1; mode=block
X-Content-Type-Options: nosniff
ETag: W/"53830a75ef520df8ad8e1894cf1e5003"
[...]
```

You get a `304 Not Modified` in response. Let's look at the Rails log.

```
Started HEAD "/companies" for 127.0.0.1 at 2018-01-27 18:36:25 +0100
```

```
Processing by CompaniesController#index as */*
  (0.2ms)  SELECT COUNT(*) AS "size", MAX("companies"."updated_at") AS
  timestamp FROM "companies"
Completed 304 Not Modified in 24ms (ActiveRecord: 0.2ms)
```

Rails took only 24ms on my machine to process the request. Plus, you have saved bandwidth again. The user will be happy with the speedy web application.

 Find more generic information about `etag` headers at https://en.wikipedia.org/wiki/HTTP_ETag.

current_user and Other Potential Parameters

As the basis for generating an `etag`, you can pass not just an object but also an array of objects. This way, you can solve the problem with the logged-in user who might get different content than a non-logged-in user. Let's assume that a logged-in user is output with the method `current_user`.

You have to add `etag { current_user.try :id }` in `app/controllers/application_controller.rb` to make sure that all `etags` in the application include the `current_user.id` value, which is `nil` if nobody is logged in, as shown in Listing 14-9.

Listing 14-9. app/controllers/application_controller.rb

```
class ApplicationController < ActionController::Base
  etag { current_user.try :id }
end
```

You can chain other objects in this array too and use this approach to define when a page has not changed.

The Magic of touch

What happens if an employee is edited or deleted? Then the `show` view and potentially the `index` view would have to change as well. That is the reason for the following line in the employee model:

```
belongs_to :company, touch: true
```

Every time an object of the class `Employee` is saved in edited form and if `touch: true` is used, `ActiveRecord` updates the superordinate `Company` element in the database. The `updated_at` field is set to the current time. In other words, it is "touched."

This approach ensures that the correct content is delivered.

stale?

Up to now, I was assuming that only HTML pages are being delivered. So, I showed how to use `fresh_when` and then do without the `respond_to do |format|` block. But HTTP caching is not limited to HTML pages. What if you want to render JSON, for example, as well and want to deliver it via HTTP caching? You need to use the method `stale?`. Using `stale?` resembles using the method `fresh_when`. Here's an example:

```ruby
def show
  if stale? @company
    respond_to do |format|
      format.html
      format.json { render json: @company }
    end
  end
end
```

Using Proxies (public)

I have also been assuming you were using a cache on the web browser. But on the Internet, there are many proxies that are often closer to the user and can therefore be useful for caching in the case of nonpersonalized pages. If the example is a publicly accessible phone book, then you can activate the free services of the proxies with the parameter `public: true` in `fresh_when` or with `stale?`.

Here's an example:

```ruby
# GET /companies/1
# GET /companies/1.json
def show
  fresh_when @company, public: true
end
```

You can go to the web page and get the output, as shown here:

```
$ curl -I http://localhost:3000/companies/1
HTTP/1.1 200 OK
X-Frame-Options: SAMEORIGIN
X-XSS-Protection: 1; mode=block
X-Content-Type-Options: nosniff
ETag: W/"f37a06dbe0ee1b4a2aee85c1c326b737"
Last-Modified: Sat, 27 Jan 2018 17:16:53 GMT
Content-Type: text/html; charset=utf-8
Cache-Control: public
[...]
```

The header `Cache-Control: public` tells all proxies that they can also cache this web page.

⚠️   Using proxies always has to be done with great caution. On the one hand, they are brilliantly suited for delivering your own web page quickly to more users, but on the other hand, you have to be absolutely sure that no personalized pages are cached on public proxies. For example, CSRF tags and flash messages should never end up in a public proxy. For CSRF tags, it is a good idea to make the output of `csrf_meta_tag` in the default app/views/layouts/application.html. erb layout dependent on the question of whether the page may be cached publicly, as shown here:

```
<%= csrf_meta_tag unless response.cache_control[:public] %>
```

Cache-Control with Time Limit

When using `etag` and `Last-Modified`, you can assume that the web browser definitely checks once more with the web server if the cached version of a web page is still current. This is a very safe approach.

But you can take the optimization one step further by predicting the future: if you am already sure when delivering the web page that this web page is not going to change in the next two minutes, hours, or days, then you can tell the web browser this directly. It then does not need to check back again within this specified period of time. This overhead savings has advantages, especially with mobile web browsers with relatively high latency. Plus, you save server load on the web server.

In the output of the HTTP header, you may already have noticed the corresponding line in the etag and Last-Modified examples, shown here:

```
Cache-Control: max-age=0, private, must-revalidate
```

The item must-revalidate tells the web browser that it should definitely check back with the web server to see whether a web page has changed in the meantime. The second parameter, private, means that only the web browser is allowed to cache this page. Any proxies on the way are not permitted to cache this page.

If you decide for the phone book that the web page is going to stay unchanged for at least two minutes, then you can expand the code example by adding the method expires_in. The controller app/controllers/companies.rb will then contain the following code for the method show:

```
# GET /companies/1
# GET /companies/1.json
def show
  expires_in 2.minutes
  fresh_when @company, public: true
end
```

Now you get a different cache control information in response to a request.

```
$ curl -I http://localhost:3000/companies/1
HTTP/1.1 200 OK
X-Frame-Options: SAMEORIGIN
X-XSS-Protection: 1; mode=block
X-Content-Type-Options: nosniff
Date: Sat, 27 Jan 2018 17:58:56 GMT
ETag: W/"f37a06dbe0ee1b4a2aee85c1c326b737"
Last-Modified: Sat, 27 Jan 2018 17:16:53 GMT
```

```
Content-Type: text/html; charset=utf-8
Cache-Control: max-age=120, public
[...]
```

The two minutes are specified in seconds (max-age=120), and you no longer need must-revalidate. So, in the next 120 seconds, the web browser does not need to check back with the web server to see whether the content of this page has changed.

> 🛈 This mechanism is also used by the asset pipeline. Assets created there in the Production environment can be identified clearly by the checksum in the file name and can be cached for a long time both in the web browser and in public proxies. That's why you have the following section in the Nginx configuration file:

```
location ^~ /assets/ {
  gzip_static on;
  expires max;
  add_header Cache-Control public;
}
```

Fragment Caching

With fragment caching, you can cache individual parts of a view. You can safely use it in combination with HTTP caching and page caching. The advantages, once again, are a reduction of server load and faster web page generation, which means increased usability.

Please create a new example application (see "The Example Application").

Enabling Fragment Caching in Development Mode

Fragment caching is by default disabled in the Development environment. You can activate it with the command rails dev:cache, which touches the file tmp/caching-dev.txt.

```
$ rails dev:cache
Development mode is now being cached.
```

To deactivate caching, run the same command again (this will delete the file tmp/caching-dev.txt).

```
$ rails dev:cache
Development mode is no longer being cached.
```

 In production mode, fragment caching is enabled by default.

Caching the Table of the Index View

On the page http://localhost:3000/companies, a computationally intensive table with all the companies is rendered. You can cache this table as a whole. To do so, you need to enclose the table in a <% cache('name_of_cache') do %> ... <% end %> block.

```
<% cache('name_of_cache') do %>

[...]

<% end %>
```

Please edit the file app/views/companies/index.html.erb as shown in Listing 14-10.

Listing 14-10. app/views/companies/index.html.erb

```erb
<h1>Companies</h1>

<% cache('table_of_all_companies') do %>
<table>
  <thead>
    <tr>
      <th>Name</th>
      <th>Number of employees</th>
      <th colspan="3"></th>
    </tr>
  </thead>

  <tbody>
    <% @companies.each do |company| %>
      <tr>
```

```
      <td><%= company.name %></td>
      <td><%= company.employees.count %></td>
      <td><%= link_to 'Show', company %></td>
      <td><%= link_to 'Edit', edit_company_path(company) %></td>
      <td><%= link_to 'Destroy', company, method: :delete, data: { confirm:
      'Are you sure?' } %></td>
    </tr>
  <% end %>
  </tbody>
</table>
<% end %>

<br />

<%= link_to 'New Company', new_company_path %>
```

Then you can start the Rails server with `rails server` and go to the URL `http://localhost:3000/companies`.

The first time, a page that has a fragment cache is a little bit slower because the cache has to be written. The second time it is a lot of faster.

Deleting the Fragment Cache

With the method `expire_fragment`, you can clear specific fragment caches. Basically, you can build this idea into the model in the same way as shown in the section "Deleting Page Caches Automatically."

The model file app/models/company.rb will look like Listing 14-11.

Listing 14-11. app/models/company.rb

```
class Company < ActiveRecord::Base
  validates :name,
            presence: true,
            uniqueness: true

  has_many :employees, dependent: :destroy

  after_create    :expire_cache
  after_update    :expire_cache
  before_destroy  :expire_cache
```

```ruby
  def to_s
    name
  end

  def expire_cache
    ActionController::Base.new.expire_fragment('table_of_all_companies')
  end
end
```

Because the number of employees also has an effect on this table, you also have to expand the file app/models/employees.rb accordingly, as shown in Listing 14-12.

Listing 14-12. app/models/employees.rb

```ruby
class Employee < ActiveRecord::Base
  belongs_to :company, touch: true

  validates :first_name,
            presence: true

  validates :last_name,
            presence: true

  validates :company,
            presence: true

  after_create   :expire_cache
  after_update   :expire_cache
  before_destroy :expire_cache

  def to_s
    "#{first_name} #{last_name}"
  end

  def expire_cache
    ActionController::Base.new.expire_fragment('table_of_all_companies')
  end
end
```

Deleting specific fragment caches often involves a lot of effort in terms of programming. First, you often miss things; second, in big projects it's not easy to keep track of all the different cache names. Often it is easier to automatically create names via the method cache_key. These then expire automatically in the cache.

Auto-expiring Caches

Managing fragment caching is rather complex with the naming convention used in the section "Caching the Table of the Index View." On the one hand, you can be sure that the cache does not have any superfluous ballast if you have programmed neatly, but on the other, it does not really matter. A cache is structured in such a way that it deletes old and no longer required elements on its own. If you use a mechanism that gives a fragment cache a unique name, as in the asset pipeline, then you do not need to go to the trouble of deleting fragment caches.

Rails has you covered. And it is pretty easy to do.

Let's edit the index view in the file app/views/companies/index.html.erb, as shown in Listing 14-13.

Listing 14-13. app/views/companies/index.html.erb

```
<h1>Companies</h1>

<% cache(@companies) do %>
<table>
  <thead>
    <tr>
      <th>Name</th>
      <th>Number of employees</th>
      <th colspan="3"></th>
    </tr>
  </thead>

  <tbody>
    <% @companies.each do |company| %>
      <tr>
        <td><%= company.name %></td>
        <td><%= company.employees.count %></td>
```

```
      <td><%= link_to 'Show', company %></td>
      <td><%= link_to 'Edit', edit_company_path(company) %></td>
      <td><%= link_to 'Destroy', company, method: :delete, data: { confirm:
      'Are you sure?' } %></td>
    </tr>
  <% end %>
  </tbody>
</table>
<% end %>

<br />

<%= link_to 'New Company', new_company_path %>
```

You ask Rails to generate a cache key for @companies and use it. If you want to see the name of that cache key in your log, you have to add `config.action_controller.enable_fragment_cache_logging = true` in the file `config/environments/development.rb`.

ℹ️   There is no general answer to the question of how much detail you should use fragment caching. Do some experimenting with it and then look in the log to see how long things take.

Russian Doll Caching

In the previous example, you created one fragment cache for the whole table of companies. If one company within that table changes, the whole table has to be re-rendered. Depending on the kind of data, that might take a lot of time.

The idea of Russian doll caching is that you cache not only the whole table but each row of the table too. So, when one row changes, just this row has to be rendered; all other rows can be fetched from the cache. When done well, this can save a lot of resources.

Please take a look at the updated example, as shown in Listing 14-14.

Listing 14-14. app/views/companies/index.html.erb

```
<h1>Companies</h1>

<% cache(@companies) do %>
<table>
  <thead>
    <tr>
      <th>Name</th>
      <th>Number of employees</th>
      <th colspan="3"></th>
    </tr>
  </thead>

  <tbody>
    <% @companies.each do |company| %>
      <% cache(company) do %>
      <tr>
        <td><%= company.name %></td>
        <td><%= company.employees.count %></td>
        <td><%= link_to 'Show', company %></td>
        <td><%= link_to 'Edit', edit_company_path(company) %></td>
        <td><%= link_to 'Destroy', company, method: :delete, data: {
        confirm: 'Are you sure?' } %></td>
      </tr>
      <% end %>
    <% end %>
  </tbody>
</table>
<% end %>

<br />

<%= link_to 'New Company', new_company_path %>
```

Change the Code in the View Results in an Expired Cache

Rails tracks an MD5 sum of the view you use. So if you change the file (e.g., `app/views/companies/index.html.erb`), the MD5 changes, and all the old caches will expire.

Cache Store

The cache store manages the stored fragment caches. If not configured otherwise, this is the Rails `MemoryStore`. This cache store is good for developing but less suitable for a production system because it acts independently for each Ruby on Rails process. So, if you have several Ruby on Rails processes running in parallel in the production system, each process holds its own `MemoryStore`.

MemCacheStore

Most production systems use memcached (`http://memcached.org/`) as a cache store. To enable memcached as a cache store in your production system, you need to add the line shown in Listing 14-15 in the file `config/environments/production.rb`.

Listing 14-15. config/environments/production.rb

```
config.cache_store = :mem_cache_store
```

The combination of appropriately used auto-expiring caches and memcached is an excellent recipe for a successful web page.

Other Cache Stores

In the official Rails documentation you will find a list of other cache stores; see `http://guides.rubyonrails.org/caching_with_rails.html#cache-stores`.

Page Caching

Page caching was removed from the core of Rails 4.0, but it is still available as a gem, and it is powerful.

To do page caching, you need a bit of knowledge to configure your web server (e.g., Nginx or Apache). Page caching is not for the faint-hearted.

With page caching, it's all about placing a complete HTML page (in other words, the render result of a view) into a subdirectory of the public directory and having it delivered directly from there by the web server (for example, Nginx) whenever the web page is visited next. Additionally, you can also save a compressed .gz version of the HTML page there. A production web server will automatically deliver files under public itself and can also be configured so that any .gz files present are delivered directly.

In complex views, that may take 500ms or even more for rendering; the amount of time you save is of course considerable. As a web page operator, you once more save valuable server resources and can service more visitors with the same hardware. The web page user profits from a faster delivery of the web page.

When programming your Rails application, please ensure that you also update this page or delete it! You will find a description of how to do this in the section "Deleting the Page Caches Automatically." Otherwise, you will end up with an outdated cache later.

Please also ensure that page caching rejects all URL parameters by default. For example, if you try to go to `http://localhost:3000/companies?search=abc`, this automatically becomes `http://localhost:3000/companies`. But that can easily be fixed with different route logic.

Please install a fresh example application (see the section "The Example Application") and add the gem with the following line in Gemfile:

```
gem 'actionpack-page_caching'
```

Now install it with the command `bundle install`.

```
$ bundle install
[...]
```

Lastly, you have to tell Rails where to store the cache files. Please add the line shown in Listing 14-16 in your `config/application.rb` file.

Listing 14-16.   config/application.rb

```
config.action_controller.page_cache_directory =
"#{Rails.root.to_s}/public/deploy"
```

Activating Page Caching in Development Mode

First you need to go to the file config/environments/development.rb and set the item config.action_controller.perform_caching to true, as shown in Listing 14-17.

Listing 14-17.   config/environments/development.rb

```
config.action_controller.perform_caching = true
```

Otherwise, you cannot try page caching in development mode. In production mode, page caching is enabled by default.

Configure Your Web Server

Now you have to tell your web server (e.g., Nginx or Apache) that it should check the /public/deploy directory first before hitting the Rails application. You have to configure it so that it will deliver a .gz file if one is available.

There is no one perfect way of doing it. You have to find the best way of doing it in your environment on your own.

As a quick and dirty hack for development, you can set page_cache_ directory to public. Then your development system will deliver the cached page.

```
config.action_controller.page_cache_directory = "#{Rails.root.to_s}/public"
```

Caching the Company Index and Show View

Enabling page caching happens in the controller. If you want to cache the show view for Company, you need to go to the controller app/controllers/companies_controller.rb and enter the command caches_page :show at the top, as shown in Listing 14-18.

Listing 14-18. app/controllers/companies_controller.rb

```
class CompaniesController < ApplicationController
  caches_page :show
```

[...]

Before starting the application, the public directory looks like this:

```
public/
├── 404.html
├── 422.html
├── 500.html
├── apple-touch-icon-precomposed.png
├── apple-touch-icon.png
├── favicon.ico
└── robots.txt
```

After starting the application with rails server and going to the URLs http://localhost:3000/companies and http://localhost:3000/companies/1 via a web browser, it looks like this:

```
public
├── 404.html
├── 422.html
├── 500.html
├── apple-touch-icon-precomposed.png
├── apple-touch-icon.png
├── deploy
│   └── companies
│       └── 1.html
├── favicon.ico
└── robots.txt
```

The file public/deploy/companies/1.html has been created by page caching.

From now on, the web server will only deliver the cached versions when these pages are accessed.

gz Versions

If you use page caching, you should also cache directly zipped .gz files. You can do this via the option :gzip ⇒ true or use a specific compression parameter as a symbol instead of true (for example, :best_compression).

The controller app/controllers/companies_controller.rb will look like Listing 14-19 at the beginning.

Listing 14-19. app/controllers/companies_controller.rb

```
class CompaniesController < ApplicationController
  caches_page :show, gzip: true

[...]
```

This automatically saves a compressed version and an uncompressed version of each page cache.

```
public
├── 404.html
├── 422.html
├── 500.html
├── apple-touch-icon-precomposed.png
├── apple-touch-icon.png
├── deploy
│   └── companies
│       ├── 1.html
│       └── 1.html.gz
├── favicon.ico
└── robots.txt
```

The File Extension .html

Rails saves the page accessed at http://localhost:3000/companies under the file name companies.html. So, the upstream web server will find and deliver this file if you go to http://localhost:3000/companies.html, but not if you try to go to http://localhost:3000/companies because the extension .html at the end of the URL is missing.

If you are using the Nginx server, the easiest way to do this is to adapt the `try_files` instruction in the Nginx configuration file as follows:

```
try_files $uri/index.html $uri $uri.html @unicorn;
```

Nginx then checks if a file with the extension `.html` of the currently accessed URL exists.

Deleting Page Caches Automatically

As soon as the data used in the view changes, the saved cache files have to be deleted. Otherwise, the cache would no longer be up-to-date.

According to the official Rails documentation, the solution for this problem is the class `ActionController::Caching::Sweeper`. But this approach, described at `http://guides.rubyonrails.org/caching_with_rails.html#sweepers`, has a big disadvantage: it is limited to actions that happen within the controller. So, if an action is triggered via URL by the web browser, the corresponding cache is also changed or deleted. But if an object is deleted in the console, for example, the sweeper would not realize this. For that reason, I will show you an approach that does not use a sweeper but works directly in the model with `ActiveRecord` callbacks.

In the phone book application, you always need to delete the cache for `http://localhost:3000/companies` and `http://localhost:3000/companies/company_id` when editing a company. When editing an employee, you also have to delete the corresponding cache for the relevant employee.

Models

You still need to fix the models so that the corresponding caches are deleted automatically as soon as an object is created, edited, or deleted, as shown in Listing 14-20 and Listing 14-21.

Listing 14-20. app/models/company.rb

```ruby
class Company < ActiveRecord::Base
  validates :name,
            presence: true,
            uniqueness: true

  has_many :employees, dependent: :destroy
```

```
  after_create    :expire_cache
  after_update    :expire_cache
  before_destroy :expire_cache

  def to_s
    name
  end

  def expire_cache
    ActionController::Base.expire_page(Rails.application.routes.url_
    helpers.company_path(self))
    ActionController::Base.expire_page(Rails.application.routes.url_
    helpers.companies_path)
  end

end
```

Listing 14-21. app/models/employee.rb

```
class Employee < ActiveRecord::Base
  belongs_to :company, touch: true

  validates :first_name,
            presence: true

  validates :last_name,
            presence: true

  validates :company,
            presence: true

  after_create    :expire_cache
  after_update    :expire_cache
  before_destroy :expire_cache

  def to_s
    "#{first_name} #{last_name}"
  end
```

```
def expire_cache
  ActionController::Base.expire_page(Rails.application.routes.url_
  helpers.employee_path(self))

  ActionController::Base.expire_page(Rails.application.routes.url_
  helpers.employees_path)
  self.company.expire_cache
end

end
```

Preheating

Now that you have read your way through this chapter, here is a final tip: preheat your cache!

For example, if you have a web application in a company and you know that at 9 a.m. all employees are going to log in and then access this web application, then it's a good idea to let your web server go through all those views a few hours in advance with a cron job. At night, your server is probably bored anyway.

Check out the behavior patterns of your users. With public web pages, this can be done, for example, via Google Analytics (www.google.com/analytics/). You will find that at certain times of the day, there is a lot more traffic going in. If you have a quiet phase prior to this, you can use it to warm up your cache.

The purpose of preheating is to save server resources and achieve better quality for the user because the web page is displayed more quickly.

Further Information

The best source of information on this topic is in the Rails documentation at http://guides.rubyonrails.org/caching_with_rails.html. There you can find additional information (e.g., low-level caching).

## CHAPTER 15

Action Cable

Most modern web pages are not just static. They often get updates from the server without interaction from the user. For example, your Twitter or Gmail browser client will display new tweets or e-mails without you reloading the page. The server pushes the information via WebSockets (`https://en.wikipedia.org/wiki/WebSocket`), and Action Cable provides the tools you need to use these mechanisms without diving deep into the technical aspects of WebSockets.

The use of Action Cable always includes JavaScript, and this book is about Ruby and Ruby on Rails. So, I will only show you a minimal Hello World example of how Action Cable works to give you an idea of how to proceed.

Hello World Action Cable Example

In the first example, you will push content from the Rails console into a browser that shows the `page#index` view.

The Rails Application

Please create the following Rails application:

```
$ rails new hello-world-action-cable
  [...]
$ cd hello-world-action-cable
$ rails db:migrate
$ rails generate controller page index
  [...]
```

Add a root route so that you can access the page at `http://localhost:3000`, as shown in Listing 15-1.

© Stefan Wintermeyer 2018
S. Wintermeyer, *Learn Rails 5.2*, https://doi.org/10.1007/978-1-4842-3489-1_15

Listing 15-1. config/routes.rb

```
Rails.application.routes.draw do
  get 'page/index'
  root 'page#index'
end
```

Listing 15-2 shows the content of the view.

Listing 15-2. app/views/page/index.html.erb

```
<h1>Action Cable Example</h1>

<div id="messages"></div>
```

Setting Up jQuery

You will now append HTML to `<div id="messages"></div>` in the DOM. To do that, you will use jQuery, which is not installed by default in Rails anymore. There are two ways of installing jQuery. The old way was to use the command gem `'jquery-rails'` followed by `bundle`. This still works, but Rails 5.2 has Yarn built-in, which is the new way. If you haven't installed Yarn yet, take a look at `https://yarnpkg.com/en/docs/install`.

If you are using macOS and Homebrew, you can install Yarn via `brew install yarn`, as shown here:

```
brew install yarn
```

Within Rails 5.2, you can use Yarn now to install jQuery, as shown here:

```
$ bin/yarn add jquery
yarn add v1.3.2
info No lockfile found.
[1/4] 🔍    Resolving packages...
[2/4] 🚚    Fetching packages...
[3/4] 🔗    Linking dependencies...
[4/4] 📃    Building fresh packages...
success Saved lockfile.
success Saved 1 new dependency.
└─ jquery@3.3.1
✨    Done in 0.52s.
```

To load jQuery, you have to add it in the app/assets/javascripts/application.js file, as shown in Listing 15-3.

Listing 15-3. app/assets/javascripts/application.js

```
//= require jquery
//= require rails-ujs
//= require activestorage
//= require turbolinks
//= require_tree .
```

Creating a Channel

Rails provides a handy generator to create a new WebSockets channel that you need in order to push information to the client. For this example, you will call the channel WebNotifications, as shown here:

```
$ rails generate channel WebNotifications
Running via Spring preloader in process 13267
      create  app/channels/web_notifications_channel.rb
    identical  app/assets/javascripts/cable.js
      create  app/assets/javascripts/channels/web_notifications.coffee
```

Whenever somebody requests the page#index view, you want the user to automatically subscribe to the WebNotificationsChannel channel. You do this by adding the piece of CoffeeScript that's shown in Listing 15-4.

Listing 15-4. app/assets/javascripts/page.coffee

```
App.room = App.cable.subscriptions.create "WebNotificationsChannel",
  received: (data) ->
    $('#messages').append data['message']
```

Lastly, you have to add the code shown in Listing 15-5 to the channel.

Listing 15-5. app/channels/web_notifications_channel.rb

```
class WebNotificationsChannel < ApplicationCable::Channel
  def subscribed
    stream_from "web_notifications_channel"
```

```
  end

  def unsubscribed
  end
end
```

You will start a `rails server` command and a `rails console` command in separate terminals. You need to use the Redis gem to make this work. This is not the default in the development setup.

To activate the Redis gem, include the line shown in Listing 15-6 in the `Gemfile`.

Listing 15-6. Gemfile

```
gem 'redis', '~> 4.0'
```

After that change, you have to run `bundle` once more.

```
$ bundle
```

Obviously, you need a running Redis server. If you are running macOS with Homebrew, you can install Redis with `brew install redis` and start it with `brew services start redis`. Don't forget to stop it with `brew services stop redis` after using it.

Further, you have to configure the use of Redis, as shown in Listing 15-7.

Listing 15-7. config/cable.yml

```
redis: &redis
  adapter: redis
  url: redis://localhost:6379/1

production: *redis
development: *redis
test: *redis
```

To make things a little bit more complicated, you have to configure the Content-Security-Policy in `config/initializers/content_security_policy.rb` to allow the use of Action Cable in the development environment by adding `p.connect_src :self, :https, 'ws://localhost:3000'`, as shown in Listing 15-8.

Listing 15-8. config/initializers/content_security_policy.rb

```
Rails.application.config.content_security_policy do |p|
  p.default_src :self, :https
  p.font_src    :self, :https, :data
  p.img_src     :self, :https, :data
  p.object_src  :none
  p.script_src  :self, :https
  p.style_src   :self, :https, :unsafe_inline
  p.connect_src :self, :https, 'ws://localhost:3000'
end
```

Take a look at https://developer.mozilla.org/en-US/docs/Web/HTTP/Headers/Content-Security-Policy for more information about Content-Security-Policy (CSP).

Finally, it's time to start up your development Rails server in the first terminal.

```
$ rails server
```

Load http://localhost:3000 in your web browser. In the log, you'll see this entry:

```
Started GET "/" for 127.0.0.1 at 2018-01-27 23:30:56 +0100
Processing by PageController#index as HTML
  Rendering page/index.html.erb within layouts/application
  Rendered page/index.html.erb within layouts/application (1.5ms)
Completed 200 OK in 236ms (Views: 221.8ms | ActiveRecord: 0.0ms)

Finished "/cable/" [WebSocket] for 127.0.0.1 at 2018-01-27 23:30:56 +0100
WebNotificationsChannel stopped streaming from web_notifications_channel
Started GET "/cable" for 127.0.0.1 at 2018-01-27 23:30:56 +0100
Started GET "/cable/" [WebSocket] for 127.0.0.1 at 2018-01-27 23:30:56 +0100
Successfully upgraded to WebSocket (REQUEST_METHOD: GET, HTTP_CONNECTION:
Upgrade, HTTP_UPGRADE: websocket)
WebNotificationsChannel is transmitting the subscription confirmation
WebNotificationsChannel is streaming from web_notifications_channel
```

Now start a second terminal and go to the directory where your Rails project is located. Fire up the console and use `ActionCable.server.broadcast` to broadcast a message to `web_notifications_channel`.

```
$ rails console
Running via Spring preloader in process 19706
Loading development environment (Rails 5.2.0)
>> ActionCable.server.broadcast 'web_notifications_channel',
message: '<p>Hello World!</p>'
[ActionCable] Broadcasting to web_notifications_channel:
{:message=>"<p>Hello World!</p>"}
=> 1
```

Now you can see the update in your browser window, as shown in Figure 15-1.

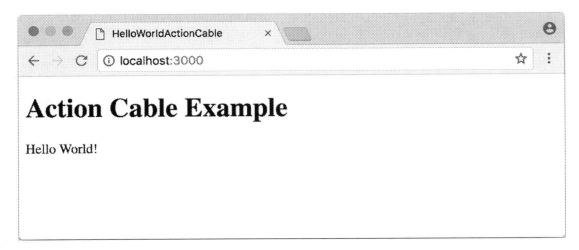

Figure 15-1. *Hello World example in browser*

You can add other messages by calling `ActionCable.server.broadcast` `'web_notifications_channel', message: '<p>Hello World!</p>'` again.

Congratulations! You have your first working Action Cable application.

By using `$('#messages').replaceWith data['message']` in `app/assets/javascripts/page.coffee`, you can replace the HTML content instead of appending it. See `http://api.jquery.com/replaceWith/`.

CHAPTER 16

Credentials

Deploying secret API keys or other secret configuration credentials to a production environment can become quite a hassle. You normally don't want to commit them unencrypted to your repository, but you also want to share them with other developers. Rails 5.1 introduced the concept of secrets, but Rails 5.2 deprecated them and introduced the concept of credentials.

You still have to store one central encryption key on your server and on all development systems, but that's it. All other secrets/credentials are encrypted with that key and can be stored safely in your code repository.

Credentials are identical in all environments. In other words, there is no difference between them in the Development and Production environments.

Let's start with a new Rails application, as shown here:

```
$ rails new shop
$ cd shop
```

Setup

In a new Rails 5.2 application, you'll find the master key, which is used to encrypt all credentials in the file `config/master.key`. Save this in your team password manager so that your team can access it.

⚠️ If you lose the key, no one, including you, can access any encrypted credentials.

It is important to keep this key secure. Anyone who has it can decrypt your credentials, and if you lose it, you cannot decrypt your credentials anymore.

© Stefan Wintermeyer 2018
S. Wintermeyer, *Learn Rails 5.2*, https://doi.org/10.1007/978-1-4842-3489-1_16

Editing Credentials

The encrypted credentials are stored in config/credentials.yml.enc. But because they are encrypted, you cannot edit them in that file with an editor. You have to use rails credentials:edit. If you are using the bash shell and don't have the environment variable EDITOR already set, you can edit your credentials with this command:

```
$ EDITOR=vim rails credentials:edit
```

Credentials are saved in the YAML format, as shown here:

```
# aws:
#   access_key_id: 123
#   secret_access_key: 345

# Used as the base secret for all MessageVerifiers in Rails, including the
one protecting cookies.
secret_key_base: 9846dad34a3168...68d634f
test: foobar
```

Accessing a Key

You can access a credential with the format AppName::Application.credentials.name_ of_the_credential. Here is an example for the previous configuration:

```
$ rails console
Running via Spring preloader in process 19662
Loading production environment (Rails 5.2.0)
>> Shop::Application.credentials.test
=> "foobar"
>> exit
```

Using the Credentials on the Production Web Server

To use the credentials in the production web server system, you have to copy the file config/master.key to that system.

CHAPTER 17

Active Storage

Ruby on Rails 5.2 introduced Active Storage, which can be used to attach files (e.g., avatar images) to objects and store those files on the server or in the cloud.

Not only can Active Storage store files, but it can also convert and resize them. In this chapter, I will show you how to attach a file to give you the basic idea of how Active Storage works.

Avatar Example

First, I'm sorry for not coming up with a more original example! Everybody uses avatars to describe how to attach something, but I will do it too because it is such a common use case.

Let's create a new phone book application that stores basic user information in the User model, as shown here:

```
$ rails new phone_book
  [...]
$ cd phone_book
$ rails generate scaffold User first_name last_name email_address
$ rails db:migrate
```

For this example, you want to add an avatar image to each user. To work with images, you need to have access to the Imagemagick software (`https://www.imagemagick.org/`). Please install it with the package manager of your choice (for macOS Homebrew users, the command `brew install imagemagick` will do the trick). On the Rails side, you have to activate the mini_magick gem. Please open your `Gemfile` and search for it. You can activate it by deleting the prefixed #, as shown in Listing 17-1.

© Stefan Wintermeyer 2018
S. Wintermeyer, *Learn Rails 5.2*, https://doi.org/10.1007/978-1-4842-3489-1_17

Listing 17-1. Gemfile

```
[...]
# Use ActiveStorage variant
gem 'mini_magick', '~> 4.8'
[...]
```

After that, run the command `bundle`.

```
$ bundle
```

To use Active Storage, you have to add a migration with `rails active_storage:install`, as shown here:

```
$ rails active_storage:install
$ rails db:migrate
== 20180128074248 CreateActiveStorageTables: migrating
========================
-- create_table(:active_storage_blobs)
   -> 0.0020s
-- create_table(:active_storage_attachments)
   -> 0.0018s
== 20180128074248 CreateActiveStorageTables: migrated (0.0040s)
===============
```

This table will take care of all the storage information. You don't have to change the user table at all to add an avatar. You can do that in the model, as shown in Listing 17-2.

Listing 17-2. app/models/user.rb

```
class User < ApplicationRecord
  has_one_attached :avatar
end
```

Now you have access to the `avatar` method in the `User` model, which is the key for working with it. Let's create a new user in the console and attach an image from the local file system as an avatar to it.

```
$ rails console
Loading development environment (Rails 5.2.0)
>> user = User.create(first_name: "Stefan", last_name: "Wintermeyer")
```

```
  (0.1ms)  begin transaction
User Create (1.4ms)  INSERT INTO "users" ("first_name", "last_name",
"created_at", "updated_at") VALUES (?, ?, ?, ?) [["first_name",
"Stefan"], ["last_name", "Wintermeyer"], ["created_at", "2018-01-28
09:47:23.769721"], ["updated_at", "2018-01-28 09:47:23.769721"]]
  (1.5ms)  commit transaction
=> #<User id: 1, first_name: "Stefan", last_name: "Wintermeyer", email_address:
nil, created_at: "2018-01-28 09:47:23", updated_at: "2018-01-28 09:47:23">
>> user.avatar.attach(io: File.open("/Users/xyz/Desktop/stefan-wintermeyer.
jpg"), filename: "stefan-wintermeyer.jpg", content_type: "image/jpg")
ActiveStorage::Attachment Load (0.5ms)  SELECT  "active_storage_
attachments".* FROM "active_storage_attachments" WHERE "active_storage_
attachments"."record_id" = ? AND "active_storage_attachments"."record_type" = ?
AND "active_storage_attachments"."name" = ? LIMIT ?  [["record_id", 1],
["record_type", "User"], ["name", "avatar"], ["LIMIT", 1]]
Disk Storage (3.1ms) Uploaded file to key: C8uKHdsuSemKP1iJXDcB5Kcf
(checksum: FW5KA5+afBfLJ+HMFEtVfA==)
  (0.1ms)  begin transaction
ActiveStorage::Blob Create (1.0ms)  INSERT INTO "active_storage_blobs"
("key", "filename", "content_type", "byte_size", "checksum", "created_at")
VALUES (?, ?, ?, ?, ?, ?)  [["key", "C8uKHdsuSemKP1iJXDcB5Kcf"],
["filename", "stefan-wintermeyer.jpg"], ["content_type", "image/jpg"],
["byte_size", 199263], ["checksum", "FW5KA5+afBfLJ+HMFEtVfA=="],
["created_at", "2018-01-28 09:48:15.946522"]]
  (0.9ms)  commit transaction
  (0.1ms)  begin transaction
ActiveStorage::Attachment Create (0.9ms)  INSERT INTO "active_storage_
attachments" ("name", "record_type", "record_id", "blob_id", "created_at")
VALUES (?, ?, ?, ?, ?)  [["name", "avatar"], ["record_type", "User"],
["record_id", 1], ["blob_id", 1], ["created_at", "2018-01-28 09:48:15.971930"]]
User Update All (0.1ms)  UPDATE "users" SET "updated_at" = '2018-01-28
09:48:15.974030' WHERE "users"."id" = ?  [["id", 1]]
  (1.1ms)  commit transaction
```

```
Enqueued ActiveStorage::AnalyzeJob (Job ID: 9c978cdf-4517-445a-a45b-
11194be8f0e7) to Async(default) with arguments: #<GlobalID:0x007ff7a42fef10
@uri=#<URI::GID gid://phone-book/ActiveStorage::Blob/1>>
 ActiveStorage::Blob Load (0.2ms)  SELECT  "active_storage_blobs".* FROM
 "active_storage_blobs" WHERE "active_storage_blobs"."id" = ? LIMIT
 ?  [["id", 1], ["LIMIT", 1]]
=> #<ActiveStorage::Attachment id: 1, name: "avatar", record_type: "User",
record_id: 1, blob_id: 1, created_at: "2018-01-28 09:48:15">
>> Performing ActiveStorage::AnalyzeJob (Job ID: 9c978cdf-4517-
445a-a45b-11194be8f0e7) from Async(default) with arguments:
#<GlobalID:0x007ff7a42c7268 @uri=#<URI::GID gid://phone-book/
ActiveStorage::Blob/1>>
  (0.1ms)  begin transaction
 ActiveStorage::Blob Update (0.5ms)  UPDATE "active_storage_blobs" SET
 "metadata" = ? WHERE "active_storage_blobs"."id" = ?  [["metadata",
 "{\"width\":1280,\"height\":1280,\"analyzed\":true}"], ["id", 1]]
  (0.9ms)  commit transaction
Performed ActiveStorage::AnalyzeJob (Job ID: 9c978cdf-4517-445a-a45b-
11194be8f0e7) from Async(default) in 96.79ms
```

You can use the `avatar.attached?` method to check whether a given user object has an avatar attached.

```
>> user.avatar.attached?
  ActiveStorage::Attachment Load (0.2ms)  SELECT  "active_storage_
  attachments".* FROM "active_storage_attachments" WHERE "active_storage_
  attachments"."record_id" = ? AND "active_storage_attachments"."record_type" = ?
  AND "active_storage_attachments"."name" = ? LIMIT ?  [["record_id", 1],
  ["record_type", "User"], ["name", "avatar"], ["LIMIT", 1]]
  ActiveStorage::Blob Load (0.1ms)  SELECT  "active_storage_blobs".* FROM
  "active_storage_blobs" WHERE "active_storage_blobs"."id" = ? LIMIT ?
  [["id", 1], ["LIMIT", 1]]
=> true
```

To see that avatar, you have to update your show view to the code shown in Listing 17-3.

Listing 17-3. app/views/users/show.html.erb

```erb
<p id="notice"><%= notice %></p>

<% if @user.avatar.attached? %>
<p>
  <%= image_tag(url_for(@user.avatar)) %>
<p>
<% end %>

<p>
  <strong>First name:</strong>
  <%= @user.first_name %>
</p>

<p>
  <strong>Last name:</strong>
  <%= @user.last_name %>
</p>

<p>
  <strong>Email address:</strong>
  <%= @user.email_address %>
</p>

<%= link_to 'Edit', edit_user_path(@user) %> |
<%= link_to 'Back', users_path %>
```

`url_for(@user.avatar)` will create a URL for the avatar. The image itself is stored in the database as a blob. Active Storage does all the magic needed to make this possible.

Uploading from the console is nice, but normally you want to have a way to upload something from within a form. So, let's update the form to make this happen, as shown in Listing 17-4.

Listing 17-4. app/views/users/_form.html.erb

```erb
<%= form_with(model: user, local: true) do |form| %>
  <% if user.errors.any? %>
    <div id="error_explanation">
      <h2><%= pluralize(user.errors.count, "error") %> prohibited this user
      from being saved:</h2>
```

```
    <ul>
    <% user.errors.full_messages.each do |message| %>
      <li><%= message %></li>
    <% end %>
    </ul>
  </div>
<% end %>

<div class="field">
  <%= form.label :first_name %>
  <%= form.text_field :first_name %>
</div>

<div class="field">
  <%= form.label :last_name %>
  <%= form.text_field :last_name %>
</div>

<div class="field">
  <%= form.label :email_address %>
  <%= form.text_field :email_address %>
</div>

<div class="field">
  <%= form.label :avatar %>
  <%= form.file_field :avatar %>
</div>

<div class="actions">
  <%= form.submit %>
</div>
<% end %>
```

But that is not enough. You have to add the part where you attach the avatar to the user object in the create and update methods in the users controller, as shown in Listing 17-5.

Listing 17-5. app/controllers/users_controller.rb

```ruby
[...]
def create
  @user = User.new(user_params)
  avatar = params[:user][:avatar]

  respond_to do |format|
    if @user.save
      if avatar
        @user.avatar.attach(avatar)
      end
      format.html { redirect_to @user, notice: 'User was successfully
      created.' }
      format.json { render :show, status: :created, location: @user }
    else
      format.html { render :new }
      format.json { render json: @user.errors, status: :unprocessable_entity }
    end
  end
end

def update
  avatar = params[:user][:avatar]

  respond_to do |format|
    if @user.update(user_params)
      if avatar
        @user.avatar.attach(avatar)
      end
      format.html { redirect_to @user, notice: 'User was successfully
      updated.' }
      format.json { render :show, status: :ok, location: @user }
    else
      format.html { render :edit }
```

```
      format.json { render json: @user.errors, status: :unprocessable_
      entity }
    end
  end
end
[...]
```

Now you can use the web GUI to upload new avatars.

Active Storage can do a lot more. It can resize the images and store them in the cloud automatically. Please take a look at `http://guides.rubyonrails.org/active_storage_overview.html` for an overview and the complete documentation.

Ruby on Rails Installation

This chapter describes how to install Ruby on Rails for development systems.

Ruby on Rails 5.2 on Debian 9.3 (Stretch)

There are two main reasons for installing a Ruby on Rails system with Ruby Version Manager (RVM).

- You do not have any root rights on the system, so you have no other option.

- You want to run several Rails systems that are separated cleanly, and perhaps also separate Ruby versions. This can be easily done with RVM.

ℹ️   You can find detailed information about RVM on the RVM home page at `https://rvm.io`.

This description assumes you have a freshly installed instance of Debian GNU/Linux 9.3 (Stretch). You will find an ISO image for the installation at `www.debian.org`. I recommend the approximately 250MB net installation CD image. For instructions on how to install Debian GNU/Linux, please go to `www.debian.org/distrib/netinst`.

Preparations

If you have root rights on the target system, you can use the following commands to ensure that you have all the required programs for a successful installation of RVM.

© Stefan Wintermeyer 2018
S. Wintermeyer, *Learn Rails 5.2*, https://doi.org/10.1007/978-1-4842-3489-1

If you do not have root rights, you have to either hope that your admin has already installed everything you need or send your admin a quick e-mail with the corresponding lines.

Log in as root, update the package lists, and upgrade the system, as shown here:

```
root@debian:~# apt-get update
[..]
root@debian:~# apt-get upgrade
```

Install the packages required for the RVM installation, as shown here:

```
root@debian:~# apt-get -y install curl gawk g++ \
make libreadline6-dev zlib1g-dev libssl-dev \
libyaml-dev libsqlite3-dev sqlite3 autoconf \
libgdbm-dev libncurses5-dev libtool bison nodejs \
pkg-config libffi-dev libgmp-dev libgmp-dev git \
dirmngr
```

Now is a good time to log out as root, as shown here:

```
root@debian:~# exit
logout
xyz@debian:~$
```

Installing Ruby 2.5 and Ruby on Rails 5.2 with RVM

Log in with your normal user account (in this case, it's the user xyz).

RVM, Ruby, and Ruby on Rails can be installed in various ways. I recommend using the following commands and getting at least one cup of tea or coffee:

```
xyz@debian:~$ gpg --keyserver hkp://keys.gnupg.net --recv-keys \
409B6B1796C275462A1703113804BB82D39DC0E3 \
7D2BAF1CF37B13E2069D6956105BD0E739499BDB
[...]
xyz@debian:~$ curl -sSL https://get.rvm.io | bash
[...]
```

To be able to use RVM, you need to run a script first. RVM will tell you which script to run (its path depends on the username).

```
xyz@debian:~$ source /home/xyz/.rvm/scripts/rvm
```

Now you can use RVM to install Ruby 2.5 and after that the current Rails version with gem, as shown here:

```
xyz@debian:~$ rvm install 2.5
[...]
xyz@debian:~$ gem install rails
[...]
xyz@debian:~$
```

gem install rails installs the current stable Rails version. You can use the format gem install rails -v 5.2.0 to install a specific version and can use gem install rails --pre to install the current beta version.

RVM, Ruby 2.6, and Rails 5.2 are now installed. You can check this with the following commands:

```
xyz@debian:~$ ruby -v
ruby 2.5.0p0 (2017-12-25 revision 61468) [x86_64-linux]
xyz@debian:~$ rails -v
Rails 5.2.0
xyz@debian:~$
```

Ruby on Rails 5.2 on macOS 10.13 (High Sierra)

macOS 10.13 includes Ruby by default, which is not what you need here. You want Ruby 2.5 and Rails 5.2. To avoid interfering with the existing Ruby and Rails installation and therefore the packet management of Mac OS X, you will install Ruby 2.5 and Rails 5.2 with RVM.

With RVM, you can install and run any number of Ruby and Rails versions as a normal user (without root rights and in your home directory).

You can find detailed information about RVM on the RVM home page at `https://rvm.io/`.

Xcode Installation or Upgrade

Before you start installing Ruby on Rails, you must install the *latest* Apple Xcode tools on your system. The easiest way to do this is via the Mac App Store (search for *xcode*) or via the web site at `https://developer.apple.com/xcode/`.

 Please take care to install all the command-line tools!

Installing Ruby 2.5 and Ruby on Rails 5.2 with RVM

RVM can be installed in various ways. I recommend using the following monster command (please copy it exactly) that installs the latest RVM, Ruby, and Ruby on Rails in your home directory:

```
$ gpg --keyserver hkp://keys.gnupg.net --recv-keys \
409B6B1796C275462A1703113804BB82D39DC0E3 \
7D2BAF1CF37B13E2069D6956105BD0E739499BDB
[...]
$ curl -sSL https://get.rvm.io | bash
[...]
```

RVM will give you a source command that you can run to set up RVM for your current shell/terminal. Usually it is just easier to close the current shell and open a new terminal window. Then everything in the new terminal will be set up properly.

```
$ rvm install 2.5
[...]
$ gem install rails
[...]
$
```

gem install rails installs the current stable Rails version. You can use the format gem install rails -v 5.2.0 to install a specific version and can use gem install rails --pre to install the current beta version.

RVM, Ruby 2.5, and Rails 5.2 are now fully installed. You can check this with the following commands:

```
$ ruby -v
ruby 2.5.0p0 (2017-12-25 revision 61468) [x86_64-darwin17]
$ rails -v
Rails 5.2.0
```

Web Server in Production Mode

This chapter walks you through the process of setting up a production server. This example will run Nginx as a reverse proxy web server and Puma as the Ruby on Rails web server behind Nginx. This chapter will start with a fresh Debian system and show how to install all the software you need. The Rails 5.2 project will be run with Ruby 2.5, which gets installed with RVM and runs for a user named `deployer`.

The example Rails application you will use is called `blog`. It will contain a `post` scaffold.

⚠️ **If you have never set up an Nginx or Apache web server by yourself on a Linux system before, you will likely get lost somewhere in this chapter.**

Debian 9.3

You will build your production web server on a minimal Debian 9.3 system. To carry out this installation, you need to have root rights on the web server.

This description assumes that you have a freshly installed Debian GNU with Linux 8.7 (Jessie). You will find an ISO image for the installation at `www.debian.org`. I recommend downloading the approximately 250MB net installation CD image. For instructions on how to install Debian GNU/Linux, please go to `www.debian.org/distrib/netinst`.

💡 **VMware or any other virtual PC system is a great playground for you to get a feeling for how this works.**

© Stefan Wintermeyer 2018
S. Wintermeyer, *Learn Rails 5.2*, https://doi.org/10.1007/978-1-4842-3489-1

Build the System

Log in as root, update the package lists, and upgrade the system, as shown here:

```
root@debian:~# apt-get update
[..]
root@debian:~# apt-get upgrade
```

Install the packages required for the RVM installation.

```
root@debian:~# apt-get -y install curl gawk g++ \
make libreadline6-dev zlib1g-dev libssl-dev \
libyaml-dev libsqlite3-dev sqlite3 autoconf \
libgdbm-dev libncurses5-dev libtool bison nodejs \
pkg-config libffi-dev libgmp-dev libgmp-dev git \
dirmngr
```

Nginx

Nginx will be the web server to the outside world.

```
root@debian:~# apt-get -y install nginx
```

User Deployer

The Rails project will use RVM in the user space. So, create a new user with the name deployer, as shown here:

```
root@debian:~# adduser deployer
Adding user `deployer' ...
Adding new group `deployer' (1001) ...
Adding new user `deployer' (1001) with group `deployer' ...
Creating home directory `/home/deployer' ...
Copying files from `/etc/skel' ...
Enter new UNIX password:
Retype new UNIX password:
passwd: password updated successfully
```

```
Changing the user information for deployer
Enter the new value, or press ENTER for the default
  Full Name []: Deployer
  Room Number []:
  Work Phone []:
  Home Phone []:
  Other []:
Is the information correct? [Y/n] Y
root@debian:~#
```

Database

In this setup, you will use PostgreSQL as the production database.

PostgreSQL Installation

You need to install the database software.

```
root@debian:~# apt-get -y install postgresql postgresql-client libpq-dev
```

To create a database user named deployer and a database named blog_production, you need to do the following steps:

```
root@debian:~# su - postgres
postgres@debian:~$ createuser -W --createdb deployer
Password:
postgres@debian:~$ createdb blog_production
postgres@debian:~$ exit
logout
root@debian:~#
```

For this example, you will use a password of 123456. It should be obvious that this is a bad idea for your application to use on a production system.

Setting Up the Rails Environment for the User Deployer

With su - deployer, you'll become the user deployer.

```
root@debian:~# su - deployer
```

As the user `deployer`, please carry out the steps for installing Ruby 2.5 and Rails 5.2 via RVM, as shown here:

```
deployer@debian:~$ gpg --keyserver hkp://keys.gnupg.net --recv-keys \
409B6B1796C275462A1703113804BB82D39DC0E3 \
7D2BAF1CF37B13E2069D6956105BD0E739499BDB
[...]
deployer@debian:~$ curl -sSL https://get.rvm.io | bash
[...]
deployer@debian:~$ source /home/deployer/.rvm/scripts/rvm
deployer@debian:~$ rvm install 2.5 --autolibs=read-only
[...]
deployer@debian:~$ gem install rails
[...]
deployer@debian:~$
```

> You need to run `gem install rails --pre` if Rails 5.2 is still in beta when you follow these steps.

Setting Up a New Rails Project

To keep this guide as simple as possible, you will create a simple blog in the home directory of the user `deployer`, as shown here:

```
deployer@debian:~$ rails new blog --database=postgresql
[...]
deployer@debian:~$ cd blog
deployer@debian:~/blog$ rails generate scaffold post subject content:text
[...]
deployer@debian:~/blog$
```

> `--database=postgresql` takes care of installing the pg gem for using PostgreSQL. If you already have a Rails application, you need to add the line gem `'pg'` to your `Gemfile` and run a `bundle install` command afterward.

Production Database Configuration

In the file config/database.yml, you need to change the production database user to deployer, as shown in Listing B-1.

Listing B-1. config/database.yml

```
[...]

production:
  <<: *default
  database: blog_production
  username: deployer
  password: <%= ENV['BLOG_DATABASE_PASSWORD'] %>
```

rails db:migrate

You still need to create the production database tables, as shown here:

```
deployer@debian:~/blog$ rails db:migrate RAILS_ENV=production
BLOG_DATABASE_PASSWORD=123456
[...]
deployer@debian:~/blog$
```

> ⚠ You probably want to set BLOG_DATABASE_PASSWORD as an environment variable in your .bash_profile file because it is not a good idea to have the database password in your bash history.

rails assets:precompile

rails assets:precompile ensures that all assets in the asset pipeline are made available to the Production environment.

```
deployer@debian:~/blog$ rails assets:precompile
```

Puma PID

Puma needs the tmp/puma directory to store a PID file, as shown here:

```
deployer@debian:~/blog$ mkdir tmp/puma
deployer@debian:~/blog$ exit
logout
root@debian:~#
```

Puma init Script

The Puma web server has to be started automatically at every booting process. Plus, it has to be killed when the server shuts down. That's been taken care of by an init script.

Please do the following commands as root:

```
$ cd /etc/init.d
$ wget https://raw.githubusercontent.com/puma/puma/master/tools/jungle/
init.d/puma
$ chmod a+x puma
$ cd /usr/local/bin
$ wget https://raw.githubusercontent.com/puma/puma/master/tools/jungle/
init.d/run-puma
$ chmod a+x run-puma
$ touch /etc/puma.conf
$ chmod 640 /etc/puma.conf
$ update-rc.d -f puma defaults
```

Now you have to create the configuration for the production instance. It includes the environment variables BLOG_DATABASE_PASSWORD and SECRET_KEY_BASE, as shown in Listing B-2.

To create a new SECRET_KEY_BASE, you should run `rails secret` in your Rails project directory.

Listing B-2. /etc/puma.conf

```
/home/deployer/blog,deployer,/home/deployer/blog/config/puma.rb,/home/
deployer/blog/log/production.log,RAILS_ENV=production;PORT=3001;BLOG_
DATABASE_PASSWORD=123456;SECRET_KEY_BASE=AASD...ASDF
```

If you don't want to store the environment variables in /etc/puma.conf, you can use the bin/rails secrets:setup mechanism.

It's time to start Puma.

```
$ /etc/init.d/puma start
[ ok ] Starting puma (via systemctl): puma.service.
$
```

Now Puma runs and is available at http://localhost:3001. To make it available to the Internet, you have to set up Nginx.

Nginx Configuration

For the Rails project, add a new configuration file called /etc/nginx/sites-available/blog.conf with the content shown in Listing B-3.

Listing B-3. /etc/nginx/sites-available/blog.conf

```
server {
  listen 80 default deferred;
  # server_name example.com;

  root /home/deployer/blog/public;

  location / {
    gzip_static on;
    try_files $uri/index.html $uri @puma;
  }
```

```
location ^~ /assets/ {
  gzip_static on;
  expires max;
  add_header Cache-Control public;
}

location @puma {
  proxy_set_header X-Forwarded-For $proxy_add_x_forwarded_for;
  proxy_set_header Host $http_host;
  proxy_redirect off;
  proxy_pass http://localhost:3001;
}

error_page 500 502 503 504 /500.html;
client_max_body_size 4G;
keepalive_timeout 10;
}
```

You link this configuration file into the /etc/nginx/sites-enabled/ directory to have it loaded by Nginx. The default file can be deleted. After that, you restart Nginx and are all set. You can access the Rails application through the IP address of this server.

```
$ ln -s /etc/nginx/sites-available/blog.conf /etc/nginx/sites-enabled/
$ rm /etc/nginx/sites-enabled/default
$ /etc/init.d/nginx restart
[ ok ] Restarting nginx (via systemctl): nginx.service.
$
```

You're all set. Your new Rails project is online. You can access the posts. You'll have to configure the root path in config/routes.rb to get a proper root path URL.

Loading Updated Versions of the Rails Project

If you want to activate updates to the Rails project, you need to copy them into the directory /home/deployer/blog and log in as the user deployer to run rails assets:precompile (see Chapter 13).

```
deployer@debian:~/blog$ rails assets:precompile
[...]
deployer@debian:~/blog$
```

If you bring in new migrations, you of course also need to run a `rails db:migrate RAILS_ENV=production` command, as shown here:

```
deployer@debian:~/blog$ rails db:migrate RAILS_ENV=production
[...]
deployer@debian:~/blog$
```

Then you need to restart Puma as the user root, as shown here:

```
root@debian:~# /etc/init.d/puma restart
```

Performance

If performance is key for your production web server, you will want to use a socket connection instead of the TCP connection.

Misc

Here are some miscellaneous topics.

Alternative Setups

This method of using RVM, Puma, and Nginx is fast and makes it possible to set up different Ruby versions on one server. But many admins prefer an easier installation process, which is promised by Phusion Passenger. Take a look at `https://www.phusionpassenger.com` for more information about Passenger. It is a good and reliable solution.

What Else There Is to Do

Please always consider the following points, although you have to decide for yourself what works for your situation and implement the best practices accordingly:

- Set up automatic and regular backups of the database and the Rails project.

- Set up log rotations of log files.

- Set up monitoring for the system load and hard drive space.

- Regularly install Debian security updates as soon as they become available.

404 and Co.

Finally, please look into the `public` directory in your Rails project and adapt the HTML pages saved there to your own requirements. Primarily, this is about the design of the pages. With the default settings, they are somewhat sparse and do not have any relation to the rest of your web site. If you decide to update your web page and shut down your Puma server to do so, Nginx will deliver the web page `public/500.html` in the meantime.

You will find a list of HTTP error codes at `http://en.wikipedia.org/wiki/List_of_HTTP_status_codes`.

Multiple Rails Servers on One System

You can run several Rails servers on one system without any problems. You need to set up a separate Puma for each Rails server. You can then distribute to it from Nginx. With Nginx you can also define on which IP address a Rails server is accessible from the outside.

The Cloud Platform as a Service Provider

If you do not have a web server available on the Internet or want to deploy to a Platform as a Service (PaaS) system right from the start, you should take a look at what the various providers have to offer. The two U.S. market leaders are currently Heroku (`www.heroku.com/`) and Engine Yard (`www.engineyard.com/`).

Going with PaaS as a platform usually offers fewer options than your own server. But you have 24/7 support for this platform if something does not work properly.

APPENDIX C

Further Rails Reading Material

You made it through the whole book. Congratulations!

Probably you are wondering what other Rails resources are available to read, watch, or listen. Here is a list of important web sites on the topic of Ruby on Rails:

`http://guides.rubyonrails.org`: This site has a couple of good official guides.

`http://rubyonrails.org/`: The project page of Ruby on Rails offers many links for further documentation. Please note that some parts of the documentation are now obsolete. Therefore, always check whether what you are reading is related specifically to Rails 3.2 or to older Rails versions.

`http://railscasts.com/`: Ryan Bates used to publish a screencast every Monday on a topic associated with Rails. Unfortunately, he hasn't published screencasts for some time now, but the page still has valuable old ones.

`https://rubyweekly.com`: Peter Cooper's *Ruby Weekly* newsletter is popular in the Ruby community.

`https://www.wintermeyer-consulting.de/newsletters/`: This is my monthly Ruby on Rails newsletter.

© Stefan Wintermeyer 2018
S. Wintermeyer, *Learn Rails 5.2*, https://doi.org/10.1007/978-1-4842-3489-1

Index

A

a 1:n association
    belongs_to options, 131
    Category model, 121, 123
    foreign key, 121
    fruits category
        access records, 126–128
        build method, 125–126
        create, 123–125
        delete and destroy, 130–131
        includes method, 129–130
        joins method, 129
        search for records, 128
    has_many options, 132–133
    Product model, 121–122
Action Cable, 393
    Hello World
        creating channel, 395–398
        Rails application, 393
        setting up jQuery, 394–395
Active Job
    create new, 295–296
    set method, 297
    Sidekiq, 297
ActiveRecord, list of countries (Europe)
    create database/model
        app/models/country.rb, 86
        configuration file, 89–90
        created_at, 86
        decimal, 88

        field types, 87–88
        getters and setters, 87
        attributes id, 86
        naming conventions, 89
        rails db, 86
        rails generate model, 84–85
        updated_at, 86
    first, last, and all, 94–97
    records
        create, 90
        new, 92–93
        new_record? method, 93–94
        syntax, 91
    seeds.rb file
        from existing data, 99
        rails db:reset, 98
        Ruby program, 98
Active Storage, 401
    avatar example
        console, 402–405
        Gemfile, 401–402
        migration, 402
        resources, 425
        User model, 401
        users controller, 406, 408
Album
    ActiveModel::Dirty
        _changed? method, 117
        changed? method, 116–117
        update method, 118

© Stefan Wintermeyer 2018
S. Wintermeyer, *Learn Rails 5.2*, https://doi.org/10.1007/978-1-4842-3489-1

V

Validation
custom, 167, 169
new shop application
create, 152
create empty record,
152, 154
error message, 154
exclusion, 165
format, 165–166
inclusion, 163–164
length, 157–159
numericality, 159–161
presence, 156–157
save(validate: false), 155
uniqueness, 161, 163
valid? method, 154
options
allow_blank, 166

allow_nil, 166
if and unless, 167
Variables
naming conventions, constants, 25
scope of, 26
global variables, 27
instance variables, 27–28
local variables, 26

W, X, Y, Z

Web console, 77–78
Web page, 67, 69
Web shop, user in
create, 280
fixtures_tests, 282–283
test suite, 280–282
unit tests, 288–290
UsersControllerTest, 285
where method, 102–103

Get the eBook for only $5!

Why limit yourself?

With most of our titles available in both PDF and ePUB format, you can access your content wherever and however you wish—on your PC, phone, tablet, or reader.

Since you've purchased this print book, we are happy to offer you the eBook for just $5.

To learn more, go to http://www.apress.com/companion or contact support@apress.com.

Apress®

Printed in the United States
By Bookmasters